Lecture Notes in Computer Science 12069

More information about this subseries at http://www.springer.com/series/7412

Huazhu Fu · Mona K. Garvin ·
Tom MacGillivray · Yanwu Xu ·
Yalin Zheng (Eds.)

Ophthalmic Medical Image Analysis

7th International Workshop, OMIA 2020
Held in Conjunction with MICCAI 2020
Lima, Peru, October 8, 2020
Proceedings

 Springer

Editors
Huazhu Fu (iD)
Inception Institute of Artificial Intelligence
Abu Dhabi, United Arab Emirates

Mona K. Garvin (iD)
University of Iowa
Iowa City, IA, USA

Tom MacGillivray (iD)
University of Edinburgh
Edinburgh, UK

Yanwu Xu (iD)
Baidu Inc.
Beijing, China

Yalin Zheng (iD)
University of Liverpool
Liverpool, UK

ISSN 0302-9743   ISSN 1611-3349   (electronic)
Lecture Notes in Computer Science
ISBN 978-3-030-63418-6   ISBN 978-3-030-63419-3   (eBook)
https://doi.org/10.1007/978-3-030-63419-3

LNCS Sublibrary: SL6 – Image Processing, Computer Vision, Pattern Recognition, and Graphics

This Springer imprint is published by the registered company Springer Nature Switzerland AG
The registered company address is: Gewerbestrasse 11, 6330 Cham, Switzerland

Preface

The 7th International Workshop on Ophthalmic Medical Image Analysis (OMIA 2020) was held in Lima, Peru, on October 8, 2020, in conjunction with the 23rd International Conference on Medical Image Computing and Computer-Assisted Intervention (MICCAI 2020). Due to the outbreak of COVID-19, this was the first time OMIA was held as a fully virtual conference.

Age-related macular degeneration, diabetic retinopathy, and glaucoma are the main causes of blindness in both developed and developing countries. The cost of blindness to society and individuals is huge, and many cases can be avoided by early intervention. Early and reliable diagnosis strategies and effective treatments are therefore a global priority. At the same time, there is mounting research on the retinal vasculature and neuro-retinal architecture as a source of biomarkers for several high-prevalence conditions like dementia, cardiovascular disease, and of course complications of diabetes. Automatic and semi-automatic software tools for retinal image analysis are being used widely in retinal biomarkers research, and increasingly percolating into clinical practice. Significant challenges remain in terms of reliability and validation, number and type of conditions considered, multi-modal analysis (e.g., fundus, optical coherence tomography, scanning laser ophthalmoscopy), novel imaging technologies, and the effective transfer of advanced computer vision and machine learning technologies, to mention a few. The workshop addressed all these aspects and more, in the ideal interdisciplinary context of MICCAI.

This workshop aimed to bring together scientists, clinicians, and students from multiple disciplines in the growing ophthalmic image analysis community, such as electronic engineering, computer science, mathematics, and medicine, to discuss the latest advancements in the field. A total of 34 full-length papers were submitted to the workshop in response to the call for papers. All submissions were double-blind peer-reviewed by at least three members of the Program Committee. Paper selection was based on methodological innovation, technical merit, results, validation, and application potential. Finally, 21 papers were accepted at the workshop and chosen to be included in this Springer LNCS volume.

We are grateful to the Program Committee for reviewing the submitted papers and giving constructive comments and critiques, to the authors for submitting high-quality papers, to the presenters for excellent presentations, and to all the OMIA 2020 attendees from all around the world.

August 2020

Huazhu Fu
Mona K. Garvin
Tom MacGillivray
Yanwu Xu
Yalin Zheng

Organization

Workshop Organizers

Huazhu Fu   Inception Institute of Artificial Intelligence, UAE
Mona K. Garvin   The University of Iowa, USA
Tom MacGillivray   The University of Edinburgh, UK
Yanwu Xu   Baidu Inc., China
Yalin Zheng   The University of Liverpool, UK

Program Committee

Bhavna Antony   IBM Research. Australia
Guozhen Chen   Shenzhen University, China
Min Chen   University of Pennsylvania, USA
Qiang Chen   Nanjing University of Science and Technology, China
Jun Cheng   UBTECH Robotics Corp Ltd., China
Dongxu Gao   The University of Liverpool, UK
Mohammad Hamghalam   Shenzhen University, China
Baiying Lei   Shenzhen University, China
Xiaomeng Li   The Chinese University of Hong Kong, Hong Kong
Dwarikanath Mahapatra   IBM Research, Australia
Emma Pead   The University of Edinburgh, UK
Suman Sedai   IBM Research, Australia
Fei Shi   Soochow University, China
Raphael Sznitman   University of Bern, Switzerland
Mingkui Tan   South China University of Technology, China
Ruwan Tennakoon   RMIT University, Australia
Jui-Kai Wang   The University of Iowa, USA
Dehui Xiang   Soochow University, China
Mengdi Xu   Yitu Technology, China
Yuguang Yan   South China University of Technology, China
Jiong Zhang   University of Southern California, USA
Yitian Zhao   Cixi Institute of Biomedical Engineering,
     Chinese Academy of Sciences, China

Yuanjie Zheng   Shandong Normal University, China
Weifang Zhu   Soochow University, China

Preface

The 7th International Workshop on Ophthalmic Medical Image Analysis (OMIA 2020) was held in Lima, Peru, on October 8, 2020, in conjunction with the 23rd International Conference on Medical Image Computing and Computer-Assisted Intervention (MICCAI 2020). Due to the outbreak of COVID-19, this was the first time OMIA was held as a fully virtual conference.

Age-related macular degeneration, diabetic retinopathy, and glaucoma are the main causes of blindness in both developed and developing countries. The cost of blindness to society and individuals is huge, and many cases can be avoided by early intervention. Early and reliable diagnosis strategies and effective treatments are therefore a global priority. At the same time, there is mounting research on the retinal vasculature and neuro-retinal architecture as a source of biomarkers for several high-prevalence conditions like dementia, cardiovascular disease, and of course complications of diabetes. Automatic and semi-automatic software tools for retinal image analysis are being used widely in retinal biomarkers research, and increasingly percolating into clinical practice. Significant challenges remain in terms of reliability and validation, number and type of conditions considered, multi-modal analysis (e.g., fundus, optical coherence tomography, scanning laser ophthalmoscopy), novel imaging technologies, and the effective transfer of advanced computer vision and machine learning technologies, to mention a few. The workshop addressed all these aspects and more, in the ideal interdisciplinary context of MICCAI.

This workshop aimed to bring together scientists, clinicians, and students from multiple disciplines in the growing ophthalmic image analysis community, such as electronic engineering, computer science, mathematics, and medicine, to discuss the latest advancements in the field. A total of 34 full-length papers were submitted to the workshop in response to the call for papers. All submissions were double-blind peer-reviewed by at least three members of the Program Committee. Paper selection was based on methodological innovation, technical merit, results, validation, and application potential. Finally, 21 papers were accepted at the workshop and chosen to be included in this Springer LNCS volume.

We are grateful to the Program Committee for reviewing the submitted papers and giving constructive comments and critiques, to the authors for submitting high-quality papers, to the presenters for excellent presentations, and to all the OMIA 2020 attendees from all around the world.

August 2020

Huazhu Fu
Mona K. Garvin
Tom MacGillivray
Yanwu Xu
Yalin Zheng

Organization

Workshop Organizers

Huazhu Fu   Inception Institute of Artificial Intelligence, UAE
Mona K. Garvin   The University of Iowa, USA
Tom MacGillivray   The University of Edinburgh, UK
Yanwu Xu   Baidu Inc., China
Yalin Zheng   The University of Liverpool, UK

Program Committee

Bhavna Antony   IBM Research. Australia
Guozhen Chen   Shenzhen University, China
Min Chen   University of Pennsylvania, USA
Qiang Chen   Nanjing University of Science and Technology, China
Jun Cheng   UBTECH Robotics Corp Ltd., China
Dongxu Gao   The University of Liverpool, UK
Mohammad Hamghalam   Shenzhen University, China
Baiying Lei   Shenzhen University, China
Xiaomeng Li   The Chinese University of Hong Kong, Hong Kong
Dwarikanath Mahapatra   IBM Research, Australia
Emma Pead   The University of Edinburgh, UK
Suman Sedai   IBM Research, Australia
Fei Shi   Soochow University, China
Raphael Sznitman   University of Bern, Switzerland
Mingkui Tan   South China University of Technology, China
Ruwan Tennakoon   RMIT University, Australia
Jui-Kai Wang   The University of Iowa, USA
Dehui Xiang   Soochow University, China
Mengdi Xu   Yitu Technology, China
Yuguang Yan   South China University of Technology, China
Jiong Zhang   University of Southern California, USA
Yitian Zhao   Cixi Institute of Biomedical Engineering,
                            Chinese Academy of Sciences, China
Yuanjie Zheng   Shandong Normal University, China
Weifang Zhu   Soochow University, China

Contents

Bio-inspired Attentive Segmentation of Retinal OCT Imaging

Georgios Lazaridis[1,4]([✉]), Moucheng Xu[1], Saman Sadeghi Afgeh[2],
Giovanni Montesano[3,4,5], and David Garway-Heath[4,5]

[1] Centre for Medical Image Computing, University College London, London, UK
g.lazaridis@ucl.ac.uk
[2] Data Science Institute, City, University of London, London, UK
[3] Optometry and Visual Sciences, City, University of London, London, UK
[4] NIHR Biomedical Research Centre at Moorfields Eye Hospital NHS
Foundation Trust, London, UK
[5] Institute of Ophthalmology, University College London, London, UK

Abstract. Albeit optical coherence imaging (OCT) is widely used to assess ophthalmic pathologies, localization of intra-retinal boundaries suffers from erroneous segmentations due to image artifacts or topological abnormalities. Although deep learning-based methods have been effectively applied in OCT imaging, accurate automated layer segmentation remains a challenging task, with the flexibility and precision of most methods being highly constrained. In this paper, we propose a novel method to segment all retinal layers, tailored to the bio-topological OCT geometry. In addition to traditional learning of shift-invariant features, our method learns in selected pixels horizontally and vertically, exploiting the orientation of the extracted features. In this way, the most discriminative retinal features are generated in a robust manner, while long-range pixel dependencies across spatial locations are efficiently captured. To validate the effectiveness and generalisation of our method, we implement three sets of networks based on different backbone models. Results on three independent studies show that our methodology consistently produces more accurate segmentations than state-of-the-art networks, and shows better precision and agreement with ground truth. Thus, our method not only improves segmentation, but also enhances the statistical power of clinical trials with layer thickness change outcomes.

1 Introduction

Optical coherence tomography (OCT) is a non-invasive imaging modality that provides high-resolution scans of the structures of the human retina [1]. The retina is organized into layers and, clinically, OCT is used as a surrogate measure to evaluate retinal cell loss by measuring layer thicknesses around the optic nerve head. Thus, OCT enables us to extract this depth information from retinal layers, which is known to change with certain ophthalmic pathologies, i.e. retinal

---

G. Lazaridis and M. Xu—these authors contributed equally.

© Springer Nature Switzerland AG 2020
H. Fu et al. (Eds.): OMIA 2020, LNCS 12069, pp. 1–10, 2020.
https://doi.org/10.1007/978-3-030-63419-3_1

nerve fibre layer (RNFL) thickness for glaucoma, and is also associated with neurodegenerative and vascular disorders [2]. Therefore, accurate and precise segmentation of retinal layers is necessary to assess morphological retinal changes in order to quantify presence or progression of pathologies.

OCT layer segmentation has produced a veritable soup of methodologies trying to address this challenging task. Classical approaches attempt to formulate the problem as a topologically correct graph or as an optimization problem based on a set of predefined or heuristic rules [3–7]. While these methods achieve remarkable results, their segmentation efficiency is limited in the presence of noise and artifacts, and results are highly sensitive to the choice of initial parameters. Moreover, topological continuity and smoothness in the obtained surfaces is not always guaranteed. Meanwhile, various methods using convolutional neural networks (CNNs) have been proposed to segment retinal OCT images [8–13]. For example, in [8], CNNs have been used to segment retinal layers by modeling the position distribution of the surfaces and by using a soft-argmax method to infer the final positions. In [9], layer segmentation is achieved by extracting the boundaries from probability maps and using a shortest path algorithm to obtain the final surfaces. The authors in [10] employ a modification of the encoder-decoder paradigm to produce dense predictions for every vertical column in each slice of the OCT volume, trying to maintain spatial correlation, whereas in [13], the authors use a U-Net [14] with residual blocks and diluted convolutions to achieve retinal layer segmentation. In [11], the authors propose to segment layers by classifying each pixel into layer or background based on an hierarchy of contextual features. In [12], segmentation is achieved by uniformly dividing the image into strips and then decomposing them into a sequence of connected regions.

These works may, however, present important limitations for OCT layer segmentation. Firstly, the previous approaches have inconsistent prediction boundaries which may not have spatial continuity. Secondly, signal and noise properties in OCT images occur at different spatial scales and, therefore, these methods might not be able to capture all the necessary information needed for segmentation. Finally, the specific geometry of OCT images is not fully exploited, thus reducing the probability for accurate and topologically sound segmentations. Therefore, principled schemes accounting for boundary morphology and signal topology must be developed, in order to preserve anatomical information and allow for spatial coherency.

This paper presents a novel end-to-end trainable method to improve retinal layer segmentation. Our methodology uses efficient high-order attention descriptors leveraging on the specific anatomical OCT geometry to extract robust quantifications of all retinal layers. Our model increases feature correlation and expression learning, exploiting the horizontally-layered retinal structure and the biological knowledge that retinal surfaces can be modeled as partitioned layers along the vertical dimension. We showcase the diagnostic precision and agreement of our method with ground truth RNFL (commonly assessed layer) segmentations from two independent studies [1,15]. Finally, we demonstrate the superiority of our method in segmenting all retinal layers using the Duke dataset [16].

2   Methods

2.1   Bio-inspired Attentive Segmentation

OCT images have a very specific geometry, where layers and retinal boundaries are oriented along the horizontal and vertical directions. For this reason, we conjecture that segmentation tasks on these type of images can benefit from exploiting the orientation of the extracted features. Also, ignoring these structural priors aggravates the issue of topological inconsistencies and incorrect pixel classifications near the layer boundaries that OCT segmentation models often suffer from [11,13,17].

Instead of mathematically formulating prior anatomical knowledge or information around layer edges, we propose a method that implements these topological priors by constraining the orientation of the feature extraction layers -that is to say, by constraining the receptive field of the convolutional layers to focus separately on each direction. The features are, then, combined into an attention mask used to enhance the supervision signal for the segmentation task. Thus, our model is better able to extract features that are primarily oriented in the horizontal and vertical direction.

2.2   Low-Rank Oriented Attention (LROA)

Given an input tensor $\boldsymbol{X} \in R^{S \times S \times C}$ and a parametrized bilinear weight matrix $\boldsymbol{W} \in \mathbb{R}^{N \times M}$, the output is given by:

$$Y = \boldsymbol{X}^T \boldsymbol{W} \boldsymbol{X} \tag{1}$$

where $Y \in \mathbb{R}^{N \times M}$. Although pair-wise dependencies of discrete pixels (Eq. 1) are typically modelled as a non-local mean operation [18], the resulting computational cost is very high due to high-rank matrix product multiplications. To enable cost-efficient computing, we model spatial correlations using a low-rank approximation based on the Hadamard product [19]:

$$Y = \boldsymbol{X}^T \boldsymbol{U} \boldsymbol{V}^T \boldsymbol{X} = \mathbf{P}^T (\boldsymbol{U}^T \boldsymbol{X} \circ \boldsymbol{V}^T \boldsymbol{X}) \tag{2}$$

where $\circ$ denotes the Hadamard product. Bias terms are omitted for simplicity. In the original formulation [19], $\boldsymbol{U}, \boldsymbol{P}, \boldsymbol{V}$ are linear projections. To incorporate prior anatomical knowledge (Sect. 2.1), we replace these with different projection operations via asymmetric convolutions. More specifically, we parametrize $\boldsymbol{U}$ and $\boldsymbol{V}$ as convolutional layers with kernel size $(1, kernel\ size)$, $(kernel\ size, 1)$ and stride of $(1, 2)$, $(2, 1)$, respectively. As a result, $\boldsymbol{U}^T \boldsymbol{X} \in \mathbb{R}^{S \times \frac{S}{2} \times C}$, and focuses on the contextual information along each vertical column. $\boldsymbol{V}^T \boldsymbol{X} \in \mathbb{R}^{\frac{S}{2} \times S \times C}$, and focuses on the contextual information of the horizontally layered structures. Apart from these two structure-orientated asymmetrical convolutional operations, we also replace the original linear projection $\boldsymbol{P}$ with a third parametrized convolutional operation for feature extraction. This operation is adopted as two consecutive standard convolutional blocks; each convolutional block consists of a convolutional layer followed by a Batch Normalisation [20] and a ReLU [21]. This operation generates features as $\boldsymbol{P}^T\boldsymbol{X} \in \mathbb{R}^{\frac{S}{2} \times \frac{S}{2} \times 2C}$. The two streams of the bilinear model are multiplied together using the Hadamard product after a transpose operation to match their shapes. We, then, reshape the feature to $\mathbb{R}^{\frac{S}{2} \times \frac{S}{2} \times 2C}$ to match the shape of tensor $\mathbf{P}^T X$. Finally, we apply a Sigmoid function for normalization to generate an attention mask, which is then combined to the result of the third feature extraction stream. The higher-order low-rank attention is then given by:

$$Y = \mathbf{P}^T X \circ \sigma(\boldsymbol{U}^T \boldsymbol{X} \circ \boldsymbol{X}^T \boldsymbol{V}) + \mathbf{P}^T X \tag{3}$$

To further increase modelling efficiency and capacity, we apply a multi-scale strategy and multi-grouped channels: Let $\{P_i\}_{i=1,\dots,4}$ be sets of asymmetrical convolutional layers with kernel size of $(1, 2)$, $(1, 3)$, $(1, 5)$, $(1, 7)$, respectively and C_{out} the output channel number. Then, $\forall \{P_i\}_{i=1,\dots,4} \exists$ different numbers of groups of filters at $C_{out}//8, C_{out}//4, C_{out}//2, C_{out}$. Our proposed attention model is finally:

$$Y = \mathbf{P}^T X \circ \sigma(\sum_{k=1}^{4} \boldsymbol{U}_k^T \boldsymbol{X} \circ \sum_{k=1}^{4} \boldsymbol{X}^T \boldsymbol{V}_k) + \mathbf{P}^T X \tag{4}$$

2.3   Architectural Overview

Our architecture consists of three branches: an encoder-decoder main branch and two parallel attention side branches. Hereinafter, the main branch is referred to as backbone. The backbone captures multi-scale visual features and integrates low-level features with high-level ones, whereas the two side branches attend to the horizontal and vertical directions. The two side branches calculate the attention weights as described in Sect. 2.2. Figure 1 illustrates the proposed framework. Our proposed architecture is composed of downsampling and upsampling components, each alternating between a convolutional block and an oriented attention block. Each downsampling block halves the size of the feature maps in height and width and doubles the channels, while each upsampling block doubles the feature maps in height and width while halving the channels.

3   Experiments and Results

3.1   Data

We used two clinical studies, COMPASS [15] and RAPID [1], and the publicly available Duke dataset [3] to evaluate our proposed methodology, conducting both binary and multi-class segmentation. All acquisitions are circular OCT (496×796) scans. Note that our method's ability to segment all retinal layers

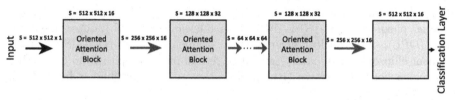

(a) Block diagram of the proposed architecture. Note that 4 blocks are shown for simplicity.

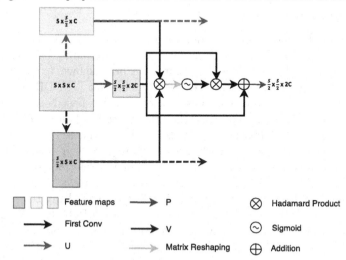

(b) Oriented attention block. Dotted lines indicate parameters sharing. S and C denote image size and number of channels, respectively. Note that all residual and skip connections are omitted for clarity.

Fig. 1. Illustration of the proposed methodology.

is illustrated in the Duke dataset; eight boundaries are annotated. The precision, repeatability and agreement of our method are evaluated independently on COMPASS and RAPID, using one layer, i.e. RNFL.

RAPID Study. The RAPID study consists of 82 stable glaucoma patients attended Moorfields Eye Hospital for up to 10 visits within a 3-month period, consisting of 502 SDOCT (SpectralisOCT, Heidelberg Engineering) images. We split the RAPID study into training, validation and testing images [1].

COMPASS Study. To test the generalizability of our method, we evaluate the trained models from RAPID on unseen cases from COMPASS. The COMPASS study consists of 943 subjects (499 patients with glaucoma and 444 healthy subjects), attended multiple centres for up to 2 years consisting of 931 SDOCT (SpectralisOCT, Heidelberg Engineering) images [15].

Duke Dataset. The Duke dataset [3] consists of 110 annotated SDOCT obtained from 10 patients suffering from Diabetic Macular Edema (DME) (11 B-scans per patient). Scans were annotated by two experts. They include: region above the retina (RaR), inner limiting membrane (ILM), nerve fiber ending to inner plexiform layer (NFL-IPL), inner nuclear layer (INL), outer plexiform layer (OPL), outer nuclear layer to inner segment myeloid (ONL-ISM), inner segment ellipsoid (ISE), outer segment to retinal pigment epithelium (OS-RPE) and region below the retina (RbR). Note that segmenting fluid is beyond the scope of this work.

3.2   Experimental Setup

To illustrate the effectiveness of our model-agnostic LROA modules, we compare each LROA-enhanced network with the corresponding backbone architecture. We use the following models that have been shown to perform well on retinal OCT segmentation tasks: U-Net [14], SegNet [22], DRUNET [13] and ReLayNet [11] to prove our hypothesis. Since LROA is based on attention mechanisms, we further include a state-of-the-art attention enhanced network, namely Attention-Unet [23]. All baselines models are re-implemented in an identical fashion as the respective papers, without pre-training, for fair comparison. Henceforth, the network using U-net [14] as backbone is referred to as "LROA-U", the network using SegNet [22] as backbone is referred to as "LROA-S", the network using DRUNET [13] as backbone is referred to as "LROA-D" and the one using RelayNet [11] as backbone is referred to as "LROA-R". We also implement two versions of LROA-S with different sized kernels in $\{P_i\}_{n=1,\dots,4}$ and $\{V_i\}_{n=1,\dots,4}$ to investigate the effect of size kernel. The first variant of LROA-S uses a larger kernel with a size of $(1,3)$, $(1,5)$, $(1,7)$ and $(1,9)$ in $\{P_i\}_{n=1,\dots,4}$, and is referred to as "LROA-SL". The second variant of LROA-S uses a larger kernel size of $(1,3)$, $(1,7)$, $(1,9)$ and $(1,15)$ in $\{P_i\}_{n=1,\dots,4}$, and is referred to as "LROA-SVL". To quantify the relative diagnostic precision, repeatability and test-retest variability, we test, independently, one layer (RNFL) as done in similar studies, i.e. predicted versus ground truth RNFL thickness on RAPID and COMPASS. To illustrate the method's segmentation improvement, we segment all layers on the Duke dataset, but the fluid region, which is beyond the scope of this work due to the very limited number of training images. All experiments are patient-independent.

Training. All images were resized to 512×512. Training images are augmented with random probability using channel ratio modification, horizontal and vertical flipping and Gaussian and speckle noise corruption. We use Standard cross-entropy loss, AdamW optimizer [24], an initial learning rate of 10^{-3}, and a minibatch size of 4 until convergence, across all experiments. All experiments were performed on a NVIDIA Titan V (12 GB) GPU using PyTorch. Code is publicly available at github.com/gelazari/MICCAI2020.

3.3   Results

Tables 1, 2 and Fig. 2 illustrate our results. Our approach improves across all experiments. Table 1 shows the 95% limits of agreement (LOA), mean difference, and the mean standard deviation (SD) of the difference for three visits

Table 1. Limits of agreement, mean difference of all methods versus ground truth, and mean SD (test-retest variability) of the first three visits difference. Results on binary RNFL segmentation on COMPASS and RAPID studies.

Method	SegNet	**LROA-S**	U-Net	**LROA-U**	SpectralisOCT
95% LOA	[4.78, −4.42]	**[3.50, −3.75]**	[4.07, −3.95]	[3.72, −3.76]	[4.70, −4.48]
Mean Diff	0.18	−0.13	0.06	**−0.02**	0.11
Mean SD	1.93	1.22	1.84	**1.13**	1.20

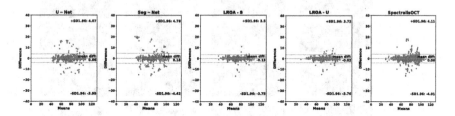

Fig. 2. Bland-Altman plots between all methods and ground truth. Note that for SpectralisOCT, repeated test-retest measurements for each eye are used.

Table 2. Multi-class segmentation results on the Duke dataset.

Networks	IoU (%)	F1 (%)	Recall (%)	Precision (%)	MSE
SegNet	45.22	52.98	58.68	53.17	0.94
LROA-S	70.20	82.33	84.43	81.98	0.31
LROA-SL	75.99	88.40	89.97	88.63	0.28
LROA-SVL	76.68	89.08	90.42	**92.81**	**0.26**
U-Net	69.08	81.47	83.38	80.77	0.39
Atten-UNet	70.52	83.52	85.07	83.16	0.41
LROA-U	76.65	89.07	90.03	89.48	0.30
ReLayNet	74.80	87.64	88.49	87.99	0.36
LROA-R	**78.59**	**91.27**	**91.57**	92.25	0.29
DRUNET	69.73	81.97	83.81	81.12	0.39
LROA-D	75.77	88.22	89.79	89.31	0.31

across all subjects on the RAPID and COMPASS study. Following similar studies, we use the average RNFL segmentation to compute these metrics. The results show that our approach outperforms all other methods: diagnostic precision and repeatability are markedly improved. Moreover, our method not only produces segmentations with high ground truth agreement, but also reduces test-retest variability. Importantly, we appreciate a statistically significant improvement in the aforementioned metrics obtained with LROA-U (best of proposed submodels) as compared to those obtained with U-Net (best baseline)$(p = 0.037$, Mann–Whitney U test), leading to a lower sample size in a clinical trial power analysis.

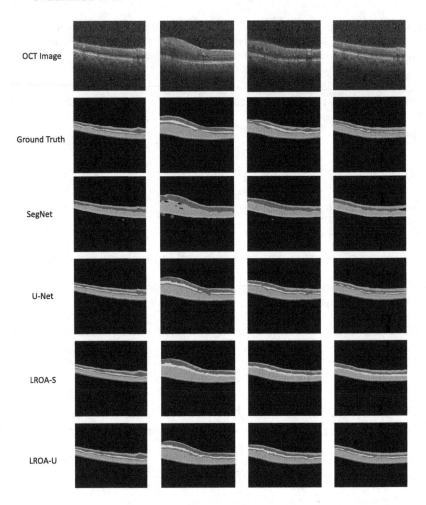

Fig. 3. Segmentation results on the Duke dataset.

Figure 2 illustrates the corresponding Bland-Altman plots; LROA leads to significantly better agreement and lower test-retest variability. Table 2 shows multiclass segmentation results on the Duke dataset, including the positive impact from larger sized asymmetrical kernels. It can be seen that the proposed method outperforms all the others by huge margins. For instance, LROA-S improves over its backbone SegNet by 55% in IoU. Figure 3 shows visual segmentation results. Note that segmenting fluid is beyond the scope of this work.

4   Discussion and Conclusion

In this paper, we present a novel, end-to-end trainable, attentive model for retinal OCT segmentation. Our contributions extend current literature as we highlight valuable features of high-level layers, efficiently combined with high-order attention information in two relevant dimensions, to guide the final segmentation. Our approach is based on feature correlation learning, exploiting the horizontally-layered retinal structure and the vertical partitioning of retinal surfaces. The proposed methodology appears robust and flexible in terms of capacity and modularity. Results show the model not only significantly improves segmentation results, but can also increase the statistical power of clinical trials with layer thickness change outcomes. Future work will focus on integrating context among different B-scans.

References

1. Garway-Heath, D.F., Quartilho, A., Prah, P., Crabb, D.P., Cheng, Q., Zhu, H.: Evaluation of visual field and imaging outcomes for glaucoma clinical trials (an American Ophthalomological Society thesis). Trans. Am. Ophthalmol. Soc. **115**, T4 (2017)
2. London, A., Benhar, I., Schwartz, M.: The retina as a window to the brain-from eye research to CNS disorders. Nat. Rev. Neurol. **9**(1), 44–53 (2013)
3. Chiu, S.J., Li, X.T., et al.: Automatic segmentation of seven retinal layers in SDOCT images congruent with expert manual segmentation. Opt. Exp. **18**(18), 19413–19428 (2010)
4. Keller, B., Cunefare, D., et al.: Length-adaptive graph search for automatic segmentation of pathological features in optical coherence tomography images. J. Biomed. Opt. **21**(7), 1–9 (2016)
5. Carass, A., Lang, A., et al.: Multiple-object geometric deformable model for segmentation of macular OCT. Biomed. Opt. Exp. **5**(4), 1062–1074 (2014)
6. Garvin, M.K., Abramoff, M.D., et al.: Automated 3-D intraretinal layer segmentation of macular spectral-domain optical coherence tomography images. IEEE Trans. Med. Imaging **28**(9), 1436–1447 (2009)
7. Lang, A., Carass, A., et al.: Retinal layer segmentation of macular OCT images using boundary classification. Biomed. Opt. Exp. **4**(7), 1133–1152 (2013)
8. He, Y., et al.: Fully convolutional boundary regression for retina OCT segmentation. In: Shen, D., et al. (eds.) MICCAI 2019. LNCS, vol. 11764, pp. 120–128. Springer, Cham (2019). https://doi.org/10.1007/978-3-030-32239-7_14
9. Ben-Cohen, A., Mark, D., et al.: Retinal layers segmentation using fully convolutional network in OCT images (2017)
10. Liefers, B., González-Gonzalo, et al.: Dense segmentation in selected dimensions: application to retinal optical coherence tomography. In: MIDL, pp. 337–346 (2019)
11. Roy, A.G., Conjeti, S., et al.: ReLayNet: retinal layer and fluid segmentation of macular optical coherence tomography using fully convolutional networks. Biomed. Opt. Exp. **8**(8), 3627–3642 (2017)
12. Qu, G., Zhang, W., et al.: StripNet: towards topology consistent strip structure segmentation. In: ACM MM, pp. 283–291 (2018)
13. Devalla, S.K., Renukanand, P.K., Sreedhar, B.K., Subramanian, G., Zhang, L., et al.: DRUNET: a dilated-residual U-Net deep learning network to segment optic nerve head tissues in optical coherence tomography images. Biomed. Opt. Exp. **9**(7), 3244–3265 (2018)
14. Ronneberger, O., Fischer, P., Brox, T.: U-Net: convolutional networks for biomedical image segmentation. In: Navab, N., Hornegger, J., Wells, W.M., Frangi, A.F. (eds.) MICCAI 2015. LNCS, vol. 9351, pp. 234–241. Springer, Cham (2015). https://doi.org/10.1007/978-3-319-24574-4_28

15. Montesano, G., Bryan, S.R., et al.: A comparison between the compass fundus perimeter and the Humphrey Field Analyzer. Ophthalmology **126**(2), 242–251 (2019)
16. Chiu, S.J., Allingham, M.J., et al.: Kernel regression based segmentation of optical coherence tomography images with diabetic macular edema. Biomed. Opt. Exp. **6**(4), 1172–1194 (2015)
17. Romero, A., Drozdzal, M., Erraqabi, A., Jégou, S., Bengio, Y.: Image Segmentation by Iterative Inference from Conditional Score Estimation. CoRR abs/1705.07450 (2017)
18. Wang, X., Girshick, R., et al.: Non-local neural networks. In: Computer Vision and Pattern Recognition (CVPR) (2017)
19. Kim, J., On, K.W., et al.: Hadamard product for low-rank bilinear pooling. In: International Conference on Learning Representations (ICLR) (2017)
20. Ioffe, S., Szegedy, C.: Batch normalization: accelerating deep network training by reducing internal covariate shift. ICML **5**(4), 1062–1074 (2015)
21. Alexe, K., Sutskever, I., Hinton, G.: ImageNet classification with deep convolutional neural networks. In: NIPS, vol. 5, no. 4, pp. 1062–1074 (2012)
22. Badrinarayanan, V., Kendall, A., et al.: SegNet: a deep convolutional encoder-decoder architecture for image segmentation. IEEE Trans. Pattern Recogn. Mach. Intell. (TPAMI) **39**, 2481–2495 (2015)
23. Oktay, O., Schlemper, J., et al.: Attention U-Net: learning where to look for the pancreas. In: Medical Imaging with Deep Learning (MIDL) (2018)
24. Loshchilov, I., Hutter, F.: Decoupled weight decay regularization. In: ICLR (2019)

DR Detection Using Optical Coherence Tomography Angiography (OCTA): A Transfer Learning Approach with Robustness Analysis

Rayna Andreeva[1]([✉]), Alessandro Fontanella[1], Ylenia Giarratano[2], and Miguel O. Bernabeu[2]

[1] School of Informatics, University of Edinburgh, Edinburgh, UK
R.Andreeva@sms.ed.ac.uk
[2] Centre for Medical Informatics, Usher Institute, University of Edinburgh, Edinburgh, UK

Abstract. OCTA imaging is an emerging modality for the discovery of retinal biomarkers in systemic disease. Several studies have already shown the potential of deep learning algorithms in the medical domain. However, they generally require large amount of manually graded images which may not always be available. In our study, we aim to investigate whether transfer learning can help in identifying patient status from a relatively small dataset. Additionally, we explore if data augmentation may help in improving our classification accuracy. Finally, for the first time, we propose a validation of our model on OCTA images acquired with a different device. OCTA scans from three different groups of participants were analysed: diabetic with and without retinopathy (DR and NoDR, respectively) and healthy subjects. We used the convolutional neural network architecture VGG16 and achieved 83.29% accuracy when classifying DR, NoDR and Controls. Our results demonstrate how transfer learning enables fairly accurate OCTA scan classification and augmentation based on geometric transformations helps in improving the classification accuracy further. Finally, we show how our model maintains consistent performance across OCTA imaging devices, without any re-training.

Keywords: Optical coherence tomography angiography · Transfer learning · OCTA devices · Diabetic retinopathy

1 Introduction

There is an estimated number of more than 20 million people in the UK suffering from at least one long-term condition [19]. If the current trend continues, this figure is projected to increase by more than 20% in the next 5 years [5]. The result of the surge would be to further aggravate the economic, social and

R. Andreeva and A. Fontanella—these authors contributed equally.

© Springer Nature Switzerland AG 2020
H. Fu et al. (Eds.): OMIA 2020, LNCS 12069, pp. 11–20, 2020.
https://doi.org/10.1007/978-3-030-63419-3_2

human burden on the National Health Service (NHS) [19]. Some of these long-term conditions could be mitigated if early detection was in place to encourage prevention methods such as changes in lifestyle and diet. Hence, there is a need for the discovery of biomarkers in the early stages of disease and therefore the latest Artificial Intelligence (AI) technologies could be utilised for identification of people who can benefit from preventative therapies, improve patients outcomes and reduce costs if implemented in clinical practice.

A potential source for disease biomarkers are the changes in microvasculature which have been linked to multiple pathological conditions like diabetes, chronic kidney disease (CKD) and Alzheimer's disease. In particular, the only place in the human body where it is possible to observe the blood vessels in a non-invasive manner with a simple instrument is the retina [19]. A number of recent studies have identified the potential of retinal imaging as a tool for early detection of systemic disease [28]. Indeed, the changes in retinal microvasculature which can be detected on the scans are indicators not only of eye disease, but also for disease of the body. Diabetic retinopathy (DR), neurodegenerative disease, cardiovascular disease and CKD are some of the diseases which have been found to leave a footprint on the retina, often prior to the development of clinically identifiable symptoms [3,10,19]. Hence, focusing on the information provided by structural changes in retinal blood vessels can be useful for early diagnosis and better medical treatment. In this work we focus on DR, a diabetes complication that may cause vision loss to the patient.

Optical coherence tomography angiography (OCTA) has emerged recently in the retina imaging domain with the advantage of being a non-invasive and rapid imaging modality. It provides *in vivo* scans of multiple layers of the retina and an insight into the microvasculature by constructing a map of the blood flow. Quantifiable features can be extracted from the OCTA images which are valuable biomarkers for various disease. Studies have identified the usefulness of candidate biomarkers for distinguishing between healthy and DR eyes. Examples include foveal avascular zone (FAZ) area, FAZ contour irregularity [13,25], vessel caliber, fractal dimension, tortuosity, density and geometric features of the vascular network [1,2,14,22]. Moreover, vessel density has been useful for identifying CKD [27] and both vessel density and perfusion density for Alzheimer's

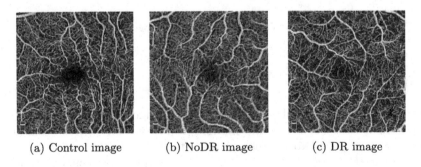

(a) Control image   (b) NoDR image   (c) DR image

Fig. 1. OCTA scans from Control, DR and NoDR patients

disease [30,31]. Example of Controls, DR and NoDR images are provided in Fig. 1, where the NoDR label refers to diabetic patients without retinopathy.

Deep learning as a subfield of machine learning has shown remarkable results in image classification tasks. The main advantage of deep learning models is that hand-crafted features are not required. In fact, features are extracted automatically in the process, saving time from doing feature engineering and removing the need for identifying disease biomarkers in advance. However, such systems require large amounts of labeled data for training. As a new imaging modality, OCTA datasets are usually small in size. Therefore, an approach known as transfer learning has been adopted, which has been established to have strong performance, especially when dealing with domains with limited data [9,24,32].

Machine learning methods have shown promising results in the quest to improve medical evaluations and patient outcomes. However, these models sometimes fail to replicate their results in real world clinical settings [4], where interoperator variability and data quality issues are more common than in highly controlled laboratory environments. In particular, the OCTA technology is based on proprietary algorithms and no standard has emerged yet for image generation, and as such different manufacturers of OCTA devices exploit different algorithms [6]. As a result, the various OCTA devices on the market differ in quality, resolution and size of the images they generate. Moreover, even images collected with the same device may present shifts in their distribution, due to interoperator variability or cooperation of patients during the examination [12,20]. Hence, a validation of the generalisation ability of the model is required to verify clinical robustness and reliability [21].

In this study we investigate the feasibility of using deep learning for determining patient status in DR, a disease with a known vascular footprint, using a small cross-sectional dataset of OCTA images. First, we investigated whether transfer learning can address the issue related to the limited size of our dataset and achieve competitive performance in disease classification. Secondly, we explored if geometric transformations improve classification performance. Thirdly, we validated our model on a dataset from a different OCTA device to test its robustness. Novel contributions of this study are the ability to independently classify diabetic eyes with and without retinopathy and the validation of the consistency in the classification accuracy of our model on a dataset composed of OCTA images collected with a different imaging device.

2   Methods

2.1   Datasets and Imaging Devices

The first dataset in the study, NHS Lothian, consists of three groups: diabetic with and without retinopathy (13 DR an 13 NoDR, respectively) and 31 age- and gender-matched healthy subjects (Controls). From each patient we considered both left and right eye whenever available, in order to increase the size of the dataset. Therefore, a total of 51 images from diabetic participants (26 DR and 25 NoDR) and 56 Control images were analysed. The scans were captured by a commercial Optovue RTVue XR Avanti system (Optovue Inc., Fremont, CA). In this study, only images of the superficial layer with 3×3 field of view (FOV) and 304×304 pixel resolution were analysed.

The second dataset used is a publicly available dataset of OCTA images, OCTAGON [8]. The dataset consists of 144 healthy and 69 diabetic OCTA images, captured using the DRI OCT Triton system (Topcon Corp, Tokyo, Japan). As in the previous analysis we used images of 3×3 FOV superficial depth level with 320×320 pixel resolution of 36 controls and 19 diabetic subjects. Scans of both eyes of the patients were used whenever they were available.

2.2 Data Augmentation and Transfer Learning

Several studies have shown the effectiveness of deep learning architectures on imaging tasks. However, these networks usually require a large amount of labeled data to avoid overfitting. In our work, we are dealing with particularly small datasets. A possible solution to this problem is data augmentation [26]. Several augmentation techniques are possible, but in our work we focused on geometric transformations on the input space. For DR classification, we selected zoom in the range $[0.8, 1.2]$ and rotations up to $40°$ as the most effective transformations. Furthermore, we performed online data augmentation, meaning that each training batch is augmented at every epoch during training, removing the constraints on the memory requirements. Performances are then computed by averaging results from a 5-fold cross-validation. To tackle the issues related to the limited size of our datasets we used a transfer learning approach: considering a convolutional neural network trained with a bottom-up approach, after pre-training with ImageNet we kept the weights of the bottom layers and re-trained only the last convolutional layers to achieve faster learning. In particular, as in [15], we fine-tuned the last 7 convolutional layers. As required by VGG16 input size, images were resized to 224×224 pixels. RmsProp optimizer with a starting learning rate of 1×10^{-5} was used to train the model for 200 epochs. Throughout the study, the metrics used to evaluate the classification performance of the models are accuracy, sensitivity, specificity and area under the Receiver operating characteristic (ROC) curve.

3 Results

3.1 Classification of Controls, DR and NoDR Patients

Evaluation metrics of the model (with and without augmentation) classifying Controls, DR and NoDR subjects on NHS Lothian are reported in Table 1.

The average ROC curves obtained with and without data augmentation are showed in Fig. 2. Data augmentation helps in improving the average classification accuracy from 78.38% to 83.29%. The effectiveness of transfer learning is then verified by comparing the model with a new one with the same CNN architecture as VGG16, but with random initialisation of the weights. The latter achieves only 50.00% accuracy.

Table 1. Table of classification performances in the DR study with standard error

	Controls		DR		NoDR	
	Without augm	With augm	Without augm	With augm	Without augm	With augm
Acc %	75.75 ± 2.30	83.03 ± 4.45	88.74 ± 2.20	85.89 ± 3.59	77.58 ± 4.66	85.89 ± 3.04
Sen %	89.70 ± 5.46	92.73 ± 3.04	60.76 ± 14.27	59.62 ± 13.88	32.67 ± 3.00	58.50 ± 11.17
Spe %	60.73 ± 2.90	72.36 ± 6.67	95.39 ± 1.82	92.04 ± 3.59	91.37 ± 3.94	96.53 ± 2.02

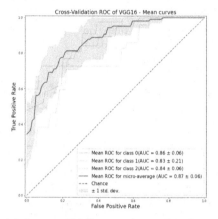

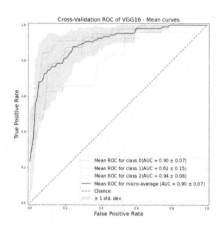

(a) Average ROC curve obtained without data augmentation

(b) Average ROC curve obtained with data augmentation

Fig. 2. Average ROC curves obtained when classifying Controls, DR and NoDR patients

3.2 Model Validation on OCTAGON Dataset

The generalisation ability of the model in classifying OCTA scans from different devices is tested using the OCTAGON dataset with the following two labels: diabetic and Control. For this reason, we classified diabetic patients, combining DR and NoDR in the same class. We repeated the previous analysis on NHS Lothian dataset by combining DR and NoDR in the same class, achieving 87.33% and 84.24% classification accuracy, with and without data augmentation respectively. Using the model without data augmentation on the OCTAGON dataset, the accuracy drops to 83.64% (Table 2a). Moreover, we test the model pre-trained on ImageNet and fine-tuned on OCTAGON without data augmentation (Table 3a).

The model trained on NHS Lothian with data augmentation achieves the classification statistics displayed in Table 2b when classifying Controls vs Diabetes on OCTAGON images. Interestingly, we can observe how in this case the accuracy drops significantly, from 87.33% achieved when classifying Controls vs Diabetes on NHS Lothian, to 63.64% when performing the same classification task on OCTAGON data. A possible explanation for this could be that data augmentation may push the images of NHS Lothian even further from the

Table 2. Classification statistics (with standard error) obtained classifying Controls vs Diabetes on OCTAGON dataset, using VGG16 pre-trained on ImageNet and fine-tuned on NHS Lothian

	Diabetes
Overall Acc %	83.64 ± 4.74
Sen %	77.50 ± 7.75
Spe %	95.00 ± 4.47

(a) Model fine-tuned on NHS Lothian without data augmentation

	Diabetes
Overall Acc %	63.64 ± 5.75
Sen %	43.57 ± 9.50
Spe %	100.00 ± 0.00

(b) Model fine-tuned on NHS Lothian with data augmentation

Table 3. Classification statistics (with standard error) obtained classifying Controls vs Diabetes on OCTAGON dataset, using VGG16 pre-trained on ImageNet and fine-tuned on OCTAGON

	Diabetes
Overall Acc %	87.27 ± 4.15
Sen %	75.00 ± 14.14
Spe %	94.64 ± 2.95

(a) Model fine-tuned on OCTAGON without data augmentation

	Diabetes
Overall Acc %	90.91 ± 3.64
Sen %	80.00 ± 10.95
Spe %	97.5 ± 2.24

(b) Model fine-tuned on OCTAGON with data augmentation

distribution of images in OCTAGON and thus worsen the classification accuracy on the latter dataset.

On the other hand, the model only pre-trained on ImageNet and fine-tuned on OCTAGON with data augmentation, achieves an accuracy of 90.91% (±3.64%), as showed in Table 3b. In this case, data augmentation helps in improving the performance since test images are from the same distribution of the training set, on which the model was fine-tuned.

4   Discussion and Conclusions

In the current study, we investigated the non-invasive detection of DR in OCTA retinal scans using deep learning. In order to address the limited size of our datasets, we employed a transfer learning approach. We also verified how our model can be successfully applied to a different dataset - OCTAGON. In particular, we achieved 83.29% (±4.31%) accuracy when classifying DR, NoDR and Controls with data augmentation and pre-training from ImageNet. On the other hand, if we start to train our model from scratch, giving a random initialisation to the weights, classification accuracy decreases significantly. For this reason, we can confidently assert that transfer learning plays a critical role in achieving a satisfactory classification performance.

Our novel contributions were the ability to independently classify diabetic eyes with and without retinopathy and the investigation of the consistency in the classification accuracy of our model on a dataset composed of OCTA images collected with a different imaging device. In particular, we verified how our model pre-trained on ImageNet and fine-tuned on NHS Lothian is able to achieve satisfactory performance in classifying OCTAGON images without re-training. Model robustness is a fundamental aspect when deploying AI screening tools to critical settings such as predictive healthcare, where it can essentially be life-critical [21].

In [15], the authors used transfer learning with VGG16 architecture to detect DR from OCTA images. They reported an accuracy of 87.28%, using a dataset of 131 OCTA images, thus achieving a slightly higher accuracy, but with a bigger dataset than in our work. Other authors have classified DR using fundus images. They achieved classification accuracy comparable to our study, but using considerably larger datasets. This imaging modality is usually not able to reveal subtle abnormalities correlated with early DR [15], as we were able when independently classifying diabetic eyes with and without retinopathy. In particular, Sayres et al. reported a 88.4% accuracy in DR classification on a dataset of 1,796 retinal fundus images from 1,612 diabetic patients using Inception-V4 architecture [23]. In [16], the authors achieved a high classification accuracy of 93.49% using Inception-V3 architecture. They had available 8,816 fundus images from 5,278 patients. Lin et al. used a CNN with 4 convolutional layers and obtained 86.10% accuracy with a datset of 21,123 fundus photographs [18]. In [17], the authors used a cross-disease attention network to grade both DR and diabetic macular edema (DME) by exploring the relationship between the two diseases. Their method, trained on the 1200 fundus images of Messidor [7] dataset, achieved 92.6% average accuracy over ten folds. Wang et al. [29] employed a network called Zoom-in-Net to generate attention maps highlighting suspicious regions and Detecting DR. They achieved 90.5 classifying referable/nonreferable DR on Messidor. Efforts in the automated classification of DR on the basis of researched biomarkers have been suggested in [1], where the authors extracted six quantitative features from the images and used them to train a support vector machine (SVM) in order to detect DR. In general, statistical learning methods rely on manual image segmentation, which lacks consistency [11] and could lead to errors, to perform feature extraction. On the other hand, deep learning methods have the advantage that they can directly process the raw images as input.

From the satisfactory results obtained when applying our model on a different dataset, we can argue that a deep learning system for automatic detection of DR, applicable to images collected with any OCTA device, can be achieved. Limitations of our work are the use of a modest dataset size and the inclusion of both left and right eye from the same participant as independent samples. Future works will validate our procedure on larger cohorts and will account for possible correlations between eyes.

In summary, we were able to verify how transfer learning techniques are useful to tackle the issue related to the limited size of OCTA datasets and achieve satisfactory performance when detecting DR and NoDR, how geometric data augmentation helps in improving the performance further and how our approach maintains consistent performance across different OCTA devices.

Acknowledgement. RA and AF are supported by the United Kingdom Research and Innovation (grant EP/S02431X/1), UKRI Centre for Doctoral Training in Biomedical AI at the University of Edinburgh, School of Informatics. YG is supported by the Medical Research Council (MRC). MOB is supported by grants from EPSRC (EP/R029598/1, EP/R021600/1, EP/T008806/1), Fondation Leducq (17 CVD 03), and the European Union's Horizon 2020 research and innovation programme under grant agreement No 801423.

References

1. Alam, M., Zhang, Y., Lim, J.I., Chan, R.V., Yang, M., Yao, X.: Quantitative optical coherence tomography angiography features for objective classification and staging of diabetic retinopathy. Retina **40**(2), 322–332 (2020)
2. Alam, M.N., Son, T., Toslak, D., Lim, J.I., Yao, X.: Quantitative artery-vein analysis in optical coherence tomography angiography of diabetic retinopathy. In: Ophthalmic Technologies XXIX, vol. 10858, p. 1085802. International Society for Optics and Photonics (2019)
3. Baker, M.L., Hand, P.J., Wang, J.J., Wong, T.Y.: Retinal signs and stroke: revisiting the link between the eye and brain. Stroke **39**(4), 1371–1379 (2008)
4. Beede, E., et al.: A human-centered evaluation of a deep learning system deployed in clinics for the detection of diabetic retinopathy. In: Proceedings of the 2020 CHI Conference on Human Factors in Computing Systems, pp. 1–12 (2020)
5. House of Commons Health Committee and others: Managing the care of people with long-term conditions. Second report of session, vol. 1, pp. 1–89 (2014)
6. Cunha-Vaz, J.G., Koh, A.: Imaging Techniques, vol. 10, pp. 52–64 (2018). https://doi.org/10.1159/000487412
7. Decencière, E., et al.: Feedback on a publicly distributed image database: the Messidor database. Image Anal. Stereol. **33**(3), 231–234 (2014)
8. Díaz, M., Novo, J., Cutrín, P., Gómez-Ulla, F., Penedo, M.G., Ortega, M.: Automatic segmentation of the foveal avascular zone in ophthalmological OCT-A images. PLOS ONE **14**(2), e0212364 (2019)
9. Donahue, J., et al.: DeCAF: a deep convolutional activation feature for generic visual recognition. In: International Conference on Machine Learning, pp. 647–655 (2014)
10. Frost, S., et al.: Retinal vascular biomarkers for early detection and monitoring of Alzheimer's disease. Transl. Psychiatry **3**(2), e233 (2013)
11. Giarratano, Y., et al.: Automated and Network Structure Preserving Segmentation of Optical Coherence Tomography Angiograms. arXiv preprint arXiv:1912.09978 (2019)
12. Hong, J.T., Sung, K.R., Cho, J.W., Yun, S.C., Kang, S.Y., Kook, M.S.: Retinal nerve fiber layer measurement variability with spectral domain optical coherence tomography. Korean J. Ophthalmol. **26**(1), 32–38 (2012)

13. Khadamy, J., Aghdam, K.A., Falavarjani, K.G.: An update on optical coherence tomography angiography in diabetic retinopathy. J. Ophthalmic Vis. Res. **13**(4), 487 (2018)
14. Le, D., Alam, M., Miao, B.A., Lim, J.I., Yao, X.: Fully automated geometric feature analysis in optical coherence tomography angiography for objective classification of diabetic retinopathy. Biomed. Opt. Exp. **10**(5), 2493–2503 (2019)
15. Le, D., Alam, M.N., Lim, J.I., Chan, R., Yao, X.: Deep learning for objective OCTA detection of diabetic retinopathy. In: Ophthalmic Technologies XXX, vol. 11218, p. 112181P. International Society for Optics and Photonics (2020)
16. Li, F., Liu, Z., Chen, H., Jiang, M., Zhang, X., Wu, Z.: Automatic detection of diabetic retinopathy in retinal fundus photographs based on deep learning algorithm. Trans. Vis. Sci. Technol. **8**(6), 4 (2019)
17. Li, X., Hu, X., Yu, L., Zhu, L., Fu, C.W., Heng, P.A.: CANet: cross-disease attention network for joint diabetic retinopathy and diabetic macular edema grading. IEEE Trans. Med. Imaging **39**(5), 1483–1493 (2019)
18. Lin, G.M., et al.: Transforming retinal photographs to entropy images in deep learning to improve automated detection for diabetic retinopathy. J. Ophthalmol. **2018**, 1–6 (2018)
19. MacGillivray, T., Trucco, E., Cameron, J., Dhillon, B., Houston, J., Van Beek, E.: Retinal imaging as a source of biomarkers for diagnosis, characterization and prognosis of chronic illness or long-term conditions. Br. J. Radiol. **87**(1040), 20130832 (2014)
20. Mwanza, J.C., Gendy, M.G., Feuer, W.J., Shi, W., Budenz, D.L.: Effects of changing operators and instruments on time-domain and spectral-domain OCT measurements of retinal nerve fiber layer thickness. Ophthalmic Surg. Lasers Imaging Retina **42**(4), 328–337 (2011)
21. Qayyum, A., Qadir, J., Bilal, M., Al-Fuqaha, A.: Secure and robust machine learning for healthcare: A survey. arXiv preprint arXiv:2001.08103 (2020)
22. Sasongko, M., Wong, T., Nguyen, T., Cheung, C., Shaw, J., Wang, J.: Retinal vascular tortuosity in persons with diabetes and diabetic retinopathy. Diabetologia **54**(9), 2409–2416 (2011)
23. Sayres, R., et al.: Using a deep learning algorithm and integrated gradients explanation to assist grading for diabetic retinopathy. Ophthalmology **126**(4), 552–564 (2019)
24. Sharif Razavian, A., Azizpour, H., Sullivan, J., Carlsson, S.: CNN features off-the-shelf: an astounding baseline for recognition. In: Proceedings of the IEEE Conference on Computer Vision and Pattern Recognition Workshops, pp. 806–813 (2014)
25. Takase, N., Nozaki, M., Kato, A., Ozeki, H., Yoshida, M., Ogura, Y.: Enlargement of foveal avascular zone in diabetic eyes evaluated by en face optical coherence tomography angiography. Retina **35**(11), 2377–2383 (2015)
26. Tanner, M.A., Wong, W.H.: The calculation of posterior distributions by data augmentation. J. Am. Stat. Assoc. **82**(398), 528–540 (1987)
27. Vadalà, M., Castellucci, M., Guarrasi, G., Terrasi, M., La Blasca, T., Mulè, G.: Retinal and choroidal vasculature changes associated with chronic kidney disease. Graefe's Arch. Clin. Exp. Ophthalmol. **257**(8), 1687–1698 (2019)
28. Wagner, S.K., et al.: Insights into systemic disease through retinal imaging-based oculomics. Trans. Vis. Sci. Technol. **9**(2), 6 (2020)

29. Wang, Z., Yin, Y., Shi, J., Fang, W., Li, H., Wang, X.: Zoom-in-Net: deep mining lesions for diabetic retinopathy detection. In: Descoteaux, M., Maier-Hein, L., Franz, A., Jannin, P., Collins, D.L., Duchesne, S. (eds.) MICCAI 2017. LNCS, vol. 10435, pp. 267–275. Springer, Cham (2017). https://doi.org/10.1007/978-3-319-66179-7_31

30. Yao, X., Alam, M.N., Le, D., Toslak, D.: Quantitative optical coherence tomography angiography: a review. Exp. Biol. Med. **245**(4), 301–312 (2020). https://doi.org/10.1177/1535370219899893. pMID: 31958986

31. Yoon, S.P., et al.: Retinal microvascular and neurodegenerative changes in Alzheimer's disease and mild cognitive impairment compared with control participants. Ophthalmol. Retina **3**(6), 489–499 (2019)

32. Yosinski, J., Clune, J., Bengio, Y., Lipson, H.: How transferable are features in deep neural networks? In: Advances in Neural Information Processing Systems, pp. 3320–3328 (2014)

What is the Optimal Attribution Method for Explainable Ophthalmic Disease Classification?

Amitojdeep Singh[1,2]([✉]), Sourya Sengupta[1,2], Jothi Balaji J.[3],
Abdul Rasheed Mohammed[1], Ibrahim Faruq[1], Varadharajan Jayakumar[1],
John Zelek[2], and Vasudevan Lakshminarayanan[1,2]

[1] Theoretical and Experimental Epistemology Lab (TEEL), School of Optometry
and Vision Science, University of Waterloo, Waterloo, Canada
amitojdeep.singh@uwaterloo.ca
[2] Department of Systems Design Engineering, University of Waterloo,
Waterloo, Canada
[3] Department of Optometry, Medical Research Foundation, Sankara Nethralaya,
Chennai, India

Abstract. Deep learning methods for ophthalmic diagnosis have shown success for tasks like segmentation and classification but their implementation in the clinical setting is limited by the black-box nature of the algorithms. Very few studies have explored the explainability of deep learning in this domain. Attribution methods explain the decisions by assigning a relevance score to each input feature. Here, we present a comparative analysis of multiple attribution methods to explain the decisions of a convolutional neural network (CNN) in retinal disease classification from OCT images. This is the first such study to perform both quantitative and qualitative analyses. The former was performed using robustness, runtime, and sensitivity while the latter was done by a panel of eye care clinicians who rated the methods based on their correlation with diagnostic features. The study emphasizes the need for developing explainable models that address the end-user requirements, hence increasing the clinical acceptance of deep learning.

Keywords: Explainability · XAI · Deep learning · Attributions · Image classification · Clinical ophthalmology · Retina · OCT

1 Introduction

There is a widespread shortage of trained medical professionals leading to longer wait times and unavailability of medical aid to remote communities. The situation is especially acute in developing countries. It is critical to have an early diagnosis for retinal diseases such as glaucoma where delayed treatment can cause irreversible vision loss. Automated screening and diagnostic assistance

© Springer Nature Switzerland AG 2020
H. Fu et al. (Eds.): OMIA 2020, LNCS 12069, pp. 21–31, 2020.
https://doi.org/10.1007/978-3-030-63419-3_3

using computer-aided methods like deep learning have been suggested as a potential solution to make the diagnosis faster and more accessible. These methods can be used to assist the clinicians in making more accurate and faster decisions.

Despite the emergence of many deep learning methods for retinal diagnosis [1,2] their adoption in clinical settings is very limited [3]. The main hurdle is the lack of trust of the expert end-users, regulators, and the patients due to the black-box nature of the algorithms. These models can detect diseases with high accuracy which is often comparable to human experts [4] but can not explain the logic for their decision. There are a very limited number of studies for explaining the retinal diagnosis performed by deep learning models [5–7]. There are studies evaluating the impact of explainability on machine learning practitioners [8] and for comparing attribution methods quantitatively [9,10]. However, to the best of our knowledge, there is no study evaluating multiple attribution methods both quantitatively and qualitatively for retinal disease diagnosis.

In this study, we performed a quantitative analysis of the attribution methods using multiple measures - robustness, runtime, and sensitivity. The quantitative analysis is important to understand the ability of an attribution method to highlight the features according to their impact on the model output. However, we strongly believe that for any explainability method to be successfully used in the field it must be evaluated by trained experts as an assistive tool. A panel of retinal experts consisting of ophthalmologists and optometrists evaluated the methods for their ability to justify the predicted class in terms of the similarity to the clinical concepts. The use of attributions as a tool to improve the models and inculcate the trust of clinician end-users through visualizations is discussed in this study.

Section 2 describes the studies on explainability and more specifically the applications for retinal diagnosis. Commonly used Inception-v3 [11] architecture was trained on the large UCSD optical coherence tomography (OCT) dataset [12] to classify images among 4 classes - choroidal neovascularization (CNV), diabetic macular edema (DME), drusen and normal. CNV refers to the formation of new leaky blood vessels in the choroid beneath the retina, DME is the accumulation of fluid in the most visually active region called the macula, and drusen are the yellowish deposits of lipids and proteins under the retina. The experiment is discussed in Sect. 3, the analyses are described in Sect. 4 and the findings are concluded in Sect. 5 with directions for future research.

2   Related Studies

It is imperative for both the machine learning practitioners and the end-users to observe the relevant features used by an artificial intelligence (AI) system for making decisions. Explaining the diagnostic and treatment decisions to all the parties involved is an integral part of the modern healthcare system. The ethical and legal challenges of the domain require decisions to be more transparent, explainable, and understandable for the users. This has lead to advances in the development of Explainable AI (XAI) systems for medical diagnosis [13].

The key challenges and opportunities for XAI are presented in [14] and a detailed categorization of the methods is provided in [15]. [16] discussed the applications of explainability in the medical imaging and highlighted a need for evaluation of these methods by end-users.

Deep learning methods are used for tasks like classification, segmentation, image enhancement, and image generation from retinal images captured by two common modalities - fundus camera and OCT scans. The classification problem deals with detection of diseases like glaucoma, diabetic retinopathy (DR), and age related macular degeneration (AMD) from retinal images. Segmentation involves identifying regions of interest such as optic cup and disc, retinal layers, drusen deposits, etc. Image enhancement refers to denoising OCT scans, increasing the details with super-resolution, and generation of synthetic data for model training. Reviews of deep learning methods for ophthalmic diagnosis are available in [1,2,17,18]. IDx-DR was a method for DR classification from fundus images [3] which received FDA approval.

In a study for weakly-supervised segmentation of lesions for AMD diagnosis [5], an extension of Integrated gradients (IG) called Expressive gradients (EG) was proposed. The EG method added the high-level attributions to the input only attributions of IG, outperforming it when applied along with a relatively small custom CNN. The impact of the model predictions and attributions generated by IG on DR grading by ophthalmologists was studied in [6]. The combination of class probabilities and attributions was found to be the most effective in improving the grading accuracy of the users compared to only the probabilities or no assistance. The grading time of the users increased initially but it reduced from the initial levels after prolonged use of the assistance showing the potential to increase the patient throughput and improve the diagnosis simultaneously.

Recent studies have looked into the quantitative analysis of multiple attribution methods [9,19] in terms of the theoretical principles. A study in the domain of brain imaging [10] performed a robustness analysis to measure the repeatability of the attributions generated by various methods. Motivated by the findings of these as well as the studies for explainable retinal diagnosis [5,6], we explore the efficacy of different attribution methods to highlight the clinically relevant regions of the images. Instead of evaluating them as a tool for weakly-supervised segmentation and then comparing with markings of a clinician, we suggest their use as a framework for understanding the model - data interactions and assisting clinical end-users.

3   Methods

The UCSD OCT dataset [12] was used to train an Inception-v3 [11] network and generate the attributions. It consisted of 83.4k training images from four classes - CNV (37.2k), DME (11.3k), drusen (8.6k) and normal (26.3k). The test set of 1000 images had 250 images from each class. The Inception-v3 model was chosen due to its prevalence in medical imaging, especially ophthalmic diagnosis [20–22], due to ease of implementation and availability of pre-trained weights.

The model was trained from random weights to avoid any irrelevant features from pre-trained models. The test accuracy for the ten training instances ranged between 99.00% and 99.90% with an average of 99.42%.

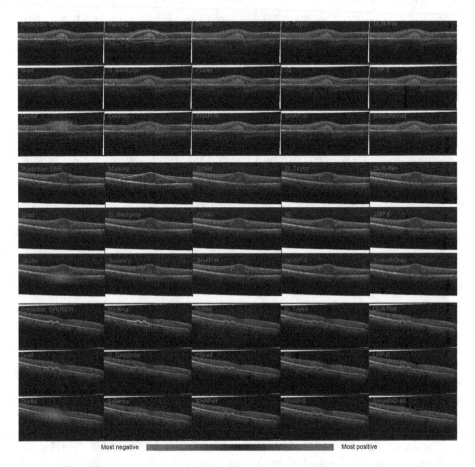

Fig. 1. Sample attributions for CNV, DME and drusen images (from top to bottom) with each original image in top left and reference clinical marking in right of 2nd row.

The attributions were generated using variants of DeconvNet [23], Saliency maps [24], Guided backpropagation (GBP) [25], Layer wise relevance propagation (LRP) [26], gradient times input, IG [27], DeepTaylor [28], Deep Learning Important FeaTures (DeepLIFT) [29], SmoothGrad [30], DeepSHapley Additive exPlanations (SHAP) [31] as well as the baselines from gradient and occlusion. Three libraries were used for implementation of these methods - Innvestigate [32], Deep Explain [19], and SHAP [31]. Some of the sample explanations for each class along with reference clinician markings are provided in Fig. 1. Note that some images of the source dataset were already cropped and rotated.

For LRP, the ϵ rule was used while DeepLIFT was used in the original rescale variant implemented by Ancona et al. [19]. The reveal cancel rule of DeepLIFT in [33] was incompatible with the bias term of the Inception model. SHAP was the only model that required background distribution and we selected a random set of 20 normal images for the same denoting it as *SHAP random*. It was observed to be sensitive to artifacts and noise in the background images. Hence, another variant with 20 normal images with low noise and artifacts was also used and denoted as *SHAP selected*. A window size of 64×64 and a step size of 16 were used for occlusion as the runtime is very high when every pixel is perturbed separately.

4   Analysis

The attributions generated by all the methods have been analyzed both quantitatively and qualitatively and are discussed in this section.

4.1   Quantitative Analysis

The quantitative evaluation of attribution methods is tedious in absence of ground truth unlike those for conventional segmentation tasks. The robustness of a given method between the trained model weights [10] and sensitivity analysis [19,34] were performed to compare the various attribution methods. All 1000 images of the test set were used for the robustness analysis to achieve better estimates while 80 images (20 per class) were used for sensitivity analysis due to computational constraints.

Robustness Between Models and Runtime: The root mean squared error (RMSE) between the attributions of a method from all pairs of 10 separately trained instances of the model was used as a measure of robustness. Ideally, the models would have learned similar features for all the runs and the attribution methods would, therefore, provide similar results. However, the stochastic nature of model training and the algorithmic differences between the attribution methods leads to non-zero RMSE values as shown in Table 1. The DeepLIFT rescale rule had the least RMSE followed by SHAP selected, while SHAP random gave similar to that of SHAP selected. SHAP random had slightly better results for drusen as it highlighted smaller areas as shown in Fig. 1. The gradient had the highest RMSE as it is directly influenced by the variation in the model's features. It should be noted that this analysis inherently favored the methods highlighting a smaller area and was affected by the difference in distributions of attributions despite normalizing them from -1 to 1. The code was run on an Intel Gold 6148 Skylake 2.4 GHz processor with 16 GB RAM and Nvidia Tesla V100 16 GB GPU to benchmark the runtimes. LRP had the least runtime while SHAP random had the most due to high computation cost incurred by having a background of normal images.

Table 1. RMSE between the attributions for different model instances and average runtime

Method	RMSE					Avg. runtime (ms)
	CNV	DME	Drusen	Normal	Total	
DeconvNet	424.74	415.37	400.05	465.75	1705.91	195.78
Deep Taylor	198.06	211.55	187.24	211.77	808.62	114.78
DeepLIFT - Rescale	**79.49**	**70.80**	93.72	**64.77**	**308.77**	181.89
Gradient	493.56	457.87	432.02	438.49	1821.93	118.00
GBP	267.25	277.97	240.25	285.48	1070.95	116.56
Input × Gradient	392.54	378.22	343.07	371.32	1485.15	255.67
IG	368.8	347.24	311.86	346.18	1374.07	629.89
LRP - ϵ	392.34	378.09	342.89	371.18	1484.50	**72.44**
Occlusion 64	196.36	306.85	441.94	598.44	1543.59	1125.65
Saliency	107.67	86.60	112.78	84.59	391.64	146.89
SHAP - Random	117.19	85.89	**93.29**	65.83	362.20	1542.67
SHAP - Selected	122.48	75.08	99.41	63.90	360.87	1136.33
SmoothGrad	465.35	429.34	405.97	409.66	1710.32	364.89

Sensitivity Analysis: It does not suffer the pitfalls of robustness and is a better indicator of the top features identified by an attribution method. The pixels in the original image were ranked by their attribution value and removed sequentially by setting them to 0. The value of a pixel provided its relative importance and was expected to have a positive correlation to its contribution

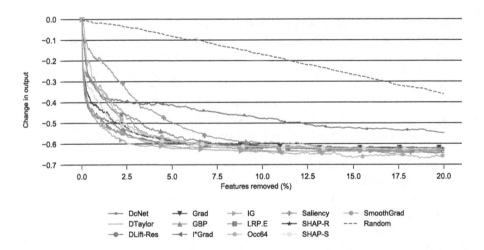

Fig. 2. Sensitivity analysis by removing the top features of each attribution map and observing the effect on the output neuron. The methods with lower curves identify the relevant features better. The random selection of features shows a linear effect.

to the output. The faster the drop in target neuron value on eliminating the top pixels, the better a method was able to rank the most important pixels and hence more sensitive to the output of the target neuron [19,35]. The analysis was performed for the top 20% of the features of the same weights. Due to the small area of pathology, it resulted in asymptotic curves beyond the 10% mark as shown in Fig. 2. The initial drop was fastest in DeepLIFT and IG but IG continued to be most sensitive till about 10% of top features beyond which occlusion 64 had the most sensitivity. Saliency and deconvnet had the worst performance which is also reflected by their noisy heatmaps as shown in Fig. 2.

4.2   Qualitative Analysis

As discussed earlier, the qualitative analysis provides an evaluation of the methods by the end-users. A method providing explanations that are both quantitatively sound and closer to the regions looked by an expert is likely to have more trust and acceptance. Three expert clinicians with different levels of experience in making diagnoses from OCT rated the explanations from all the attribution methods for 20 images from each of the 3 disease classes from a scale of 0 to 5 with 0 indicating no clinical significance. P1 has clinical optometry experience of more than 25 years and has imaged and reviewed around 2500 retinal images in the last 5 years. P2 is an optometrist with 4 years of clinical experience. P3 has over several years of clinical experience as an ophthalmologist and now as an optometrist.

Figure 3 shows box plots of the ratings given to explanations of different methods. To adjust for harshness, each clinician's ratings are normalized by the respective average and then the minimum of all clinicians' ratings is added to them. It was observed that the clinicians preferred Deep Taylor with a mean rating of 4.42 due to clinically coherent explanations, better coverage of pathology, and lack of high-frequency noise. GBP had a mean of 3.79 while SHAP-selected had marginally better mean of 2.85 compared to 2.81 of SHAP-random.

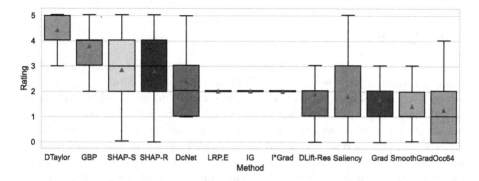

Fig. 3. The box plots of the normalized ratings of the clinicians for explanations of different methods sorted by mean (red marker). Deep Taylor and GBP had the high mean and short whiskers indicating consistently good ratings. (Color figure online)

LRP, IG, and input × gradient have a consistent but mediocre rating of around 2, and occlusion performed the worst as expected. It was observed that the ratings of methods changed over pathologies, e.g. SHAP performed close to Deep Taylor for detecting relatively small drusen deposits as it highlighted smaller areas.

It must be noted that there were differences in rating preferences between the clinicians as shown in Table 2. The clinical experience profile might have some influences on grading OCT especially in the absence of written criteria. P1, with the most experience in OCT grading, gave a lower rating to the methods and gave a more accurate diagnosis. Spearman's rank-order correlation indicated a strong correlation between the ratings of P1 and P3 despite the difference in mean and median values.

Table 2. Statistics of ratings for all data and the best rated method - Deep Taylor

Rater	Mean all	Median all	Mean best	Median best	Spearman ρ
P1	1.30	1	3.15	3	2: 0.11 3: 0.51
P2	2.30	2	4.28	4	1: 0.11 3: 0.22
P3	2.33	2	4.78	5	1: 0.51 2: 0.22

The clinicians pointed out several differences between these methods and actual areas of relevance. It was observed that some low rated methods highlighted the vitreous regions outside the retina as explanations. This is due to the system's lack of awareness about the bounds of the retinal region. P1 pointed out that CNV was the hardest to explain for the methods while drusen had the most consistent results. P2 and P3 highlighted discrepancies in the source data such as lack of information about the cross-sectional plane of scans and incomplete view of the affected region. The clinicians also found secondary diagnosis for 4 out of the 60 images indicating potential noise or confounds in the source data.

5   Conclusion

In this study, we compared 13 different attribution methods for explaining a deep learning model for retinal OCT classification. The quantitative comparison showed high robustness between the models for DeepLIFT and SHAP while IG had marginally more sensitive for detecting the features that impacted the decision the most. However, the qualitative ratings from clinicians showed a clear preference for Deep Taylor which had an above-average quantitative performance and a fast run-times. SHAP achieved a reasonable balance between robustness, sensitivity, and clinical significance but had a high run-time. Our analysis shows that quantitative measures, which are the criteria to benchmark most attribution methods may not align with the needs of the end-users. There is a need to perform more end-user focused studies and develop attribution methods to meet their needs. Another area of work can be to explain the diagnosis using both images and patient data to assimilate the diagnostic process. Overall, there is a consensus from the clinicians that explainability methods can help inculcating trust in deep learning methods and make the diagnosis process more efficient.

Acknowledgement. This work is supported by an NSERC Discovery Grant and NVIDIA Titan V GPU Grant to V.L. This research was enabled in part by Compute Canada (www.computecanada.ca).

References

1. De Fauw, J., et al.: Clinically applicable deep learning for diagnosis and referral in retinal disease. Nat. Med. **24**(9), 1342–1350 (2018)
2. Sengupta, S., Singh, A., Leopold, H.A., Gulati, T., Lakshminarayanan, V.: Ophthalmic diagnosis using deep learning with fundus images-a critical review. Artif. Intell. Med. **102**, 101758 (2020)
3. Abràmoff, M., et al.: Improved automated detection of diabetic retinopathy on a publicly available dataset through integration of deep learning. Invest. Ophthalmol. Vis. Sci. **57**(13), 5200–5206 (2016)
4. Ruamviboonsuk, P., et al.: Deep learning versus human graders for classifying diabetic retinopathy severity in a nationwide screening program. NPJ Digit. Med. **2**(1), 1–9 (2019)
5. Yang, H.L., et al.: Weakly supervised lesion localization for age-related macular degeneration detection using optical coherence tomography images. PLOS One **14**(4), e0215076 (2019)
6. Sayres, R., et al.: Using a deep learning algorithm and integrated gradients explanation to assist grading for diabetic retinopathy. Ophthalmology **126**(4), 552–564 (2019)
7. Singh, A., Sengupta, S., Abdul Rasheed, M., Zelek, J., Lakshminarayanan, V.: Interpretation of deep learning using attributions: application to ophthalmic diagnosis. In: Proceedings of the Applications of Machine Learning. International Society for Optics and Photonics (SPIE) (2020, in press)
8. Kaur, H., Nori, H., Jenkins, S., Caruana, R., Wallach, H., Wortman Vaughan, J.: Interpreting interpretability: understanding data scientists' use of interpretability tools for machine learning. In: Proceedings of the 2020 CHI Conference on Human Factors in Computing Systems, pp. 1–14 (2020). https://doi.org/10.1145/3313831.3376219
9. Wang, Z., Mardziel, P., Datta, A., Fredrikson, M.: Interpreting interpretations: Organizing attribution methods by criteria. arXiv preprint arXiv:2002.07985 (2020)
10. Eitel, F., Ritter, K.: Testing the robustness of attribution methods for convolutional neural networks in MRI-based Alzheimer's disease classification. In: Suzuki, K., et al. (eds.) ML-CDS/IMIMIC - 2019. LNCS, vol. 11797, pp. 3–11. Springer, Cham (2019). https://doi.org/10.1007/978-3-030-33850-3_1
11. Szegedy, C., et al.: Going deeper with convolutions. In: Proceedings of the IEEE Conference on Computer Vision and Pattern Recognition, pp. 1–9 (2015)
12. Kermany, D., Goldbaum, M.: Labeled optical coherence tomography (OCT) and Chest X-Ray images for classification. Mendeley Data, Version 2 (2018).https://doi.org/10.17632/RSCBJBR9SJ.2

13. Holzinger, A., Biemann, C., Pattichis, C.S., Kell, D.B.: What do we need to build explainable AI systems for the medical domain? arXiv preprint arXiv:1712.09923 (2017)
14. Arrieta, A.B., et al.: Explainable artificial intelligence (XAI): concepts, taxonomies, opportunities and challenges toward responsible AI. Inf. Fusion **58**, 82–115 (2020)
15. Stiglic, G., Kocbek, P., Fijacko, N., Zitnik, M., Verbert, K., Cilar, L.: Interpretability of machine learning based prediction models in healthcare. arXiv preprint arXiv:2002.08596 (2020)
16. Singh, A., Sengupta, S., Lakshminarayanan, V.: Explainable deep learning models in medical image analysis. J. Imaging **6**(6), 52 (2020)
17. Leopold, H., Zelek, J., Lakshminarayanan, V.: Deep learning methods applied to retinal image analysis. In: Sejdic, E., Falk, T. (eds.) Signal Processing and Machine Learning for Biomedical Big Data, pp. 329–365. CRC Press (2018)
18. Leopold, H., Sengupta, S., Singh, A., Lakshminarayanan, V.: Deep learning on optical coherence tomography for ophthalmology. In: El-Baz, A. (ed.) State-of-the-Art in Neural Networks. Elsevier, NY (2020)
19. Ancona, M., Ceolini, E., Öztireli, C., Gross, M.: Towards better understanding of gradient-based attribution methods for deep neural networks. arXiv preprint arXiv:1711.06104 (2017)
20. Kermany, D.S., et al.: Identifying medical diagnoses and treatable diseases by image-based deep learning. Cell **172**(5), 1122–1131 (2018)
21. Singh, A., Sengupta, S., Lakshminarayanan, V.: Glaucoma diagnosis using transfer learning methods. In: Proceedings of the Applications of Machine Learning, vol. 11139, p. 111390U. International Society for Optics and Photonics (SPIE) (2019)
22. Sengupta, S., Singh, A., Zelek, J., Lakshminarayanan, V.: Cross-domain diabetic retinopathy detection using deep learning. In: Applications of Machine Learning, vol. 11139, p. 111390V. International Society for Optics and Photonics (2019)
23. Zeiler, M.D., Fergus, R.: Visualizing and understanding convolutional networks. In: Fleet, D., Pajdla, T., Schiele, B., Tuytelaars, T. (eds.) ECCV 2014. LNCS, vol. 8689, pp. 818–833. Springer, Cham (2014). https://doi.org/10.1007/978-3-319-10590-1_53
24. Simonyan, K., Vedaldi, A., Zisserman, A.: Deep inside convolutional networks: Visualising image classification models and saliency maps. arXiv preprint arXiv:1312.6034 (2013)
25. Springenberg, J.T., Dosovitskiy, A., Brox, T., Riedmiller, M.: Striving for simplicity: The all convolutional net. arXiv preprint arXiv:1412.6806 (2014)
26. Bach, S., Binder, A., Montavon, G., Klauschen, F., Müller, K.R., Samek, W.: On pixel-wise explanations for non-linear classifier decisions by layer-wise relevance propagation. PLOS One **10**(7), e0130140 (2015). https://doi.org/10.1371/journal.pone.0130140
27. Sundararajan, M., Taly, A., Yan, Q.: Axiomatic attribution for deep networks. In: Proceedings of the 34th International Conference on Machine Learning, vol. 70, pp. 3319–3328. JMLR.org (2017)
28. Montavon, G., Lapuschkin, S., Binder, A., Samek, W., Müller, K.R.: Explaining nonlinear classification decisions with deep Taylor decomposition. Pattern Recogn. **65**, 211–222 (2017)
29. Shrikumar, A., Greenside, P., Shcherbina, A., Kundaje, A.: Not just a black box: Learning important features through propagating activation differences. arXiv preprint arXiv:1605.01713 (2016)
30. Smilkov, D., Thorat, N., Kim, B., Viégas, F., Wattenberg, M.: SmoothGrad: removing noise by adding noise. arXiv preprint arXiv:1706.03825 (2017)

31. Chen, H., Lundberg, S., Lee, S.I.: Explaining models by propagating Shapley values of local components. arXiv preprint arXiv:1911.11888 (2019)
32. Alber, M., et al.: iNNvestigate neural networks! J. Mach. Learn. Res. **20**(93), 1–8 (2019)
33. Shrikumar, A., Greenside, P., Kundaje, A.: Learning important features through propagating activation differences. In: Proceedings of the 34th International Conference on Machine Learning, vol. 70, pp. 3145–3153. JMLR.org (2017)
34. Ancona, M., Öztireli, C., Gross, M.: Explaining deep neural networks with a polynomial time algorithm for Shapley values approximation. arXiv preprint arXiv:1903.10992 (2019)
35. Samek, W., Binder, A., Montavon, G., Lapuschkin, S., Müller, K.R.: Evaluating the visualization of what a deep neural network has learned. IEEE Trans. Neural Netw. Learn. Syst. **28**(11), 2660–2673 (2016)

DeSupGAN: Multi-scale Feature Averaging Generative Adversarial Network for Simultaneous De-blurring and Super-Resolution of Retinal Fundus Images

Sourya Sengupta[1,2]([⊠]), Alexander Wong[2], Amitojdeep Singh[1,2], John Zelek[2], and Vasudevan Lakshminarayanan[1,2]

[1] Theoretical and Experimental Epistemology Laboratory (TEEL), School of Optometry, Waterloo, Canada
s28sengu@uwaterloo.ca
[2] Systems Design Engineering, University of Waterloo, Waterloo, Canada

Abstract. Image quality is of utmost importance for image-based clinical diagnosis. In this paper, a generative adversarial network-based retinal fundus quality enhancement network is proposed. With the advent of different cheaper, affordable and lighter point-of-care imaging or telemedicine devices, the chances of making a better and more accessible healthcare system in developing countries become higher. But these devices often lack the quality of images. This single network simultaneously takes into account two different image degradation problems that are common i.e. blurring and low spatial resolution. A novel convolutional multi-scale feature averaging block (MFAB) is proposed which can extract feature maps with different kernel sizes and fuse them together. Both local and global feature fusion are used to get a stable training of wide network and to learn the hierarchical global features. The results show that this network achieves better results in terms of peak-signal-to-noise ratio (PSNR) and structural similarity index (SSIM) metrics compared with other super-resolution, de-blurring methods. To the best of our knowledge, this is the first work that has combined multiple degradation models simultaneously for retinal fundus images analysis.

Keywords: Image quality · Retinal fundus image · Image de-blurring · Image super-resolution · Generative adversarial network

1 Introduction

Retinal imaging is widely used for the diagnosis of different retinal diseases. Major diseases like glaucoma, diabetic retinopathy (DR), age-related macular degeneration (AMD) are diagnosed by examining the retinal fundus images [1]. In the clinics, expensive fundus cameras are used to collect images but the rapid growth of

© Springer Nature Switzerland AG 2020
H. Fu et al. (Eds.): OMIA 2020, LNCS 12069, pp. 32–41, 2020.
https://doi.org/10.1007/978-3-030-63419-3_4

research in telemedicine has resulted in the development of portable, hand-held, cost-efficient fundus cameras. In addition optical attachments have been developed which make smartphones into fundus cameras. The low-cost and portable design of these cameras make them especially useful in remote areas of underdeveloped or developing countries where sufficient health-care facilities are not available [2]. But recent studies have found that sometimes the quality of the images captured by these new point-of-care imaging devices are not sufficient for clinical diagnosis purpose due to the low image quality problem namely, poor resolution, motion blur, out-of-focus blur, etc. [3]. Blurriness in the images can also be caused due to the presence of diseases like cataracts which may eventually hamper the quality of diagnosis. Quellec et al. [4] found the poor image quality of a hand-held camera (Horos DEC 200) while comparing it with one table-top camera (AFC12 330). The DR diagnosis performance was worse with the hand-held camera in comparison with table-top one. Cuadros et al. [5] also reported degraded image quality of telemedicine devices. Barritt et al. [6] made a comparative analysis of images captured with a D-Eye Digital Ophthalmoscope attached to a smartphone with an actual fundus camera and found differences in image quality which can affect clinical efficacy. In most of the telemedicine fundus image devices, the spatial resolution is 2 to 4 times lower than the clinical fundus camera images.

These degraded images can also lead to unsatisfactory results of different image post-processing tasks like image segmentation. In different diseases, various landmarks and biomarkers (hemorrhages, microaneurysms, exudates, blood vessels, optic disc and optic cup, fovea) of the retina get affected. Hence the prominence and visibility of each landmark is very important for flawless clinical diagnosis.

Image quality enhancement from a degraded image is an ill-posed inverse problem and does not have a single unique solution. Mathematically the problem can be formulated as:

$$y = (x \downarrow_s) \otimes k \qquad (1)$$

where k is a blur kernel, $\downarrow_s$ is the downsampler. x is the high-resolution high-quality image, y is the low-resolution degraded image, and $\otimes$ is the convolution operation.

The major contributions of this paper are: (1) To the best of our knowledge, this is the first work to address multiple fundus image degradation problems like low-resolution and blur. All previously published fundus image enhancement papers dealt with either super-resolution or de-blurring issues separately. (2) A novel multi-scale feature averaging block (MFAB) has been designed to fuse features with different kernel sizes.

2   Related Work

Previously published literature on retinal image enhancement dealt with either image super-resolution or image de-blurring separately. Fu et al. [7], Shen et al. [8], in some their recent works, discussed about evaluation and understanding of retinal image quality. Recently different methods have been proposed for removing blurriness, enhancing contrast and luminance of retinal fundus images. Contrast and luminosity enhancement methods have been proposed using luminance gain matrix and contrast enhancement adaptive histogram equalization (CLAHE) technique [9]. Mitra et al. [10] used the Fourier transform and CLAHE technique to remove the opacity and enhance the contrast of fundus images. Blurriness removal task was performed by Xiong et al. [11] by estimating the transmission map and background illuminance. The previously published methods needed to estimate the degradation model and hence limited to very specific cases. Recently Zhao et al. [12] proposed a data-driven model to remove blurriness from unpaired sets of original and blurry images. Williams et al. [13] proposed a hierarchical convolutional neural network based method to classify between blurred and non-blurred images and then restore the images. Neither of these methods considered spatial resolution as a degradation model nor did they experiment with different kinds of blurring issues. On the other hand, different fundus image super-resolution tasks have been performed. Mahapatra et al. [14] proposed a GAN based architecture for retinal fundus image super-resolution using saliency maps to incorporate saliency loss for better super-resolved image quality. In a later study, Mahapatra et al. [15] used a progressive generative adversarial network to upscale fundus images. These super-resolution papers did not consider other image degradation model. It can be seen that all of these works separately considered image super-resolution or blur issue and hence can not be generalized for practical applications.

3   Methodology

In this section, we discuss the proposed network architecture of and the loss function of the generative adversarial network (GAN) [16]. In Fig. 1, the schematic diagram and corresponding blocks are shown.

3.1   DeSupGAN Structure

The generator of the proposed DeSupGAN consists of 3 different parts as shown in Fig. 1 (above row): (1) feature extraction module (2) residual reconstruction module and (3) up-sampling module. The discriminator contains several convolutional layers (convolution+ batchnormalization+ LeakyReLU activation function) followed by a dense layer for final decision making. The three major parts of the generator architecture are described below:

Feature Extraction Module: The feature extraction module is made with several multi-scale feature averaging blocks (MFAB), the MFAB consists of 3 convolutional blocks (convolution+ batchnormalization+ activation function). The kernel sizes of convolutional blocks are different in sizes. The outputs of each of the blocks are averaged and the residual connection is used to add the input of MFAB to the output of the averaging layer for preserving the local structure of the feature map.

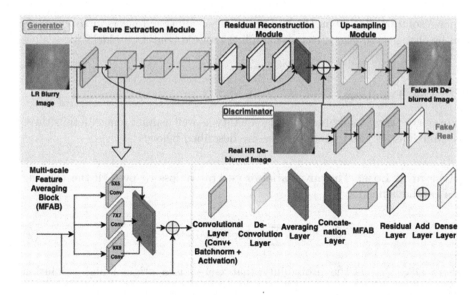

Fig. 1. Top row: the proposed architecture of DeSupGAN; Bottom: proposed MFAB and nomenclature of other layers. the generator consists of 3 different modules: feature extraction module: it consists of MFAB blocks, residual reconstruction module: it consists of residual skip connections and concatenation layers, up-sampling module: it consists of deconvolutional layers.

Often during the blurring problem, the exact size of the blur kernel is not known and it is quite difficult to estimate it. In addition the size of the blur kernel can also change in different screening experiments. The MFAB is introduced to extract multi-scale features with different kernel sizes to take care of the above mentioned problem. In the case of different blur kernels, the MFAB can produce the possible averaged result. The bottom row of Fig. 1 shows a schematic of MFAB.

Residual Reconstruction Module: The residual module consists of several residual skip connections and a concatenation layer. Every individual residual block of this module has a convolutional layer followed by a batch normalization and an activation function (ReLU). The final output of the module is concatenated with the output feature map of the first convolutional layer followed by a global skip connection as shown in Fig. 1. The complete module helps to provide a stable and better representation of the network and ensures a better flow of gradients.

Up-Sampling Module: The up-sampling module has deconvolutional layers with kernel size 3. The layer consists of an up-sampling layer followed by a convolution operation and an activation function. This block helps in increasing the spatial size of the output image. Depending on the scaling factor of the super-resolution algorithm, the number of deconvolutional layers in this module can be changed. In Fig. 1, the up-sampling module holds two blocks for scaling factor X4.

3.2   Loss Functions

To preserve perceptually better image quality as well as finer image details three loss functions are used jointly. These are described below:

Adversarial Loss: The adversarial or generative loss L_G over all the training data can be defined as

$$L_G = \sum_{n=1}^{N} -logD(G(I_D)) \tag{2}$$

Where $D(G(I_D))$ is the probability that $G(I_D)$ is a original high-resolution image.

Structural Similarity Loss: The structural similarity (SSIM) is considered as a better alternative than mean square error (MSE) as an image quality measure. For two images I and J following expression is used to calculate

$$SSIM = \frac{(2\mu_I\mu_J + C_1)(2\sigma_{IJ} + C_2)}{((\mu_I^2) + (\mu_J^2) + C_1)(\sigma_I^2 + \sigma_J^2 + C_2)} \tag{3}$$

The function is differentiable and can be written as

$$L_s = 1 - SSIM \tag{4}$$

Perceptual Loss: Perceptual loss [17] is a L_2 loss but it is based on the difference between the feature maps from a particular CNN layer. It is defined by this following equation:

$$L_p = \frac{1}{W_{i,j}H_{i,j}} \sum_{x=1}^{W_{i,j}} \sum_{x=1}^{H_{i,j}} ((\phi_{i,j}(I_O'))_{x,y} - (\phi_{i,j}G(I_D))_{x,y})^2 \tag{5}$$

$W_{i,j}$ and $H_{i,j}$ are the dimensions of the feature maps. $\phi_{i,j}$ is the feature map extracted from the jth layer of the pre-trained (on Imagenet dataset) VGG-19 network [18].

The final loss function was defined as $L = L_G + \lambda_1 * L_s + \lambda_2 * L_p$, where λ_1 and λ_2 are constant values.

4   Experiment

4.1   Dataset Generation

To evaluate the results of proposed DeSupGAN, the MESSIDOR dataset [19] was used. For each of the images corresponding degraded paired image were simulated using different blur kernels. Motion blur and de-focus blur were induced with blur kernels of randomly selected sizes from 1 to 10. For each of the blur kernels two different scaling factors (X2 and X4) were used to generate low resolution images with commonly used methods of bi-cubic interpolation.

4.2   Training Details

Data augmentation was performed by rotation, horizontal flip, and vertical flip. A total of 798 images were divided between 698 images for training and 100 images for the test. All images were resized into 512×512 size. The Adam optimizer [20] was used for both the discriminator and the combined network with a learning rate of 0.0001 with a momentum of 0.9 and decay rate of 0.1 after each epoch. This method was tested to provide better and stable convergence for the network training. The model was implemented using the tensorflow/keras [21] framework and it took approximately 6 h using a Titan V NVIDIA GPU in an i7 processor with 64 GB RAM to train for 100 epochs with a batch size of 1. The proposed DeSupGAN was compared with other several methods: (1) bicubic interpolation followed by Richardson-Lucy de-blurring algorithm [22] (2) SRRESNet [23] (3) SRGAN [23] [17] (4) SRGAN+DeBlurGAN [24]. The widely used metrics PSNR and SSIM values were calculated to measure the performance of each algorithm.

4.3   Results

The results of the experiments for two different kernels with two different scaling factors are tabulated below. The best results are shown in red.

Table 1. Results for motion blur and different scaling factors

Methods	Scaling factor			
	Scaling factor:X2		Scaling factor:X4	
	PSNR	SSIM	PSNR	SSIM
Bicubic+RL	37.32	0.650	36.56	0.740
SRRES	42.01	0.995	40.20	0.991
SRGAN	41.57	0.995	39.67	0.990
SRGAN+DeBlurGAN	41.47	0.994	40.50	0.992
DeSupGAN	42.42	0.997	41.37	0.995

Table 2. Results for de-focus blur and different scaling factors

Methods	Scaling factor			
	Scaling factor:X2		Scaling factor:X4	
	PSNR	SSIM	PSNR	SSIM
Bicubic+RL	37.01	0.635	36.67	0.740
SRRES	40.70	0.986	39.67	0.987
SRGAN	40.80	0.992	39.8	0.987
SRGAN+DeBlurGAN	40.56	0.991	39.71	0.987
DeSupGAN	41.41	0.996	40.24	0.993

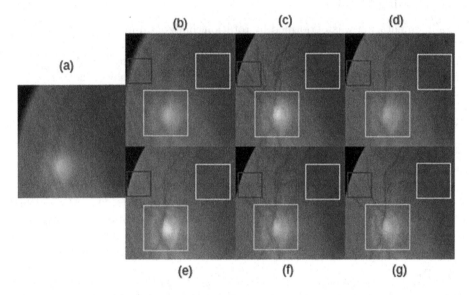

Fig. 2. Results of: (a) LR blurred image, (b) bicubic+Richardson-Lucy algorithm, (c) SRRESNet, (d) SRGAN, (e) SRGAN+DeBlurGAN, (f) DeSupGAN, (g) HR de-blrured image (ground truth). The different coloured bounding boxes show the specific parts of the images where the proposed algorithm performed better than other algorithms in image quality enhancement.

Tables 1 and 2 show the results for motion blur and de-focus blur respectively, both with two scaling factors of 2 and 4 for each. The PSNR and SSIM were considered as the metrics for assessing the quality of the generated images and it can be found that DeSupGAN outperformed other SR and de-blurring algorithms for all different tasks. DeSupGAN achieved PSNR value of 42.42, 41.37, 41.41, 40.24 and SSIM value of 0.997, 0.995, 0.996, 0.993 for motion blur scaling factor 2, motion blur scaling factor 4, de-focus blur scaling factor 2 and de-focus blur factor 4 respectively. Figure 2 shows comparative results of different algorithms, the different colored boxes show that DeSupGAN yielded better

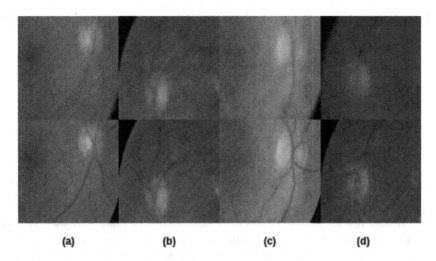

(a)   (b)   (c)   (d)

Fig. 3. Results of DeSupGAN - the top row consists of LR blurry images, bottom row consists of the results. (a) motion blur, scaling factor 4, (b) motion blur, scaling factor 2, (c) defocus blur, scaling factor 4, (d) defocus blur, scaling factor 2.

finer details of blood vessels, optic disc boundary than other methods. Figure 3 shows the results of DeSupGAN for all different scaling factors and blur kernels.

4.4 Ablation Studies

The ablation studies were carried out in which we removed two important component of the proposed network, namely the novel MFAB block and structural similarity loss (L_S), are shown. It can be seen from Tables 3 and 4 that worse results were found which proves the importance of the components in the proposed network.

Table 3. Ablation studies: results for motion blur and different scaling factors

Methods	Scaling factor			
	Scaling factor:X2		Scaling factor:X4	
	PSNR	SSIM	PSNR	SSIM
w/o structural similarity loss	42.02	0.995	40.20	0.992
w/o MFAB block	40.90	0.994	39.89	0.991

Table 4. Ablation studies: results for defocus blur and different scaling factors

Methods	Scaling factor			
	Scaling factor:X2		Scaling factor:X4	
	PSNR	SSIM	PSNR	SSIM
w/o structural similarity loss	40.29	0.993	39.67	0.989
w/o MFAB block	40.95	0.994	40.20	0.992

5   Conclusion

We proposed a network DeSupGAN which can generate high-resolution deblurred retinal fundus images from low-resolution blurry images. It uses MFAB blocks for extracting multi-scale feature and triplet loss functions to generate perceptually better results. The experimental results show that the proposed DeSupGAN outperformed other state-of-the-art methods in terms of PSNR and SSIM values.

References

1. Sengupta, S., Singh, A., Leopold, H.A., Gulati, T., Lakshminarayanan, V.: Ophthalmic diagnosis using deep learning with fundus images-a critical review. Artif. Intell. Med. **10**, 101758 (2020)
2. Panwar, N., Huang, P., Lee, J., Keane, P.A., Chuan, T.S., Richhariya, A., et al.: Fundus photography in the 21st century–a review of recent technological advances and their implications for worldwide healthcare. Telemed. e-Health **22**(3), 198–208 (2016)
3. Das, V., Dandapat, S., Bora, P.K.: A novel diagnostic information based framework for super-resolution of retinal fundus images. Comput. Med. Imaging Graph. **72**, 22–33 (2019)
4. Quellec, G., Bazin, L., Cazuguel, G., Delafoy, I., Cochener, B., Lamard, M.: Suitability of a low-cost, handheld, nonmydriatic retinograph for diabetic retinopathy diagnosis. Transl. Vis. Sci. Technol. **5**(2), 16 (2016)
5. Cuadros, J., Bresnick, G.: Can commercially available handheld retinal cameras effectively screen diabetic retinopathy? J. Diab. Sci. Technol. **11**(1), 135–137 (2017)
6. Barritt, N., Parthasarathy, M.K., Faruq, I., Zelek, J., Lakshminarayanan, V.: Fundus camera versus smartphone camera attachment: image quality analysis. In: Current Developments in Lens Design and Optical Engineering XX, vol. 11104, p. 111040A. International Society for Optics and Photonics (2019)
7. Fu, H., et al.: Evaluation of retinal image quality assessment networks in different color-spaces. In: Shen, D., et al. (eds.) MICCAI 2019. LNCS, vol. 11764, pp. 48–56. Springer, Cham (2019). https://doi.org/10.1007/978-3-030-32239-7_6
8. Shen, Z., Fu, H., Shen, J., Shao, L.: Understanding and correcting low-quality retinal fundus images for clinical analysis. arXiv preprint arXiv:2005.05594 (2020)
9. Zhou, M., Jin, K., Wang, S., Ye, J., Qian, D.: Color retinal image enhancement based on luminosity and contrast adjustment. IEEE Trans. Biomed. Eng. **65**(3), 521–527 (2017)

10. Mitra, A., Roy, S., Roy, S., Setua, S.K.: Enhancement and restoration of non-uniform illuminated fundus image of retina obtained through thin layer of cataract. Comput. Methods Programs Biomed. **156**, 169–178 (2018)
11. Xiong, L., Li, H., Xu, L.: An enhancement method for color retinal images based on image formation model. Comput. Methods Programs Biomed. **143**, 137–150 (2017)
12. Zhao, H., Yang, B., Cao, L., Li, H.: Data-driven enhancement of blurry retinal images via generative adversarial networks. In: Shen, D., et al. (eds.) MICCAI 2019. LNCS, vol. 11764, pp. 75–83. Springer, Cham (2019). https://doi.org/10.1007/978-3-030-32239-7_9
13. Williams, B.M., et al.: Fast blur detection and parametric deconvolution of retinal fundus images. In: Cardoso, M.J., et al. (eds.) FIFI/OMIA -2017. LNCS, vol. 10554, pp. 194–201. Springer, Cham (2017). https://doi.org/10.1007/978-3-319-67561-9_22
14. Mahapatra, D., Bozorgtabar, B., Hewavitharanage, S., Garnavi, R.: Image super resolution using generative adversarial networks and local saliency maps for retinal image analysis. In: Descoteaux, M., Maier-Hein, L., Franz, A., Jannin, P., Collins, D.L., Duchesne, S. (eds.) MICCAI 2017. LNCS, vol. 10435, pp. 382–390. Springer, Cham (2017). https://doi.org/10.1007/978-3-319-66179-7_44
15. Mahapatra, D., Bozorgtabar, B., Garnavi, R.: Image super-resolution using progressive generative adversarial networks for medical image analysis. Comput. Med. Imaging Graph. **71**, 30–39 (2019)
16. Goodfellow, I., Pouget-Abadie, J., Mirza, M., Xu, B., Warde-Farley, D., Ozair S., et al.: Generative adversarial nets. In: Advances in Neural Information Processing Systems, pp. 2672–2680 (2014)
17. Johnson, J., Alahi, A., Fei-Fei, L.: Perceptual losses for real-time style transfer and super-resolution. In: Leibe, B., Matas, J., Sebe, N., Welling, M. (eds.) ECCV 2016. LNCS, vol. 9906, pp. 694–711. Springer, Cham (2016). https://doi.org/10.1007/978-3-319-46475-6_43
18. Simonyan, K., Zisserman, A.: Very deep convolutional networks for large-scale image recognition. arXiv preprint arXiv:1409.1556 (2014)
19. Decencière, E., Zhang, X., Cazuguel, G., Lay, B., Cochener, B., Trone, C., et al.: Feedback on a publicly distributed image database: the Messidor database. Image Anal. Stereol. **33**(3), 231–234 (2014)
20. Kingma, D.P., Ba, J.: Adam: a method for stochastic optimization. arXiv preprint arXiv:1412.6980 (2014)
21. Abadi, M., Agarwal, A., Barham, P., Brevdo, E., Chen, Z., Citro, C., et al.: TensorFlow: large-scale machine learning on heterogeneous systems (2015). Software Available from tensorflow.org
22. Tai, Y.-W., Tan, P., Brown, M.S.: Richardson-Lucy deblurring for scenes under a projective motion path. IEEE Trans. Pattern Anal. Mach. Intell. **33**(8), 1603–1618 (2010)
23. Ledig, C., Theis, L., Huszár, F., Caballero, J., Cunningham, A., Acosta, A., et al.: Photo-realistic single image super-resolution using a generative adversarial network. In: Proceedings of the IEEE Conference on Computer Vision and Pattern Recognition, pp. 4681–4690 (2017)
24. Kupyn, O., Budzan, V., Mykhailych, M., Mishkin, D., Matas, J.: DeblurGAN: blind motion deblurring using conditional adversarial networks. In: Proceedings of the IEEE Conference on Computer Vision and Pattern Recognition, pp. 8183–8192 (2018)

Encoder-Decoder Networks for Retinal Vessel Segmentation Using Large Multi-scale Patches

Björn Browatzki[1,3], Jörn-Philipp Lies[1,2], and Christian Wallraven[1,3(✉)]

[1] Eye2you GmbH, Tübingen, Germany
{bjoern,phil,christian}@eye2you.ai
[2] University Eye Hospital Tübingen, Tübingen, Germany
[3] Department of Artificial Intelligence, Korea University, Seoul, South Korea
wallraven@korea.ac.kr

Abstract. We propose an encoder-decoder framework for the segmentation of blood vessels in retinal images that relies on the extraction of large-scale patches at multiple image-scales during training. Experiments on three fundus image datasets demonstrate that this approach achieves state-of-the-art results and can be implemented using a simple and efficient fully-convolutional network with a parameter count of less than 0.8M. Furthermore, we show that this framework - called VLight - avoids overfitting to specific training images and generalizes well across different datasets, which makes it highly suitable for real-world applications where robustness, accuracy as well as low inference time on high-resolution fundus images is required.

Keywords: Retinal vessel detection · Fundus image · Semantic segmentation · Residual networks

1 Introduction

The analysis of retinal blood vessel structure from fundus photographs can help to identify eye diseases such as diabetic retinopathy, macular degeneration, or hypertension at early stages [1]. Often the growth of new vessels, increased tortuosity, and other morphological changes can be observed in patients [4,12]. A second application domain is the use of the unique vascular structure as a landmark feature for tasks such as biometric authentication [21] or registration of multiple images of the same eye across visits to track retinal changes over time or align multiple views to obtain a larger field-of-view [8,10,34].

However, accurate tracing of the fine vascular structure is a difficult, labor-intensive and time consuming task. Numerous methods for automatic vessel segmentation have been proposed in the past. These range from early systems relying on low-level features analyzing local image statistics such as Gabor filters [30] or ridge based features [32] in combination with various types of classifiers such as support vector machines [26,38], k-NN [32], boosting [6], or neural networks [20]. In recent years, approaches relying on powerful convolutional neural

© Springer Nature Switzerland AG 2020
H. Fu et al. (Eds.): OMIA 2020, LNCS 12069, pp. 42–52, 2020.
https://doi.org/10.1007/978-3-030-63419-3_5

networks have gained popularity and have led to significant increases in segmentation performance [7,18].

Many of these deep learning approaches follow a patch-based approach in which the fundus image is split into a set of small patches and each patch is processed individually [13,17,18,22]. These methods offer high performance in terms of pixelwise accuracy but are unable to capture semantic and contextual information as only a small image neighborhood is observed. In addition, these approaches are computationally expensive even for low-resolution images since a high number of patches has to be processed.

In contrast, several methods have been proposed that take the entire fundus image as input and produce the segmentation result in one pass [7,19,31]. These methods typically operate much faster and are also able to produce high quality segmentation masks. Another advantage of this approach is that image-wide knowledge about the shape of the vessel structure across the retina becomes available and can be even incorporated explicitly in the model as, for example, in [31]. A core limitation of this approach, however, is that they almost always also learn the specific "appearance" of a particular training set given that public datasets typically only contain a low number of fundus images. Therefore these methods struggle to generalize to new images from different sources, as retinal images may vary drastically in terms of image resolution, field-of-view, illumination, sharpness, and recording artefacts.

In the present paper, we propose a hybrid approach in order to bridge the gap between local patch-based and global image-based methods. Specifically, we make use of large patches that are extracted at multiple image scales. Our experiments show that this combination is able to achieve state-of-the-art segmentation performance combined with excellent generalizability across different types of fundus images.

Importantly, we also show that accurate vessel segmentation does not require large and computationally expensive models. By employing a ResNet-based [9] encoder-decoder architecture and incorporating building blocks of modern efficient networks [11,28,29], we show that it is possible to downscale model complexity and processing time by an order of magnitude without a loss in performance, culminating in our VLight architecture.

Source code and pre-trained models are available at https://github.com/browatbn2/VLight.

2   Studying Patch Size and Model Architecture

In the following section we want to first shed light on how the choice of patch size in training and test affects segmentation performance. Next, we will study how much computational complexity is required to achieve high quality results.

Datasets. As test bed for our evaluations serve three common fundus image datasets: DRIVE, CHASE_DB1, and HRF. The DRIVE dataset [32] is currently the most widely used benchmark in this field. It contains 40 RGB fundus images of size 565×584 pixels, split into 20 images for training and 20 images for testing. Annotations of the first human observer serve as ground truth. CHASE_DB1 [25] contains only 28 images but of higher resolution (999×964 px) than DRIVE. Since there is no fixed training/test split and choices are inconsistent throughout the literature, we follow the majority of the recent methods we compare against [2,17,37,40] by selecting the first 20 images as training images and use the remaining 8 images for testing. The HRF dataset [15] contains 45 high-resolution (3504×2336 px) fundus images split into 3 sets of 15 images from healthy patients, patients with diabetic retinopathy, and patients with glaucoma. We follow Orlando et al. [23] using the first five images in each set (healthy, glaucoma, diabetic retinopathy) for training and the remaining 30 images for testing.

Training Procedure. We do not employ any preprocessing or post-processing steps. We apply common data augmentations of rotation ($\pm 60°$), horiz./vert. flipping as well as RGB color (± 20), brightness/contrast ($\pm 50\%$), and gamma ($\pm 20\%$) shifts. All models are trained for 100k samples where one sample constitutes a dynamically selected random crop.

We use the Adam optimizer [14] ($\beta_1 = 0.9, \beta_2 = 0.999$) with a learning rate of 0.001 (reduced to 0.0002 after 80k samples) and a batch size of 10. We minimize the binary cross entropy loss between sample ground truth segmentations and predicted vessel probabilities.

Evaluation Metrics. We evaluate the quality of vessel predictions by reporting Area Under Curve for Receiver Operating Characteristic (ROC), Area Under Curve for the Precision-Recall Curve (PR), and F1 measure (or Dice coefficient). For binarized results we also report accuracy (ACC). Vessel probability maps are converted to binary masks by applying a fixed threshold of 0.5. Please note that segmentations contain many more non-vessel pixels than vessel pixels. Accuracy is therefore a less suitable measure for performance in comparison to threshold-free metrics like Precision-Recall or ROC.

As is common practice, we only consider pixels inside the field-of-view for calculating the above metrics and discard black borders surrounding the visible part of the retina. Field-of-view masks are supplied by DRIVE and HRF. For CHASE_DB1, masks were determined by thresholding median-filtered grayscale images.

2.1 Effective Patch Sizes

Methods that operate on image patches for retinal vessel segmentation use small patches of, for example, 48×48 pixels [13]. These patches only cover a local region of the typically very large fundus images lacking larger-scale contextual information. To study the influence of the selected patches on segmentation performance we train a baseline U-Net model [27] with different patch selection strategies for training and test. We opt for the U-Net model since it has become immensely popular in recent years for medical image segmentation. Numerous methods have been propose for vessel segmentation that build upon the basic U-Net architecture by adding, for example, residual and recurrent blocks [2], deformable convolutions [13], or efficient bottleneck blocks [16]. We compare against these methods explicitly in Sect. 3.

Table 1. Evaluating the effect of different patch sizes within and across datasets.

Method	Patch-size	Scale train/test	Patches (test)	Time GPU	F1 DRIVE	F1 CHASE	F1 HRF
U-Net	544×544	1/1	1	**0.04 s**	0.8305	0.7724	0.7478
U-Net [13]	48×48	1/1	14916	3.1 s	0.8175	–	–
U-Net	48×48	1/1	342	1.65 s	0.8172	0.5290	0.4809
U-Net	96×96	1/1	64	0.32 s	0.8281	0.5355	0.3935
U-Net	128×128	1/1	36	0.25 s	0.8304	0.5192	0.3831
U-Net	256×256	1/1	9	0.08 s	**0.8316**	0.4824	0.2607
U-Net	256×256	1/2	25	0.25 s	0.7253		
U-Net	512×512	2/2	9	0.295 s	0.8302	0.7722	0.7704
U-Net	256×256	[1-2]/1	9	0.08 s	0.8173	0.7125	0.7561
U-Net	256×256	[1-2]/2	36	0.28 s	0.8248		
U-Net	256×256	[1-2]/1 + 2	45	1.96 s	0.8261		
U-Net	512×512	[2-4]/2	9	0.29 s	0.8283	**0.7745**	**0.7954**
U-Net	512×512	[2-4]/3	16	0.51 s	0.8190		
U-Net	512×512	[2-4]/4	36	1.13	0.8273		
U-Net	512×512	[2-4]/2 + 3 + 4	61	1.96 s	0.8299		

Results are listed in Table 1. We distinguish between three types of approaches here: Full images as inputs (equivalent to a single patch of 544×544 pixels), fixed size patches, and varying patch sizes. We make three important observations here: First, we see that models trained with large fixed size patches produce excellent results when tested on the same dataset (DRIVE) but do not generalize well to images from other datasets (CHASE_DB1 and HRF). Second, multi-scale testing leads to a significant increase in accuracy if trained on varying resolutions. Lastly, processing time decreases considerably as patch sizes are increased.

2.2   Efficient Architecture

As studied in the previous section, we can obtain a highly accurate segmentation results by employing a vanilla U-Net architecture. However, the model size and computational costs make it unsuitable for mobile or embedded devices. Our goal in this section is to show that accuracy can be maintained (or even increased) while at the same time reducing processing time by an order of magnitude.

While leaving training and testing procedures untouched, we replace the U-Net with a ResNet-based encoder-decoder model similar to the Simple Baseline architecture of [36]. This model consists of the first three ResNet layers of a standard ResNet-18 architecture and an inverted counterpart in which 2-strided convolutions are replaced by 4×4 deconvolutions.

A common approach for activation upsizing in a decoder pipeline consists in simple bilinear upscaling. In our experiments this, however, led to decreased accuracy and no increase in runtime performance. Shi et al. [29] proposed an alternative upscaling method in the context of image super-resolution which has also been used successfully for semantic segmentation tasks [3]. Their so-called Pixel Shuffle operation transforms a $H \times W \times Cr^2$ tensor into a $rH \times rW \times C$ tensor by simply rearranging element positions as shown in Fig. 2 d). This efficient operation leads a reduction in decoder parameters and a processing speed-up without suffering a significant loss in performance (Table 2).

Table 2. Comparison between different model architectures on DRIVE.

Method	Patch-size	Scale	Params	Time	F1
U-Net	512×512	[2-4] /2 + 3 + 4	31.03M	1.96 s	0.8299
Simple Baseline (SB) [36]	512×512	[2-4]/2 + 3 + 4	18.96M	1.03 s	**0.8312**
SB + Bilinear	512×512	[2-4]/2 + 3 + 4	16.39M	1.21 s	0.8311
SB + Pixel Shuffle [29]	512×512	[2-4]/2 + 3 + 4	13.45M	0.83 s	0.8309
SB + Pixel Shuffle + DWC [5]	512×512	[2-4]/2 + 3 + 4	1.83M	0.72 s	0.8307
VLight	512×512	[2-4]/2	0.74M	**0.08 s**	0.8184
VLight	512×512	[2-4]/3	0.74M	0.15 s	0.8276
VLight	512×512	[2-4]/4	0.74M	0.34 s	0.8261
VLight	512×512	[2-4]/2 + 3 + 4	0.74M	0.56 s	0.8299

Next, we make use depthwise separable convolutions (DWCs), introduced in Xception [5], and replace ResNet blocks with blocks akin to MobileNet [11,28]. See Figs. 1 and 2 for more details. A similar approach is also used by M2U-Net [16] to create an extremely efficient segmentation model for embedded devices. We observe a drastic reduction in parameter count while only noticing a small decrease in accuracy.

For our final model, VLight, we replace the costly first 7×7 convolution followed by maxpooling with two 3×3 convolutions and trade model depth for

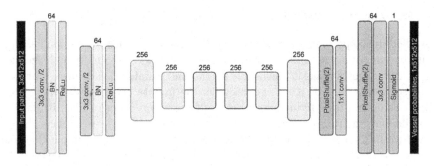

Fig. 1. VLight network overview. Numbers on top of layers and blocks denote number of output channels.

model width. This tradeoff has been motivated by recent studies, for example in [35]. We half the number of residual blocks and the set all channel sizes to 256.

3 Comparison with State-of-the-Art

We first compare our approach with other methods on the two common evaluation benchmarks DRIVE and CHASE_DB1. In addition, we present results for high-resolution fundus images from HRF in Sect. 3.2.

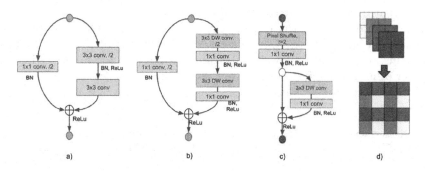

Fig. 2. VLight network blocks. (a) Original ResNet downsampling block containing two convolutional layers; (b) Residual downsampling block with depthwise convolutional layers; (c) Residual upsampling block with Pixel Shuffle; (d) Upscaling using Pixel Shuffle operation

3.1 Results

Table 3 shows the performance of our approach in comparison to recent state-of-the-art methods on DRIVE and CHASE_DB1. VLight achieves best non-binarized results on both datasets, outperforming much more complex and slower

Table 3. Comparison against other recent approaches on DRIVE and CHASE_DB1.

Method	Year	DRIVE				CHASE_DB1			
		F1	ACC	ROC	PR	F1	ACC	ROC	PR
Li [17]	2015	–	0.9527	0.9738	–	–	0.9581	0.9716	–
DRIU [19]	2016	0.8210	0.9541	0.9793	0.9064	–	–	–	–
V-GAN [31]	2017	0.8277	0.9560	0.9803	0.9142	–	–	–	–
DUNet [13]	2018	0.8237	0.9566	0.9802	–	–	0.9610	0.9804	–
M2U-Net [16]	2018	0.8091	**0.9630**	0.9714	–	0.8006	**0.9703**	0.9666	–
R2U-Net [2]	2018	0.8171	0.9556	0.9784	–	0.7928	0.9634	0.9815	–
Yan [37]	2018	–	0.9542	0.9752	–	–	0.9610	0.9781	–
LadderNet [40]	2019	0.8202	0.9561	0.9703	–	0.8031	0.9656	0.9839	–
VLight	2020	**0.8299**	0.9565	**0.9820**	**0.9168**	**0.8194**	0.9671	**0.9873**	**0.9057**

methods. Only M2U-Net [16] reports higher accuracy - however at considerably lower F1/ROC/PR rates. It is unclear, whether this stems from differences in the training process or a different thresholding method. Our fixed threshold of 0.5 does not necessarily produce the highest possible accuracy. However, we refrain from optimizing this threshold since it easily results in overfitting the (small) test set and may lead to less robust results in practice.

3.2 High-Resolution Fundus Images

Table 4 summarises segmentation results for our and other methods on the HRF dataset that contains high-resolution fundus images of 3504×2336 pixel. On HRF we test only using the original image scale and use Otsu thresholding [24] to obtain binary masks. Our efficient model outperforms the previous top-performing method (DUNet) while processing the high-resolution fundus images an order of magnitude faster. M2U-Net offers faster runtimes at, however, significantly reduced performance.

Table 4. Segmentation results and runtime performance on the high-resolution HRF dataset (3504×2336 px). *CPU (Xeon E5-2690), GPU †‡GTX 1080Ti ¶TITAN X.

Method	Year	Time	F1	SE	SP	ACC	ROC	PR
Orlando [23]	2017	5.8 s*	0.7158	0.7874	0.9584	–	–	–
Yan et al. [37]	2018	–	0.7212	**0.7881**	0.9592	0.9437	–	–
M2U-Net [16]	2018	**19.9 ms**†	0.7814	–	–	0.9635	–	–
DUNet [16]	2018	-[>1min]‡	–	0.7464	**0.9874**	0.9651	0.9831	–
VLight	2020	460 ms¶	**0.8145**	0.7537	0.9873	**0.9656**	**0.9850**	**0.8977**

3.3 Cross-Dataset Evaluation

Due to the high human effort involved in creating ground truth annotations for retinal vessel segmentations, available datasets are very small. DRIVE, CHASE_DB1, and HRF only contain 40, 28, and 45 images respectively. Modern deep networks are easily able to fit closely to the data distribution of the training set which poses a high risk of overfitting. Furthermore, there exists a clear danger of test set overfitting through repeated hyper-parameter tuning.

To study the robustness and generalizability of our method, we evaluate segmentation performance across datasets. We use our previously trained models and predict vessels on another unseen dataset without any adaptation to the new dataset. Table 5 shows that our multi-scale training scheme leads to a high degree of adaptability to the different images sizes and appearance across the three tested datasets. Our simple and efficient approach even outperforms ADCM, a method explicitly dedicated to domain adaptation.

Table 5. Evaluation of cross-dataset segmentation performance to study generalizability of our and other methods. D = DRIVE, C = CHASE_DB1, H = HRF.

Metric	Method	DRIVE			CHASE			HRF		
		D	C	H	D	C	H	D	C	H
F1	ErrorNet [33]	–	–	–	73.20	81.5	68.6	–	–	–
	V-GAN [31]	–	–	–	69.30	79.7	66.4	–	–	–
	U-Net [39]	–	50.69	–	65.05	–	–	–	–	–
	AMCD [39]	82.33	73.95	–	78.60	80.15	–			
	VLight	**82.84**	**76.00**	**79.21**	**81.65**	**81.94**	**81.31**	**80.31**	**75.37**	**81.45**
ROC	Li [17]	97.38	96.28	–	96.05	97.16	–	–	–	–
	U-Net [39]	–	68.89	–	92.18	–	–	–	–	–
	AMCD [39]	97.77	96.43	–	96.91	97.85	–	–	–	–
	VLight	**98.12**	**97.70**	**98.10**	**97.80**	**98.73**	**98.44**	**97.16**	**96.89**	**98.50**

Figure 3 shows example segmentations for an image from the HRF dataset segmented with two models: one trained on the same HRF dataset and another trained on the DRIVE dataset. First, we note that segmentation performance of the two models is comparable (F1: 88.88% vs 86.98%). Second, and most importantly, the model trained on DRIVE actually was trained with much lower resolution images, but is still able to generalize to the image material of HRF by making use of our multi-patch, multi-scale framework.

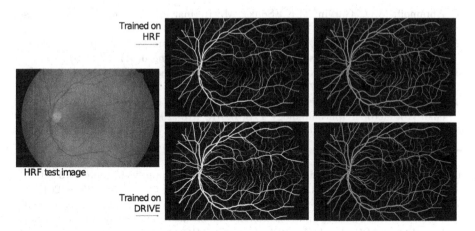

Fig. 3. Segmentation result for an HRF test image for models trained on HRF (upper row) and DRIVE (lower row). Second column shows ground truth in white. Third column in green: correct vessels, red: misses, blue: false positives (zoom in for details). (Color figure online)

4   Conclusion

Our experiments on retinal vessel segmentation have shown that a hybrid framework with large patch sizes extracted at multiple image scales is able to achieve state-of-the-art performance. The combination of these two approaches is able to leverage contextual, large-range image dependencies while at the same time preserving short-range, high-resolution image information. In addition, the framework can better generalize across different datasets as it avoids overfitting on a specific training set's visual appearance.

The overall network structure consists of a simple encoder-decoder structure with ResNet blocks, which provide highly efficient performance at reduced parameter count compared to a U-Net architecture, for example. Our experiments have demonstrated that it possible to reduce the number of parameters even further at minimal loss of segmentation accuracy. It is possible to provide good performance with only 0.8M parameters, which makes our hybrid approach suitable not only for high-precision segmentation, but also for a wide variety of computation-time-sensitive applications.

Acknowledgements. This work was supported by Institute of Information & Communications Technology Planning & Evaluation (IITP) grant funded by the Korean government (MSIT) (No. 2019-0-00079, Dept. of Artificial Intelligence, Korea University).

References

1. Abràmoff, M.D., Garvin, M.K., Sonka, M.: Retinal imaging and image analysis. IEEE Rev. Biomed. Eng. **3**, 169–208 (2010)
2. Alom, M.Z., Yakopcic, C., Hasan, M., Taha, T.M., Asari, V.K.: Recurrent residual U-Net for medical image segmentation. J. Med. Imaging **6**(01), 1 (2019)
3. Cai, X., Pu, Y.F.: FlatteNet: a simple and versatile framework for dense pixelwise prediction. IEEE Access **7**, 179985–179996 (2019)
4. Cheung, C.Y.L., et al.: Retinal vascular tortuosity, blood pressure, and cardiovascular risk factors. Ophthalmology **118**(5), 812–818 (2011)
5. Chollet, F.: Xception: deep learning with depthwise separable convolutions. In: Proceedings - 30th IEEE Conference on Computer Vision and Pattern Recognition, CVPR 2017 2017-January, pp. 1800–1807 (2017)
6. Fraz, M.M., et al.: An ensemble classification-based approach applied to retinal blood vessel segmentation. IEEE Trans. Biomed. Eng. **59**(9), 2538–2548 (2012)
7. Fu, H., Xu, Y., Lin, S., Kee Wong, D.W., Liu, J.: DeepVessel: retinal vessel segmentation via deep learning and conditional random field. In: Ourselin, S., Joskowicz, L., Sabuncu, M.R., Unal, G., Wells, W. (eds.) MICCAI 2016. LNCS, vol. 9901, pp. 132–139. Springer, Cham (2016). https://doi.org/10.1007/978-3-319-46723-8_16
8. Gharabaghi, S., Daneshvar, S., Sedaaghi, M.H.: Retinal image registration using geometrical features. J. Digit. Imaging **26**(2), 248–258 (2013)
9. He, K., Zhang, X., Ren, S., Sun, J.: Deep residual learning for image recognition. arXiv.Org **7**(3), 171–180 (2015)
10. Hervella, Á.S., Rouco, J., Novo, J., Ortega, M.: Multimodal registration of retinal images using domain-specific landmarks and vessel enhancement. Procedia Comput. Sci. **126**, 97–104 (2018)
11. Howard, A.G., et al.: MobileNets: efficient convolutional neural networks for mobile vision applications (2017)

12. Hubbard, L.D., et al.: Methods for evaluation of retinal microvascular abnormalities associated with hypertension/sclerosis in the atherosclerosis risk in communities study. Ophthalmology **106**(12), 2269–2280 (1999)
13. Jin, Q., Meng, Z., Pham, T.D., Chen, Q., Wei, L., Su, R.: DUNet: a deformable network for retinal vessel segmentation. Knowl.-Based Syst. **178**, 149–162 (2019)
14. Kingma, D.P., Ba, J.: Adam: a method for stochastic optimization, pp. 1–15 (2014)
15. Köhler, T., Budai, A., Kraus, M.F., Odstrčilik, J., Michelson, G., Hornegger, J.: Automatic no-reference quality assessment for retinal fundus images using vessel segmentation. In: Proceedings - IEEE Symposium on Computer-Based Medical Systems, pp. 95–100 (2013)
16. Laibacher, T., Weyde, T., Jalali, S.: M2U-Net: effective and efficient retinal vessel segmentation for resource-constrained environments (2018)
17. Li, Q., Feng, B., Xie, L., Liang, P., Zhang, H., Wang, T.: A cross-modality learning approach for vessel segmentation in retinal images. IEEE Trans. Med. Imaging **35**(1), 109–118 (2016)
18. Liskowski, P., Krawiec, K.: Segmenting retinal blood vessels with deep neural networks. IEEE Trans. Med. Imaging **35**(11), 2369–2380 (2016)
19. Maninis, K.-K., Pont-Tuset, J., Arbeláez, P., Van Gool, L.: Deep retinal image understanding. In: Ourselin, S., Joskowicz, L., Sabuncu, M.R., Unal, G., Wells, W. (eds.) MICCAI 2016. LNCS, vol. 9901, pp. 140–148. Springer, Cham (2016). https://doi.org/10.1007/978-3-319-46723-8_17
20. Marín, D., Aquino, A., Gegúndez-Arias, M.E., Bravo, J.M.: A new supervised method for blood vessel segmentation in retinal images by using gray-level and moment invariants-based features. IEEE Trans. Med. Imaging **30**(1), 146–158 (2011)
21. Mariño, C., Penedo, M.G., Penas, M., Carreira, M.J., Gonzalez, F.: Personal authentication using digital retinal images. Pattern Anal. Appl. **9**(1), 21–33 (2006)
22. Oliveira, A., Pereira, S., Silva, C.A.: Retinal vessel segmentation based on fully convolutional neural networks. Expert Syst. Appl. **112**, 229–242 (2018)
23. Orlando, J.I., Prokofyeva, E., Blaschko, M.B.: A discriminatively trained fully connected conditional random field model for blood vessel segmentation in fundus images. IEEE Trans. Biomed. Eng. **64**(1), 16–27 (2017)
24. Otsu, N.: Threshold selection method from gray-level histograms. IEEE Trans. Syst. Man Cybern. SMC **9**(1), 62–66 (1979)
25. Owen, C.G., et al.: Measuring retinal vessel tortuosity in 10-year-old children: validation of the computer-assisted image analysis of the retina (CAIAR) program. Invest. Ophthalmol. Vis. Sci. **50**(5), 2004–2010 (2009)
26. Ricci, E., Perfetti, R.: Retinal blood vessel segmentation using line operators and support vector classification. IEEE Trans. Med. Imaging **26**(10), 1357–1365 (2007)
27. Ronneberger, O., Fischer, P., Brox, T.: U-Net: convolutional networks for biomedical image segmentation. In: Navab, N., Hornegger, J., Wells, W.M., Frangi, A.F. (eds.) MICCAI 2015. LNCS, vol. 9351, pp. 234–241. Springer, Cham (2015). https://doi.org/10.1007/978-3-319-24574-4_28
28. Sandler, M., Howard, A., Zhu, M., Zhmoginov, A., Chen, L.C.: MobileNetV2: inverted residuals and linear bottlenecks. In: Proceedings of the IEEE Computer Society Conference on Computer Vision and Pattern Recognition pp. 4510–4520 (2018)
29. Shi, W., et al.: Real-time single image and video super-resolution using an efficient sub-pixel convolutional neural network. In: Proceedings of the IEEE Computer Society Conference on Computer Vision and Pattern Recognition, December 2016, pp. 1874–1883 (2016)

30. Soares, J.V., Leandro, J.J., Cesar, R.M., Jelinek, H.F., Cree, M.J.: Retinal vessel segmentation using the 2-D Gabor wavelet and supervised classification. IEEE Trans. Med. Imaging **25**(9), 1214–1222 (2006)

31. Son, J., Park, S.J., Jung, K.H.: Retinal vessel segmentation in fundoscopic images with generative adversarial networks (2017)

32. Staal, J., Abràmoff, M.D., Niemeijer, M., Viergever, M.A., Van Ginneken, B.: Ridge-based vessel segmentation in color images of the retina. IEEE Trans. Med. Imaging **23**(4), 501–509 (2004)

33. Tajbakhsh, N., Lai, B., Ananth, S.P., Ding, X.: ErrorNet: learning error representations from limited data to improve vascular segmentation. In: Proceedings - International Symposium on Biomedical Imaging, April 2020, pp. 1364–1368 (2020)

34. Tian, J., Deng, K., Zheng, J., Zhang, X., Dai, X., Xu, M.: Retinal fundus image registration via vascular structure graph matching. Int. J. Biomed. Imaging **2010**, Article ID 906067 (2010)

35. Wu, Z., Shen, C., van den Hengel, A.: Wider or deeper: revisiting the ResNet model for visual recognition. Pattern Recogn. **90**, 119–133 (2019)

36. Xiao, B., Wu, H., Wei, Y.: Simple baselines for human pose estimation and tracking. In: Ferrari, V., Hebert, M., Sminchisescu, C., Weiss, Y. (eds.) ECCV 2018. LNCS, vol. 11210, pp. 472–487. Springer, Cham (2018). https://doi.org/10.1007/978-3-030-01231-1_29

37. Yan, Z., Yang, X., Cheng, K.T.: Joint segment-level and pixel-wise losses for deep learning based retinal vessel segmentation. IEEE Trans. Biomed. Eng. **65**(9), 1912–1923 (2018)

38. You, X., Peng, Q., Yuan, Y., Cheung, Y.M., Lei, J.: Segmentation of retinal blood vessels using the radial projection and semi-supervised approach. Pattern Recogn. **44**(10–11), 2314–2324 (2011)

39. Zhuang, J., Chen, Z., Zhang, J., Zhang, D., Cai, Z.: Domain adaptation for retinal vessel segmentation using asymmetrical maximum classifier discrepancy. In: ACM International Conference Proceeding Series (2019)

40. Zhuang, J.: LadderNet: multi-path networks based on U-Net for medical image segmentation, pp. 2–5 (2018)

Retinal Image Quality Assessment via Specific Structures Segmentation

Xinqiang Zhou[1,2,3], Yicheng Wu[2], and Yong Xia[1,2(✉)]

[1] Research and Development Institute of Northwestern Polytechnical University in Shenzhen, Shenzhen 518057, China
`yxia@nwpu.edu.cn`
[2] National Engineering Laboratory for Integrated Aero-Space-Ground-Ocean Big Data Application Technology, School of Computer Science and Engineering, Northwestern Polytechnical University, Xi'an 710072, China
[3] Institute of Medical Research, Northwestern Polytechnical University, Xi'an 710072, China

Abstract. Quality of retinal image plays an essential role in ophthalmic disease diagnosis. However, most of the existing models neglect the potential correlation between retinal structure segmentation and retinal image quality assessment (RIQA), since the segmentation result is able to provide the region of interests (ROIs) and the RIQA model can extract more discriminative features. Therefore, in this paper, we incorporate the retinal structure segmentation process into RIQA tasks and thus propose a structure-guided deep neural network (SG-Net) for better image quality assessment. The SG-Net consists of a vessel segmentation module, an optic disc segmentation module, and a quality assessment module. The vessel segmentation module and optic disk segmentation module generate the segmentation results of important retinal structures (i.e., vessel and optic disc) that provide supplementary knowledge to support the quality assessment module. The quality assessment module is a three-branches classification network to extract and fuse features to estimate image quality. We evaluated our proposed SG-Net on the Eye-Quality (EyeQ) database, and the experiment results demonstrated that the proposed SG-Net outperforms other existing state-of-the-art methods. Our ablation studies also indicated that each structure segmentation module is able to achieve impressive performance gain on the EyeQ database.

Keywords: Retinal image quality assessment · Image segmentation · Deep learning

1 Introduction

Due to the low-cost and easy-access, retinal imaging is widely used to diagnose ophthalmic diseases, including glaucoma, diabetic retinopathy (DR), and macular degeneration. The diagnosis relies heavily on the quality of retinal images [7],

H. Fu et al. (Eds.): OMIA 2020, LNCS 12069, pp. 53–61, 2020.
https://doi.org/10.1007/978-3-030-63419-3_6

which, however, varies a lot with the imaging devices and/or the screening conditions [13]. Therefore, retinal image quality assessment (RIQA), particularly no-reference RIQA, is considered an essential step before computer-aided diagnosis (CAD).

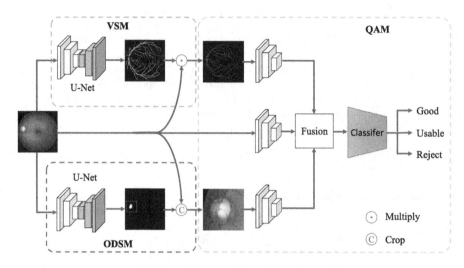

Fig. 1. Pipeline of the proposed SG-Net. The vessel segmentation module generates vessel regions. The optic disc segmentation module generates optic disk regions. The quality assessment module extracts and fuses the features to predict the quality grade of an image. VSM: vessel segmentation module, ODSM: optic disc segmentation module, QAM: quality assessment module.

No-reference RIQA has been extensively studied [5,13,15]. Traditional methods usually extract handcraft features, including the contrast, illumination, and sharpness descriptors, and then use them to train a classifier. For instance, Abdel-Hamid et al. [2] proposed a wavelet-based method to extract generic features (i.e., contrast, blur, and noise) for image quality assessment. Wang et al. [15] extracted features based on three characteristics of the human visual system and employed a support vector machine (SVM) and a decision tree to assess the image quality. The performance of these methods, however, is limited by the discriminatory power of handcrafted features.

Nowadays, deep learning techniques have widely applied to medical image processing tasks, including RIQA. Mahapatra et al. [6] proposed a deep model to combine the local and global image information for image quality assessment. Zago et al. [19] employed a deep neural network pre-trained on ImageNet to detect low-quality retinal images. Fu et al. [3] designed a multiple color-space fusion network (MCF-Net) for RIQA, which makes full use of the information in three color spaces. Shen et al. [12] proposed a multi-task deep learning framework to assess image quality for DR screening. Despite their prevalence, these deep learning models' major strength is the powerful learning-based extraction of the features about image quality factors. However, not all quality factors described by those features interfere with the diagnosis in clinical practice. Comparing to the contrast, illumination, and sharpness of an retinal image, ophthalmologists care more about the visibility and morphology of essential structures, such as the vessel and optic disk [10]. Therefore, we advocate that a diagnosis-oriented RIQA method should focus the image quality assessment on those structures, instead of the whole image. Apparently, there is a potential correlation between RIQA and retinal structure segmentation, since the segmentation results provide the region of interests (ROIs) and the features extracted in these ROIs are more effective for RIQA. As early attempts, Kohler et al. [5] and Welikala et al. [16] analyzed quantitatively the topology and size of retinal vessel based on the segmentation results produced by traditional methods and employed the analytical values to assist the RIQA task. In contrast, we suggest using deep learning techniques to explore the correlation between RIQA and segmentation to further improve the performance of RIQA.

In this paper, we incorporate retinal structure segmentation into RIQA and thus propose a deep learning-based structure-guided model (SG-Net), which is composed of a vessel segmentation module, an optic disc segmentation module, and a quality assessment module (see Fig. 1). For each input retinal image, two segmentation modules are able to produce the ROIs of vessel and optic disk, based on which the quality assessment module extract features and predict its quality grade. Two segmentation modules are trained on two databases with pixel-level labels, and the quality assessment module is trained on the database with image-level quality labels. We evaluated the proposed SG-Net on the Eye-Quality (EyeQ) database [3] and achieved state-of-the-art performance.

2   Database

For this study, we evaluated the proposed SG-Net on the EyeQ database. The EyeQ database contains 12543 training and 16249 testing color retinal images. Each image was selected from the EyePACS database [1] and was manually anno-tated by experts using a three-level quality grading system (i.e., 'Good', 'Usable', and 'Reject'). The quality grading system considers four common quality fac-tors (i.e., blur, illumination, contrast, and artifact) to grade the quality of color retinal images.

The detailed criteria of quality grading system are listed as follows [3]:

'Good': There are no low-quality factors in the retinal image, and all retinopathy characteristics are clearly visible.

'Usable': There are some slight low-quality factors in the retinal image. The retinal image cannot be used by CAD systems. However, ophthalmologists can identify important structures and retinopathy characteristics.

'Reject': There are some serious low-quality factors in the retinal image, and the retinal image cannot be used by CAD systems and ophthalmologists. If the optic disc or macula region is invisible, the retinal image is also graded as 'Reject'.

3 Method

The proposed SG-Net consists of three modules: a vessel segmentation module, an optic disc segmentation module, and a quality assessment module. The pipeline of this model is shown in Fig. 1. We now delve into the details of each module.

3.1 Segmentation Modules

In the vessel segmentation module and optic disc segmentation module, we employ U-Net [9] model to segment important retinal structures, since it has shown promising performance on many medical image segmentation tasks. The architecture of the U-Net model used for this study is illustrated in Fig. 2. In the encoder path, each block consists of two 3×3 convolutional layers, each followed by a rectified linear unit (ReLU), and a 2×2 max-pooling layer with a stride of two. In the decoder path, each block consists of an up-sampling of 2×2 by strides of two and two 3×3 convolutional layers, each followed by a ReLU. The skip connections from the encoder to decoder provide essential high-resolution features. In the last layer, 1×1 convolutions are utilized to reduce the number of output channels to the number of labels. Note that a dropout layer with a rate of 20% is embedded into two adjacent convolutional layers to relieve over-fitting.

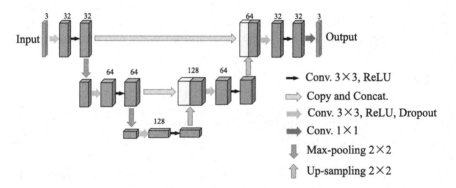

Fig. 2. Architecture of the U-Net used for specific structure segmentation.

For each obtained vessel mask, we multiply it to the retinal image on a pixel-by-pixel basis to filter out non-vessel regions. Based on each obtained optic disk mask, we first generate a preliminary localization of optic disk and then crop the optic disk region from the retinal image. The purpose of cropping is to reduce the influence of redundant background. Finally, we feed each vessel region, optic disk region, and retinal image to the quality assessment module to predict the quality grade.

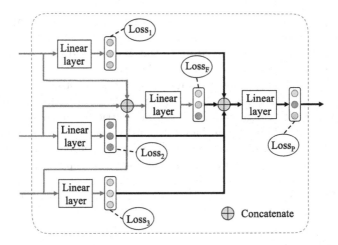

Fig. 3. Illustration of the fusion architecture. The $Loss_i$ denotes the cross-entropy loss of i-th branch in the quality assessment module, $Loss_F$ and $Loss_P$ denote the cross-entropy loss of the two feature fusion results.

3.2 Quality Assessment Module

The quality assessment module consists of three branches. Each branch is a DenseNet-121 [4] model, which has been pre-trained on the ImageNet database. We removed the fully connected linear layers in the branches and replaced them with a fusion architecture (see Fig. 3) [3], which fuses the features from three branches at a feature-level and decision-level simultaneously.

To optimize the quality assessment module, we used the following loss function,

$$Loss = \sum_{i=1}^{3} w_i Loss_i + w_F Loss_F + w_P Loss_P \qquad (1)$$

where $Loss_i$ denotes the cross-entropy loss of i-th branch in the quality assessment module, $Loss_F$ or $Loss_P$ denotes the cross-entropy loss of the fusion results via feature-level ensemble strategy or prediction-level ensemble strategy, respectively. The weight parameters including ω_1, ω_2, ω_3, ω_F, and ω_P are used to balance the five outputs of our proposed SG-Net.

3.3 Implementation Detail

In the proposed SG-Net, the vessel segmentation module, optic disk segmentation module and quality assessment module are trained on DRIVE [14], ORIGA-650 [20] and EyeQ database, respectively.

To train the U-Nets in the vessel segmentation module and optic disk segmentation module, retinal images were pre-processed by using the CLAHE [11], gamma adjusting, and database normalization algorithms. In the training stage, we first randomly extracted 48×48 patches in each pre-processed retinal image, and then adopted the Adam algorithm with a batch size of 32 as the optimizer and the cross-entropy loss as the loss function. In the testing stage, we regularly extracted the retinal patches from testing images and then recompose the predicted patches into the intact results as [17,18].

To train the quality assessment module, we resized the original images, vessel regions and optic disk regions to the size of 224×224. For each input image, we performed random data augmentation, including vertical and horizontal flipping, and rotation. We adopted the mini-batch stochastic gradient descent (mini-batch SGD) algorithm to optimize the quality assessment module and set the batch size to 32, the learning rate to 0.01, and the maximum epoch number to 100. Tack into account that each feature has a variable impact on the final prediction, we empirically set weight parameters ω_1, ω_2, ω_3, ω_F, and ω_P to 0.15, 0.1, 0.05, 0.1, and 0.6, respectively.

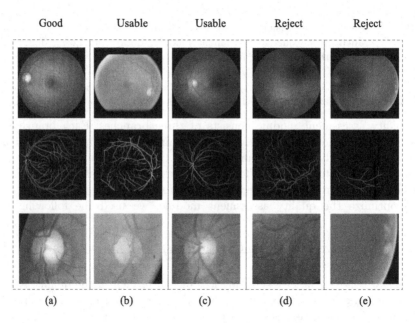

Fig. 4. Five retinal images and their corresponding intermediate results generated by two segmentation modules. The top is the quality degree of each sample.

4   Results

4.1   Comparative Studies

To qualitatively compare the segmentation results of retinal images with different quality degrees, the segmentation results of five retinal images are shown in Fig. 4. It reveals that retinal structure segmentation results are closely related to image quality.

Specifically, we can obtain most of vessels from high-quality retinal images (see Fig. 4 (a)) and get fragmentary vessel from low-quality retinal images (see Fig. 4 (d, e)). The segmentation results of optic disks are interfered with by local illumination conditions. The low illumination makes it difficult to detect optic disks. Meanwhile, other high illumination regions and artifacts will be misjudged as optic disk due to the bad image quality (see Fig. 4 (d, e)).

Next, we compared our model to the backbone network (DenseNet-121) and two existing state-of-the-art models (i.e., MFQ-Net [8] and MCF-Net) using four performance metrics, including the average accuracy, recall, precision, and F1-score. Comparing to existing models, our proposed SG-Net, using both the vessel segmentation module and optic disk segmentation module, is able to lead to a 0.64% increase of accuracy, a 0.17% gain of recall, a 1.43% increase of precision and a 1.12% gain of F1-score. As a result, the SG-Net sets the new state of the art on the EyeQ database (Table 1).

Table 1. The performance of several existing state-of-the-art models on the EyeQ testing database.

Method	Accuracy	Recall	Precision	F1-score
DenseNet-121	0.8943	0.8194	0.8114	0.8152
MFQ-Net	0.8565	0.8564	0.8564	0.8564
MCF-Net	0.9175	0.8645	0.8497	0.8551
Ours	**0.9239**	**0.8662**	**0.8707**	**0.8676**

4.2 Ablation Studies

We carried out an ablation study to show each performance gain caused by the vessel segmentation module and optic disk segmentation module of the proposed SG-Net. In the ablation experiment, we implemented three variants of our SG-Net, including (1) the SG-Net without the optic disk segmentation module, (2) the SG-Net without the vessel segmentation module, and (3) the SG-Net without both segmentation modules. The results obtained by applying the proposed SG-Net and its three variants to the EyeQ database were given in Table 2. It shows that the vessel segmentation module and optic disk segmentation module substantially improves the assessment accuracy.

4.3 Computational Complexity

We implemented the proposed SG-Net and performed all experiments based on the PyTorch (Version: 1.3.1) on a desktop with two Intel(R) Xeon(R) E5-2690 v3 2.60 GHz ×12 CPUs, 128 GB memory and four Nvidia GeForce GTX 2080Ti 11 GB GPUs. The training time cost of the vessel segmentation module, optic disc segmentation module, and quality assessment module is about 4, 4 and 15 h, respectively. In the inference stage, it costs about 12 s to assess a retinal image.

Table 2. The performance of ablation studies of our model on the EyeQ testing database. "✓ , ✗" represents the corresponding module is kept and removed, respectively. VSM: vessel segmentation module, ODSM: optic disc segmentation module.

Segmentation module		Accuracy	Recall	Precision	F1-score
ODSM	VSM				
✗	✗	0.8943	0.8194	0.8114	0.8152
✗	✓	0.9191	0.8595	0.8581	0.8560
✓	✗	0.9109	0.8495	0.8447	0.8435
✓	✓	**0.9239**	**0.8662**	**0.8707**	**0.8676**

5   Conclusion

In this paper, we propose the SG-Net for RIQA tasks, which utilizes discriminative features extracted from specific retinal structures to guide the RIQA task. We evaluated our model on a large scale EyeQ database and achieved state-of-the-art performance. Our results show that the retinal structure segmentation could be a useful clue for the evaluation of the retinal image quality. In our future work, we plan to design a mutual-assisting model, which not only utilizes retinal structure segmentation to assist RIQA tasks but also utilizes the RIQA results to support retinal structure segmentation, aiming to mutually boost the performance on two sub-tasks.

Acknowledgment. This work was supported in part by the Science and Technology Innovation Committee of Shenzhen Municipality, China, under Grants JCYJ20180306171334997, and in part by the National Natural Science Foundation of China under Grants 61771397. We appreciate the efforts devoted to collect and share the DRIVE, ORIGA-650, and EyeQ datasets for comparing retinal image analysis algorithms.

References

1. https://www.kaggle.com/c/diabetic-retinopathy-detection/leaderboard
2. Abdel-Hamid, L.S., El-Rafei, A., El-Ramly, S., Michelson, G., Hornegger, J.: No-reference wavelet based retinal image quality assessment. In: Computational Vision and Medical Image Processing V: VIPImage, pp. 123–129 (2015)
3. Fu, H., et al.: Evaluation of retinal image quality assessment networks in different color-spaces. In: Shen, D., et al. (eds.) MICCAI 2019. LNCS, vol. 11764, pp. 48–56. Springer, Cham (2019). https://doi.org/10.1007/978-3-030-32239-7_6
4. Huang, G., Liu, Z., van der Maaten, L., Weinberger, K.Q.: Densely connected convolutional networks. In: The IEEE Conference on Computer Vision and Pattern Recognition (CVPR), pp. 4700–4708, July 2017
5. Köhler, T., Budai, A., Kraus, M.F., Odstrčilik, J., Michelson, G., Hornegger, J.: Automatic no-reference quality assessment for retinal fundus images using vessel segmentation. In: Proceedings of the 26th IEEE International Symposium on Computer-Based Medical Systems, pp. 95–100 (2013)

6. Mahapatra, D., Roy, P.K., Sedai, S., Garnavi, R.: Retinal image quality classification using saliency maps and CNNs. In: Wang, L., Adeli, E., Wang, Q., Shi, Y., Suk, H.-I. (eds.) MLMI 2016. LNCS, vol. 10019, pp. 172–179. Springer, Cham (2016). https://doi.org/10.1007/978-3-319-47157-0_21

7. Patton, N., et al.: Retinal image analysis: concepts, applications and potential. Prog. Retinal Eye Res. **25**(1), 99–127 (2006)

8. Pérez, A.D., Perdomo, O., González, F.A.: A lightweight deep learning model for mobile eye fundus image quality assessment. In: 15th International Symposium on Medical Information Processing and Analysis, vol. 11330, pp. 151–158 (2020)

9. Ronneberger, O., Fischer, P., Brox, T.: U-Net: convolutional networks for biomedical image segmentation. In: Navab, N., Hornegger, J., Wells, W.M., Frangi, A.F. (eds.) MICCAI 2015. LNCS, vol. 9351, pp. 234–241. Springer, Cham (2015). https://doi.org/10.1007/978-3-319-24574-4_28

10. Salazar-Gonzalez, A., Kaba, D., Li, Y., Liu, X.: Segmentation of the blood vessels and optic disk in retinal images. IEEE J. Biomed. Health Inform. **18**(6), 1874–1886 (2014)

11. Setiawan, A.W., Mengko, T.R., Santoso, O.S., Suksmono, A.B.: Color retinal image enhancement using CLAHE. In: International Conference on ICT for Smart Society, pp. 1–3 (2013)

12. Shen, Y., et al.: Multi-task fundus image quality assessment via transfer learning and landmarks detection. In: Shi, Y., Suk, H.-I., Liu, M. (eds.) MLMI 2018. LNCS, vol. 11046, pp. 28–36. Springer, Cham (2018). https://doi.org/10.1007/978-3-030-00919-9_4

13. Shen, Y., Sheng, B., Fang, R., Li, H., Dai, L., Stolte, S., Qin, J., Jia, W., Shen, D.: Domain-invariant interpretable fundus image quality assessment. Med. Image Anal. **61**, 101654 (2020)

14. Staal, J., Abramoff, M.D., Niemeijer, M., Viergever, M.A., van Ginneken, B.: Ridge-based vessel segmentation in color images of the retina. IEEE Trans. Med. Imaging **23**(4), 501–509 (2004)

15. Wang, S., Jin, K., Lu, H., Cheng, C., Ye, J., Qian, D.: Human visual system-based fundus image quality assessment of portable fundus camera photographs. IEEE Trans. Med. Imaging **35**(4), 1046–1055 (2016)

16. Welikala, R., et al.: Automated retinal image quality assessment on the UK biobank dataset for epidemiological studies. Comput. Biol. Med. **71**, 67–76 (2016)

17. Wu, Y., Xia, Y., Song, Y., Zhang, Y., Cai, W.: Multiscale network followed network model for retinal vessel segmentation. In: Frangi, A.F., Schnabel, J.A., Davatzikos, C., Alberola-López, C., Fichtinger, G. (eds.) MICCAI 2018. LNCS, vol. 11071, pp. 119–126. Springer, Cham (2018). https://doi.org/10.1007/978-3-030-00934-2_14

18. Wu, Y., Xia, Y., Song, Y., Zhang, Y., Cai, W.: NFN+: a novel network followed network for retinal vessel segmentation. Neural Netw. **126**, 153–162 (2020)

19. Zago, G.T., Andreão, R.V., Dorizzi, B., Salles, E.O.T.: Retinal image quality assessment using deep learning. Comput. Biol. Med. **103**, 64–70 (2018)

20. Zhang, Z., et al.: ORIGA-light: an online retinal fundus image database for glaucoma analysis and research. In: 2010 Annual International Conference of the IEEE Engineering in Medicine and Biology, pp. 3065–3068 (2010)

Cascaded Attention Guided Network for Retinal Vessel Segmentation

Mingxing Li, Yueyi Zhang$^{(\boxtimes)}$, Zhiwei Xiong, and Dong Liu

University of Science and Technology of China, Hefei, China
mxli@mail.ustc.edu.cn, zhyuey@ustc.edu.cn

Abstract. Segmentation of retinal vessels is of great importance in the diagnosis of eye-related diseases. Many learning-based methods have been proposed for this task and get encouraging results. In this paper, we propose a novel end-to-end Cascaded Attention Guided Network (CAG-Net) for retinal vessel segmentation, which can generate more accurate results for retinal vessel segmentation. Our CAG-Net is a two-step deep neural network which contains two modules, the prediction module and the refinement module. The prediction module is responsible for generating an initial segmentation map, while the refinement module aims at improving the initial segmentation map. The final segmentation result is obtained by integrating the outputs of the two modules. Both of the two modules adopt an Attention UNet++ (AU-Net++) to boost the performance, which employs Attention guided Convolutional blocks (AC blocks) on the decoder. The experimental results show that our proposed network achieved state-of-the-art performance on the three public retinal datasets DRIVE, CHASE_DB1 and STARE.

Keywords: Retinal vessel segmentation · Channel attention · Cascaded network

1 Introduction

Retinal vessel segmentation plays a key role in early diagnosis of eye-related diseases, such as diabetes, hypertension and arteriosclerosis [3]. Manual segmentation for retinal vessel is significantly laborious and requires professional skills. A lot of approaches have been proposed for automatic retinal vessel segmentation to save the time of ophthalmologists. However, it is still challenging to accomplish accurate and fine segmentation for the retinal vessel.

Image processing and machine learning are two widely employed traditional methods in the retinal vessel segmentation. For instance, Soares et al. [13] applied Gabor wavelet transform to denoise vessels and classified pixels by the gaussian mixture model (GMM). Ricci et al. [11] developed two orthogonal line detectors to extract a feature vector and classified pixels by support vector machines (SVM). Recently, deep learning based neural networks, especially fully convolutional networks (FCNs), have shown outstanding performance in the field of

© Springer Nature Switzerland AG 2020
H. Fu et al. (Eds.): OMIA 2020, LNCS 12069, pp. 62–71, 2020.
https://doi.org/10.1007/978-3-030-63419-3_7

image segmentation. Many approaches based on the U-Net structure [12] are proposed for retinal vessels segmentation, such as [15,19,23], which demonstrate remarkable performance. In [18], Yan et al. classified the retinal vessels into a thick group and a thin group according to the pixel width of the vessels. Then they proposed a two-stage approach for segmentation of the thick and think vessels respectively. Inspired by the previous works, we plan to design a two-stage neural network for the task of retinal vessel segmentation. For the basic architecture, we attempt to revised UNet++ [21], which is a popular variant of U-Net. Although UNet++ is very successful in many bio-medical segmentation tasks, from our perspective, it has two main limitations for retinal vessel segmentation: 1) the extensive usage of BatchNorm layers in UNet++ is not conducive to the convergence of the network in the experiments when mixing dark samples in a random-cropped batch. Here, the dark samples are randomly cropped patches with the almost pure background. 2) The simple 1×1 convolutional layer is not able to fully fuse the various scale information of the decoder, which can be further improved by the channel attention mechanism.

In this paper, we introduce a Cascaded Attention Guided Network (CAG-Net) for retinal vessel segmentation. CAG-Net accomplishes the segmentation task in two steps. First, the prediction module predicts the initial segmentation map based on the color retinal image. Then the refinement module further refines segmentation map leveraging the color retinal image and the initial segmentation map. The outputs of the two modules are concatenated together to generate the final segmentation result. Inside the CAG-Net, we introduce an Attention U-Net++ (AU-Net++), which is used in both of the two modules. AU-Net++ includes Attention Guided Convolutional blocks (AC blocks) to fuse the multi-scale information adaptively. Extensive experiments were conducted on the three public datasets: the DRIVE, CHASE_DB1 and STARE datasets. The F1-score/Area Under Curve (AUC) of our CAG-Net is 0.8298/0.9867, 0.8227/0.9880 and 0.8254/0.9894 respectively.

2   Methodology

2.1   Cascaded Deep Learning Network

Figure 1 shows the architecture of our proposed CAG-Net. In the prediction module, AU-Net++ predicts an initial segmentation map from the color retinal image. Next, the generated initial segmentation map is concatenated with the original retinal image to form a new volume, which is the input of the refinement module. Then, the refinement module also employs AU-Net++ to enhance the segmentation map especially for the slender structures. The outputs of the two modules are concatenated together. After a 1×1 convolutional layer and a softmax layer, the final segmentation map is predicted.

In the training stage, we adopt a hybrid loss function for the proposed network, which can be depicted as:

$$loss = loss_{ce}(y, \hat{y}_{pred}) + loss_{dice}(y, \hat{y}_{final}) \tag{1}$$

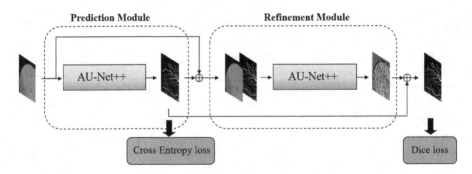

Fig. 1. The architecture of the proposed CAG-Net for retinal vessel segmentation. The proposed CAG-Net consists of a prediction module and a refinement module. '$\oplus$' denotes concatenation.

where $loss_{ce}$ denotes the cross entropy loss, $loss_{dice}$ denotes the dice loss [6], and y, $\hat{y}_{pred}$, $\hat{y}_{final}$ represent ground truth, the segmentation map generated from the prediction module and the final segmentation map respectively. Note the dice loss directly affects the final output instead of the refinement module. With this setting of loss function, the prediction module generates the segmentation map pixel-wisely close to the ground truth, meanwhile the final segmentation map is forced to approach the ground truth from the perspective of regions. The refinement module essentially learns the segmentation residual (See Fig. 3) and focuses more on the under-segmented region of the prediction module.

2.2 Attention UNet++

Inside our CAG-Net, we propose an Attention UNet++ (AU-Net++), which has the Attention Guided Convolutional block (AC block) on the decoder. An AC block has four components: a channel attention layer, a convolutional layer, an InstanceNorm layer and a ReLU layer. Here we employ the InstanceNorm layer, which is the normalization of a single image, to replace the BatchNorm layer in classical convolutional block of the UNet++. Therefore, the dark samples in a training batch will not disturb the training process and further degrade the prediction results.

The channel attention mechanism in [20] is employed for the image super-resolution task, which can adaptively enhance important channel-wise features. UNet++ simply uses the 1×1 convolutional layer to fuse the various scale information of the decoder. In our design, we utilize the channel attention layer at the beginning of the AC block to highlight critical feature maps in different scales. For the channel attention layer in each AC block, we set the reduction ratio of channel numbers as 4. In [20], the channel attention mechanism used Adaptive Average Pooling (AAP) for downsampling. Given that Max Pooling can retain more discriminative information [7], we replace Adaptive Average Pooling with Adaptive Max Pooling (AMP) in our design of the channel attention layer.

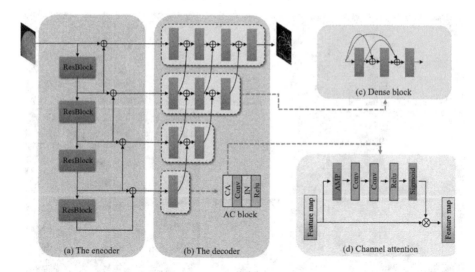

Fig. 2. The details of AU-Net++. The blue dashed lines point to the block details. '⊕' and '⊗' denote concatenation and element-wise multiplication.(Color figure online)

For each dense block of the decoder, the Conv-BatchNorm-Relu blocks in UNet++ are replaced by our proposed AC blocks. Figure 2(b) gives more details for the decoder.

3 Experiments

3.1 Datasets

We evaluate the proposed CAG-Net on three widely used retinal datasets DRIVE [14], CHASE_DB1 [10] and STARE [2]. The DRIVE dataset consists of 40 randomly selected color fundus retinal images of size 565×584. Officially, the DRIVE dataset is split into two equal groups for training and testing. The CHASE_DB1 dataset contains 28 color fundus retinal images in total. The resolution of images in the CHASE_DB1 is 999×960. The STARE dataset has 20 color fundus retinal images of size 700×605. Note the CHASE_DB1 and STARE datasets have no clear partition for training and testing. We follow the popular setting in [5] that the training/testing number is 20/8 and 16/4 on the CHASE_DB1 and STARE datasets respectively.

3.2 Implementation Details

Our CAG-Net was implemented with the Pytorch framework (version 1.1). Two NVIDIA GTX 1080Ti graphics cards were utilized for training and testing. Different from other approaches, retinal pre-processing operations (i.e., contrast limited adaptive histogram equalization and gamma adjustment) were not required

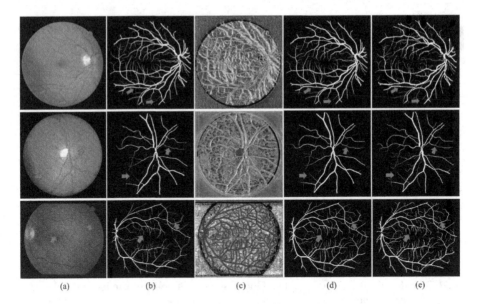

Fig. 3. (a) Test retinal images from the DRIVE, CHASE_DB1, and STARE datasets respectively. (b) The segmentation map of the prediction module. (c) The segmentation map of the refinement module (best view in contrast enhancement). (d) Final segmentation map. (e) Ground-truth of the test retinal images. The blue arrows highlight the local details. (Color figure online)

for our CAG-Net. Data augmentation, including random flipping and random contrast adjustment, was utilized to increase the training samples. To efficiently train our CAG-Net, we cropped image patches from the original images. The size of sampled patches for different datasets is not universal. It depends on the size of the original image on the dataset. For the three datasets, we adopted 0.3 as the ratio of the sample patch size to the original image size. Thus, the sampled patch sizes for the DRIVE, CHASE_DB1 and STARE datasets were 169×175, 299×288, 210×181 respectively. To fit the feature pyramid structure of our CAG-Net, we further interpolated the sampled patches to the size that was multiples of 16. Essentially, our CAG-Net is a variant of fully convolutional network. Thus in the testing stage, the patching strategy is not required. CAG-Net is able to predict the segmentation results with the input image of original resolution. In our experiments, we adopted Adam optimizer [4] with the initial learning rate 0.005, to train CAG-Net. Scheduling of the learning rate is not employed in the training process. For the three datasets, we adopted batchsize 4 and maximum number of iterations 24000 in the training process. The inference time of our proposed CAG-Net is measured. Averagely, it took 0.252, 0.270 and 0.290 seconds on the DRIVE, CHASE_DB1 and STARE datasets respectively for a single image.

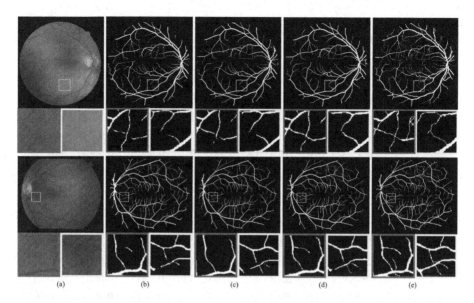

Fig. 4. (a) Test retinal images from the DRIVE and STARE datasets respectively. (b) The segmentation result of UNet++. (c) The segmentation result of AG-Net. (d) The segmentation result of our CAG-Net. (e) Ground-truth of the test images.

3.3 Evaluation Methods

To evaluate the performance of CAG-Net for retinal vessel segmentation, we compare the segmentation results of CAG-Net and other approaches in both qualitative and quantitative ways. For the qualitative comparison, we focus on the visual effects of vessel segmentation, especially for capillaries. For the quantitative comparison, we utilize five metrics for evaluation, which are F1-score, Sensitivity (SE), Specificity (SP), Accuracy (ACC) and Area Under Curve (AUC).

3.4 Results

Figure 3 shows the retinal segmentation results of CAG-Net on the three datasets. The five columns of images present the color fundus retinal image, the segmentation map generated by the prediction module, the normalized map generated by the refinement module, the final segmentation map generated by CAG-Net and the ground-truth annotation respectively. By observing the details of the segmentation maps, it can be seen that our refinement module successfully enhances the initial segmentation map, especially adding segmentation for thin vessels on the CHASE_DB1 and STARE datasets. In addition, it can be seen that our final segmentation map is very close to the ground truth annotation.

In Fig. 4, we qualitatively compare the segmentation results on the two retinal image examples from the DRIVE and STARE datasets. In addition to CAG-Net, the segmentation results of UNet++ [21] and AG-Net [19] are also shown.

Table 1. Performance of CAG-Net and other methods on the DRIVE, CHASE_DB1 and STARE datasets.

Dataset	Method	Year	F1	SE	SP	ACC	AUC
DRIVE	R2U-Net [1]	2018	0.8171	0.7792	0.9813	0.9556	0.9784
	MS-NFN [17]	2018	–	0.7844	0.9819	0.9567	0.9807
	DDNet [8]	2019	–	0.8126	0.9788	0.9594	0.9796
	Vessel-net [16]	2019	–	0.8038	0.9802	0.9578	0.9821
	DEU-Net [15]	2019	0.8270	0.7940	0.9816	0.9567	0.9772
	ACE-Net [22]	2019	–	0.7725	0.9842	0.9569	0.9742
	AG-Net [19]	2019	–	0.8100	0.9848	0.9692	0.9856
	CS-Net [9]	2019	–	0.8170	**0.9854**	0.9632	0.9798
	IterNet [5]	2020	0.8205	0.7735	0.9838	0.9574	0.9816
	CAG-Net	2020	**0.8298**	**0.8397**	0.9827	**0.9700**	**0.9867**
CHASE_DB1	R2U-Net [1]	2018	0.7928	0.7756	0.9712	0.9634	0.9815
	MS-NFN [17]	2018	–	0.7538	0.9847	0.9637	0.9825
	Vessel-Net [16]	2019	–	0.8132	0.9814	0.9661	0.9860
	AG-Net [19]	2019	–	0.8186	0.9848	0.9743	0.9863
	DEU-Net [15]	2019	0.8037	0.8074	0.9821	0.9661	0.9812
	IterNet [5]	2020	0.8073	0.7970	0.9823	0.9655	0.9851
	CAG-Net	2020	**0.8227**	**0.8520**	**0.9853**	**0.9768**	**0.9880**
STARE	UNet [5]	2015	0.7594	0.6681	0.9939	0.9736	0.9779
	DB-UNet [5]	2018	0.7691	0.6807	**0.9940**	0.9745	0.9801
	DUNet [5]	2019	0.7629	0.6810	0.9931	0.9736	0.9823
	AG-Net [19]	2019	0.8193	0.7891	0.9914	0.9787	0.9863
	IterNet [5]	2020	0.8146	0.7715	0.9919	0.9782	**0.9915**
	CAG-Net	2020	**0.8254**	**0.8127**	0.9901	**0.9791**	0.9894

To better observe the differences, we amplify two small blocks in the segmentation results and show them inside two windows with the red and yellow border. Compared with UNet++ and AG-Net, CAG-Net preserves richer vessel structures. In summary, it can be seen that CAG-Net recovers the topology tree of retinal vessel more accurately, which is beneficial for ophthalmologists to make the diagnosis for eye-related diseases.

The quantitative comparison results between our CAG-Net and other previous state-of-the-art methods on the three datasets are shown in Table 1. From Table 1, it can be summarized that our proposed CAG-Net has the best F1-score, sensitivity, accuracy and top-two AUC on the three datasets. The F1-scores of CAG-Net are 0.28%/1.54%/0.61% higher than the second best method. The sensitivity values of our CAG-Net are 2.27%/3.34%/2.36% higher than the second best method. The accuracy values of our CAG-Net are 0.08%/0.25%/0.04% higher than the second best method. From both qualitative and quantitative perspective, the proposed CAG-Net achieves state-of-the-art performance on the DRIVE, CHASE_DB1 and STARE datasets.

3.5 Ablation Study

To validate the effectiveness of each component, we performed the ablation study on the DRIVE, CHASE_DB1 and STARE datasets. We compared the segmentation performances of four networks: (1) U-Net++, (2) CAG-Net without refinement module (w/o Refinement), (3) CAG-Net without channel attention mechanism (w/o CA) and (4) CAG-Net. Here CAG-Net w/o Refinement is a single AU-Net++ (i.e. UNet++ with the AC blocks). As shown in Table 2, the F1-score/AUC of CAG-Net w/o Refinement is higher than UNet++ by 0.22%/3.32%, 0.44%/3.46% and 0.23%/3.71% on the three datasets respectively. Besides, we also analyzed the effect of channel attention mechanism in the AC block and refinement module, which also had obvious improvement.

Also we performed several experiments on the setting of loss function. DICE and CE denote dice loss and cross entropy loss respectively. The left side of "+" is the loss function of the prediction module, and the right side of " + " is the loss function of final output. Our CAG-Net utilizes the setting of CE+DICE. It can be seen that the CE+DICE setting beats other settings multiple times when comparing the F1-score and AUC metrics on the three datasets, which proves that the loss function of CAG-Net is more reasonable.

Table 2. Ablation study on the DRIVE, CHASE_DB1 and STARE datasets.

	DRIVE		CHASE_DB1		STARE	
	F1-score	AUC	F1-score	AUC	F1-score	AUC
U-Net++	0.8251	0.9515	0.8154	0.9505	0.8196	0.9487
CAG-Net w/o Refinement	0.8273	0.9847	0.8198	0.9851	0.8219	0.9858
CAG-Net w/o CA	0.8261	0.9840	0.8207	0.9874	0.8232	0.9886
CAG-Net w/ DICE+DICE	0.8283	0.9846	0.8211	0.9875	**0.8263**	0.9883
CAG-Net w/ CE+CE	0.8292	0.9844	0.8202	**0.9885**	0.8208	0.9878
CAG-Net w/ DICE+CE	0.8281	0.9863	0.8202	0.9872	0.8245	0.9872
CAG-Net	**0.8298**	**0.9867**	**0.8227**	0.9880	0.8254	**0.9894**

4 Conclusion

In this paper, we propose an end-to-end Cascaded Attention Guided Network, named CAG-Net, for retinal vessel segmentation. Within CAG-Net, a prediction module is first deployed to generate an initial segmentation map. Then we cascade a refinement module to enhance the segmentation map. Both of the two modules utilize an Attention UNet++, which extends UNet++ with AC block. Experimental results on three retinal datasets demonstrate that our proposed CAG-Net achieves the state-of-the-art performance.

Acknowledgement. This work was supported in part by Anhui Provincial Natural Science Foundation under Grant 1908085QF256 and the Fundamental Research Funds for the Central Universities under Grant WK2380000002.

References

1. Alom, M.Z., Hasan, M., Yakopcic, C., Taha, T.M., Asari, V.K.: Recurrent residual convolutional neural network based on U-Net (R2U-Net) for medical image segmentation. arXiv preprint arXiv:1802.06955 (2018)
2. Hoover, A., Kouznetsova, V., Goldbaum, M.: Locating blood vessels in retinal images by piecewise threshold probing of a matched filter response. IEEE Trans. Med. Imaging **19**(3), 203–210 (2000)
3. Kanski, J.J., Bowling, B.: Clinical Ophthalmology: A Systematic Approach. Elsevier Health Sciences, Amsterdam (2011)
4. Kingma, D.P., Ba, J.: Adam: a method for stochastic optimization. arXiv preprint arXiv:1412.6980 (2014)
5. Li, L., Verma, M., Nakashima, Y., Nagahara, H., Kawasaki, R.: IterNet: retinal image segmentation utilizing structural redundancy in vessel networks. In: The IEEE Winter Conference on Applications of Computer Vision, pp. 3656–3665 (2020)
6. Milletari, F., Navab, N., Ahmadi, S.A.: V-Net: fully convolutional neural networks for volumetric medical image segmentation. In: 2016 Fourth International Conference on 3D Vision (3DV), pp. 565–571. IEEE (2016)
7. Mishkin, D., Sergievskiy, N., Matas, J.: Systematic evaluation of convolution neural network advances on the imagenet. Comput. Vis. Image Underst. **161**, 11–19 (2017)
8. Mou, L., Chen, L., Cheng, J., Gu, Z., Zhao, Y., Liu, J.: Dense dilated network with probability regularized walk for vessel detection. IEEE Trans. Med. Imaging **39**, 1392–1403 (2019)
9. Mou, L., et al.: CS-Net: channel and spatial attention network for curvilinear structure segmentation. In: Shen, D., et al. (eds.) MICCAI 2019. LNCS, vol. 11764, pp. 721–730. Springer, Cham (2019). https://doi.org/10.1007/978-3-030-32239-7_80
10. Owen, C.G., et al.: Measuring retinal vessel tortuosity in 10-year-old children: validation of the computer-assisted image analysis of the retina (CAIAR) program. Invest. Ophthalmol. Vis. Sci. **50**(5), 2004–2010 (2009)
11. Ricci, E., Perfetti, R.: Retinal blood vessel segmentation using line operators and support vector classification. IEEE Trans. Med. Imaging **26**(10), 1357–1365 (2007)
12. Ronneberger, O., Fischer, P., Brox, T.: U-Net: convolutional networks for biomedical image segmentation. In: Navab, N., Hornegger, J., Wells, W.M., Frangi, A.F. (eds.) MICCAI 2015. LNCS, vol. 9351, pp. 234–241. Springer, Cham (2015). https://doi.org/10.1007/978-3-319-24574-4_28
13. Soares, J.V., Leandro, J.J., Cesar, R.M., Jelinek, H.F., Cree, M.J.: Retinal vessel segmentation using the 2-D gabor wavelet and supervised classification. IEEE Trans. Med. Imaging **25**(9), 1214–1222 (2006)
14. Staal, J., Abràmoff, M.D., Niemeijer, M., Viergever, M.A., Van Ginneken, B.: Ridge-based vessel segmentation in color images of the retina. IEEE Trans. Med. Imaging **23**(4), 501–509 (2004)
15. Wang, B., Qiu, S., He, H.: Dual encoding U-Net for retinal vessel segmentation. In: Shen, D., et al. (eds.) MICCAI 2019. LNCS, vol. 11764, pp. 84–92. Springer, Cham (2019). https://doi.org/10.1007/978-3-030-32239-7_10

16. Wu, Y., et al.: Vessel-Net: retinal vessel segmentation under multi-path supervision. In: Shen, D., et al. (eds.) MICCAI 2019. LNCS, vol. 11764, pp. 264–272. Springer, Cham (2019). https://doi.org/10.1007/978-3-030-32239-7_30

17. Wu, Y., Xia, Y., Song, Y., Zhang, Y., Cai, W.: Multiscale network followed network model for retinal vessel segmentation. In: Frangi, A.F., Schnabel, J.A., Davatzikos, C., Alberola-López, C., Fichtinger, G. (eds.) MICCAI 2018. LNCS, vol. 11071, pp. 119–126. Springer, Cham (2018). https://doi.org/10.1007/978-3-030-00934-2_14

18. Yan, Z., Yang, X., Cheng, K.T.: A three-stage deep learning model for accurate retinal vessel segmentation. IEEE J. Biomed. Health Inform. **23**(4), 1427–1436 (2018)

19. Zhang, S., et al.: Attention guided network for retinal image segmentation. In: Shen, D., et al. (eds.) MICCAI 2019. LNCS, vol. 11764, pp. 797–805. Springer, Cham (2019). https://doi.org/10.1007/978-3-030-32239-7_88

20. Zhang, Y., Li, K., Li, K., Wang, L., Zhong, B., Fu, Y.: Image super-resolution using very deep residual channel attention networks. In: Proceedings of the European Conference on Computer Vision (ECCV), pp. 286–301 (2018)

21. Zhou, Z., Rahman Siddiquee, M.M., Tajbakhsh, N., Liang, J.: UNet++: a nested U-Net architecture for medical image segmentation. In: Stoyanov, D., et al. (eds.) DLMIA/ML-CDS -2018. LNCS, vol. 11045, pp. 3–11. Springer, Cham (2018). https://doi.org/10.1007/978-3-030-00889-5_1

22. Zhu, Y., Chen, Z., Zhao, S., Xie, H., Guo, W., Zhang, Y.: ACE-Net: biomedical image segmentation with augmented contracting and expansive paths. In: Shen, D., et al. (eds.) MICCAI 2019. LNCS, vol. 11764, pp. 712–720. Springer, Cham (2019). https://doi.org/10.1007/978-3-030-32239-7_79

23. Zhuang, J.: LadderNet: multi-path networks based on U-Net for medical image segmentation. arXiv preprint arXiv:1810.07810 (2018)

Self-supervised Denoising via Diffeomorphic Template Estimation: Application to Optical Coherence Tomography

Guillaume Gisbert[1], Neel Dey[1(✉)], Hiroshi Ishikawa[2], Joel Schuman[2], James Fishbaugh[1], and Guido Gerig[1]

[1] Computer Science and Engineering, New York University, Brooklyn, NY, USA
neel.dey@nyu.edu
[2] Ophthalmology, New York University, New York, NY, USA

Abstract. Optical Coherence Tomography (OCT) is pervasive in both the research and clinical practice of Ophthalmology. However, OCT images are strongly corrupted by noise, limiting their interpretation. Current OCT denoisers leverage assumptions on noise distributions or generate targets for training deep supervised denoisers via averaging of repeat acquisitions. However, recent self-supervised advances allow the training of deep denoising networks using only repeat acquisitions *without* clean targets as ground truth, reducing the burden of supervised learning. Despite the clear advantages of self-supervised methods, their use is precluded as OCT shows strong structural deformations even between sequential scans of the same subject due to involuntary eye motion. Further, direct nonlinear alignment of repeats induces correlation of the noise between images. In this paper, we propose a joint diffeomorphic template estimation and denoising framework which enables the use of self-supervised denoising for motion deformed repeat acquisitions, without empirically registering their noise realizations. Strong qualitative and quantitative improvements are achieved in denoising OCT images, with generic utility in any imaging modality amenable to multiple exposures.

1 Introduction

Optical coherence tomography (OCT) is a frontline tool in the non-invasive investigation of ocular microstructure and widely informs critical decisions in Ophthalmology. However, due to the physics of its acquisition, speckle noise permeates OCT volumes and strongly limits the delineation of image structure and its signal-to-noise ratio, a problem which is especially pronounced in images acquired on clinical scanners. To this end, image restoration via denoising may be crucial in the evaluation of OCT imaging, both in a clinical setting and in enabling improved downstream analysis (e.g., segmentation of structures or detection of pathology) in research.

© Springer Nature Switzerland AG 2020
H. Fu et al. (Eds.): OMIA 2020, LNCS 12069, pp. 72–82, 2020.
https://doi.org/10.1007/978-3-030-63419-3_8

Input   Our Denoising

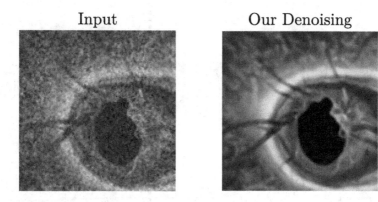

Fig. 1. Through a joint diffeomorphic template estimation and denoising framework, our methods enable the improved assessment of relevant image features in OCT.

Denoising is a foundational task in image analysis and is an active field of research. Recent years have seen the widespread adoption of supervised deep networks which train mappings between noisy images to clean ones. In OCT or Fluorescence Microscopy, these clean targets for supervised training are often obtained by averaging multiple images [10,13,24,29]. Yet, techniques based on dictionary learning [16] or non-local patch statistics in image or transform domains (e.g., BM3D [9]) remain competitive in unsupervised image denoising.

Unsupervised deep denoisers have seen rapid progress of late, and have a much lower burden of data preparation as they do not require clean targets. Cycle-consistent image translation methods [30] have been used successfully for OCT image enhancement when a dataset acquired on a high-quality scanner is available [26]. However, mappings produced by cycle-consistent methods are brittle and are subject to high-frequency adversarial noise [3,8]. In parallel, several works [4,19,20] show that noisy images can be denoised via masking of the reconstruction loss function or network receptive field. However, this family of methods is inapplicable to OCT due to their strong requirement of independent identically distributed (i.i.d.) pixel noise [14], leading to checkerboard artefacts.

Most promising for our application, Noise2Noise [21] makes no pixelwise i.i.d. assumption, and furthermore no assumption on noise following a specific distribution (e.g., Gaussian), and that a denoiser can be trained by replacing the clean target with repeat acquisitions with independent noise between the scans. However, due to eye motion in OCT, repeat scans are structurally misaligned and Noise2Noise is precluded. Even after affine alignment, a linear average of the registered images may be blurry due to nonlinear deformation of ocular microstructure. Correction for this nonlinear deformation is non-trivial as any nonlinear registration algorithm may register noise in addition to structure, breaking the assumptions of Noise2Noise. To this end, a registration and Noise2Noise method was presented in [7], but was designed for only two repeats, and did not address the registration of structure versus noise.

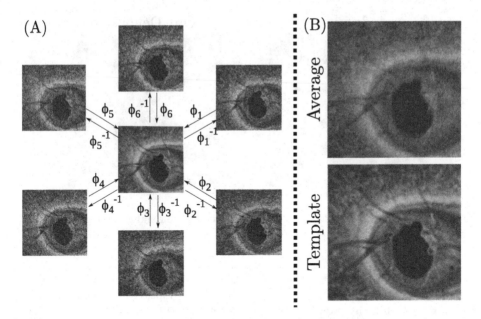

Fig. 2. (A) A high-level overview of template estimation. (B) Comparison between a linear average after affine alignment (top) and the estimated template (bottom). As templates are deformable averages, they create intrinsically sharper representations.

In this paper, we propose a joint diffeomorphic template estimation and denoising framework. Given a subject with n repeats, we first construct a diffeomorphic template [1, 2, 15] for each subject that minimizes geometric deformation to each of the n repeats while registering each acquisition to this template via careful unsupervised pre-filtering and multi-resolution registration. Once these deformation fields are obtained on the pre-filtered images, we apply these warps to the original images, which empirically ensures that only structure is registered and not noise. We then train a Noise2Noise network on paired slices to denoise the individual OCT images. The presented work is a substantial extension of our preliminary conference abstract [12], including methodological details and thorough experiments. Our approach leads to quantitative improvement of reference-free scores of image quality against several unsupervised denoising methods.

2   Methods

2.1   Problem Formulation

A high-level overview of our pipeline is given in Fig. 3. Given a dataset of m subjects with n repeats each with nonlinear deformation, the goal is to learn a denoising function f that maps noisy images to clean images.

To enable the learning of f via a Noise2Noise-like method, we co-register the n repeat 3D OCT scans for each of the m subjects to m subject-specific templates as detailed in Sect. 2.2. Once registered, f can be efficiently learned via methods detailed in Sect. 2.3 on 2D slices rather than 3D volumes given the strong anisotropy of OCT imaging.

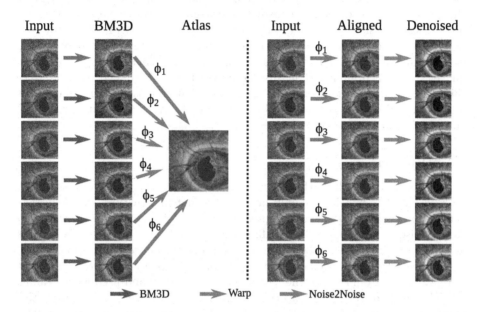

Fig. 3. Overview of the framework. The raw 3D OCT scans are denoised using BM3D and are then used to build a template with deformations Φ_i. Once obtained, each Φ_i is applied on its corresponding raw scan, thus enabling the use of Noise2Noise denoising. Deformation fields and templates are estimated in 3D to fully accommodate eye motion.

2.2 Registration

Given n repeats to be registered, a reference volume could be arbitrarily chosen to register the remaining $n-1$ volumes to. However, this approach leads to biased registration estimation as the user-selected target may require some images to deform significantly more than others depending on the choice of reference. Instead, one can estimate an unbiased template/atlas [2,15] which minimizes geometric deformation to each of the n repeats as shown in Fig. 2(a), doing this by alternating between template estimation and nonlinear registration of the individual images. Of note, template estimation is ubiquitous in neuroimaging, but is starting to find applications in Ophthalmology in both OCT [25] and retinal fluorescence microscopy [11].

To avoid the registration of noise in addition to structure, each OCT volume is first denoised via BM3D [9] applied slicewise. While BM3D does not preserve all structure, it retains sufficient clarity of fine structure for detail preservation in template estimation. We observe that the volumetric equivalent of BM3D (BM4D [22]) leads to strong block-like artefacts due to the high anisotropy of

OCT as shown in Fig. 4. For non-linear registration, we take a multi-resolution strategy, at each stage smoothing with a Gaussian kernel to avoid aliasing, which further encourages the registration of local and global structure rather than local noise. All deformation fields are diffeomorphic, ensuring that no topological changes (tearing, holes, etc.) are made to the structures during registration. This process leads to sharper estimates of image averages as shown in Fig. 2(b).

Once the deformation fields Φ_i mapping images to the template are obtained, we discard the prefiltered images and apply the deformations to the original images such that primarily structure, rather than noise, is aligned. We note that this procedure does not theoretically guarantee that no noise is correlated in the registration. However, we find it to be empirically successful towards the desired outcome in our application.

2.3 Denoising

Noise2Noise [21] is built on the assumption that if a denoising network is trained on repeat images which vary only in noise and not in structure, the clean target can be replaced by a noisy repeat if the noise is zero mean. However, if Noise2Noise is directly applied on affinely aligned images, the output is blurred as shown in Fig. 4 as the network cannot distinguish between noise and structure. Once m subject-specific templates for m subjects are built, random pairs of repeat slices from each of the n repeats are extracted and used as a training set. This leads to $(m \times {}^nP_2 \times z)$ training points for Noise2Noise where z is the number of 2D slices. As the variance of the denoising estimate decays with the square of the number of training points [21], we find that a small OCT dataset with multiple repeats trained slicewise rapidly becomes sufficient for training.

3   Experiments

3.1 Dataset

Our training dataset consists of 24 subjects who underwent 6 repeat OCT acquisitions, each. The images were of resolution $200 \times 200 \times 600$ were captured on the Cirrus HD5000. Once registered with the process detailed in Sect. 2.2, we build every pair of images to train a Noise2Noise network. We crop each slice to a 128×128 central field of view. Given 6 repeats, we have ${}^6P_2$ pairs for each z-slice for each subject. In total, this generates 432,000 training examples. No data augmentation was used in our experiments. As this work pertains to unsupervised denoising without available ground truth, we do not consider a held-out test set.

3.2 Implementation Details

Initial pre-registration denoising was performed on 2D slices with a `MATLAB` BM3D implementation[1] with default parameters and $\sigma = 0.07$. To estimate

---

[1] http://www.cs.tut.fi/~foi/GCF-BM3D/.

subject-specific diffeomorphic templates we use ANTs[2], with the local normalized cross-correlation metric in a multi-resolution fashion for $50 \times 25 \times 10 \times 10$ iterations at one-sixth, one-fourth, half, and full resolution, respectively.

For training the Noise2Noise-network, we use the TensorFlow implementation provided by the authors[3]. Briefly, it employs a U-Net architecture [27] with 5 downsampling and upsampling layers each. As in the original work, we do not use any regularization or normalization during training. The network was trained for two hundred epochs with a batch size of 4 with the Adam optimizer [17] with an L_1 loss, a learning rate of 0.0002 and $\beta_1 = 0.9$ and $\beta_2 = 0.999$. Training was performed for two days on a single NVIDIA V100 GPU. New, unseen images are denoised in seconds.

3.3 Evaluation Methods

Denoising methods and image quality improvements are popularly benchmarked by using peak signal-to-noise ratio (PSNR) or structural similarity (SSIM) [28]. However, these scores require noise-free reference images which do not exist in our applications. Further, in preliminary experiments, we found scores that rely on statistics of natural images [23] do not correlate well with human perception of denoising quality in OCT images and hence do not use them. Instead, we present two different scores that do not require reference images or training sets of high-quality images.

The first is the Q-metric [31], which selects anisotropic patches in the noisy input to attribute a score based on the singular value decomposition properties of the patch and then averages the patch scores. The second is another no-reference metric developed by [18] (hence referred to as AD), which measures the structural similarity between the noisy input and the denoised estimation, with the underlying assumption that the noise should be independent in the original image. Higher is better for each score[4]. Of note, both of these scores are image-dependent, i.e., score improvement on one image cannot be compared to another image. However, we average the scores on the same dataset for all denoising methods benchmarked, so the values are now comparable.

3.4 Results

We benchmark a variety of unsupervised denoising methods, including a simple linear average of all repeats after affine alignment, Non-Local Means [6], BM3D [9], BM4D [22], Noise2Noise (with affine alignment only), and our method. We do not compare with self-supervised methods that require only single noisy images without pairs [4,19,20] as these methods require pixelwise i.i.d. noise not satisfied

---

[2] http://stnava.github.io/ANTs/.

[3] https://github.com/NVlabs/noise2noise.

[4] For [18], Algorithm 1 in the paper suggests that lower is better. However, their code negates the final correlation value, thus making higher better. We do the same to maintain consistency with their convention.

by OCT images, thus leading to checkerboard artefacts [14] and creating an unfair comparison.

Table 1. Quantitative denoising performance benchmark based on [18,31] of all unsupervised denoising methods compared. Higher is better for each score. The linear average and Noise2Noise methods use images after affine alignment but without diffeomorphic atlas registration.

Method	Mean Q-metric [31] ($\uparrow$)	Mean AD [18] ($\uparrow$)
Linear average (affine alignment)	2.8527	0.4677
Non-local means [6]	12.2789	0.6585
BM3D (slicewise) [9]	15.7812	0.6499
BM4D [22]	12.2843	0.6858
Noise2Noise (affine alignment) [21]	16.7860	0.4646
Ours	**29.5722**	**0.7183**

Qualitative results are shown in Fig. 4 for the XY slices that our model was trained on, further including assembled XZ and *en face* mean projections commonly used in ophthalmology for completeness. We observe that while a linear average does denoise, subtle details are lost due to nonlinear deformation. Non-local 2D patch-based methods blur details that may be relevant structurally. BM4D introduces significant block-like artefacts visible in the *en face* view due to image anisotropy. A direct application of Noise2Noise on affinely aligned images significantly blurs detail. Finally, our proposed method shows a net improvement in image quality, reducing noise drastically while preserving sharp edges.

Quantitatively, we report the dataset-wide scores detailed in Table 1. We find that for both scores, the proposed framework outperforms the baselines. Interestingly, we note that the blurry reconstruction produced by a direct application of Noise2Noise (with affine alignment) is marginally preferred by the Q-metric over the slicewise application of BM3D (which is perceptually better denoised). This may suggest that AD is a more reliable score of image denoising quality for this application, as pointed out by [18].

4   Discussion

In this paper, we present a self-supervised framework to denoise repeat acquisitions of images subject to strong noise and deformation, common in OCT imaging. Strong qualitative and quantitative improvements are observed w.r.t. unsupervised baselines, denoising while maintaining fine detail and allowing for clearer morphological interpretation. Furthermore, as OCT practice often averages multiple scans to remove noise, repeated scans are typically available. Lastly, the method is generic and could be applied to other imaging modalities which are subject to deformation and noise in repeat acquisitions, e.g., live fluorescence microscopy.

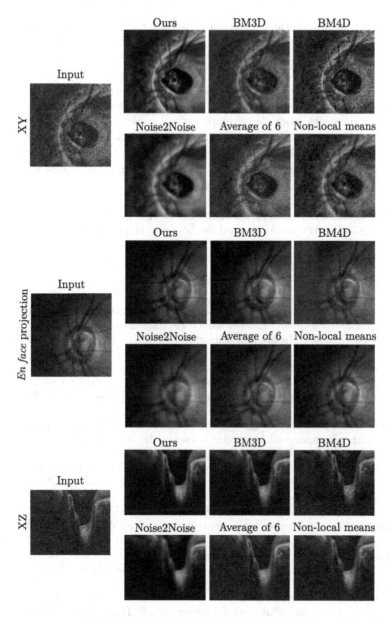

Fig. 4. A qualitative comparison of denoising quality of all benchmarked methods. Our network was trained and tested on XY-slices only, with the other views assembled and included for completeness. Readers are encouraged to zoom-in for details.

While repeat observations are required for training, the model can be directly applied to unseen individual scans from new subjects thereafter. This enables the denoising of large amounts of retrospective data, as long as there is no significant domain gap.

In future work, we will investigate the ability of deep self-supervised denoisers that require no repeat acquisitions in handling the correlated noise typical to OCT. Very recent work [5] develops such a method for handling structured noise in fluorescence microscopy, but requires a heuristic estimation of the structure of noise. Finally, our framework is not amenable to end-to-end training of registration and denoising, and such a joint method may have improved results and widespread utility in biomedical imaging.

Acknowledgments. This work was supported by NIH grants 1R01EY027948-01 and 2R01EY013178-15. HPC resources used for this research provided by grant NSF MRI-1229185.

References

1. Avants, B., Gee, J.C.: Geodesic estimation for large deformation anatomical shape averaging and interpolation. Neuroimage **23**, S139–S150 (2004)
2. Avants, B.B., et al.: The optimal template effect in hippocampus studies of diseased populations. Neuroimage **49**(3), 2457–2466 (2010)
3. Bashkirova, D., Usman, B., Saenko, K.: Adversarial self-defense for cycle-consistent GANs. In: Advances in Neural Information Processing Systems, pp. 637–647 (2019)
4. Batson, J., Royer, L.: Noise2self: blind denoising by self-supervision. In: International Conference on Machine Learning, pp. 524–533 (2019)
5. Broaddus, C., Krull, A., Weigert, M., Schmidt, U., Myers, G.: Removing structured noise with self-supervised blind-spot networks. In: 2020 IEEE 17th International Symposium on Biomedical Imaging (ISBI), pp. 159–163. IEEE (2020)
6. Buades, A., Coll, B., Morel, J.M.: A non-local algorithm for image denoising. In: 2005 IEEE Computer Society Conference on Computer Vision and Pattern Recognition (CVPR'05), vol. 2, pp. 60–65. IEEE (2005)
7. Buchholz, T.O., Jordan, M., Pigino, G., Jug, F.: Cryo-CARE: content-aware image restoration for cryo-transmission electron microscopy data. In: 2019 IEEE 16th International Symposium on Biomedical Imaging (ISBI 2019), pp. 502–506. IEEE (2019)
8. Chu, C., Zhmoginov, A., Sandler, M.: Cyclegan, a master of steganography. arXiv preprint arXiv:1712.02950 (2017)
9. Dabov, K., Foi, A., Katkovnik, V., Egiazarian, K.: Image denoising by sparse 3-D transform-domain collaborative filtering. IEEE Trans. Image Process. **16**(8), 2080–2095 (2007)
10. Devalla, S.K., et al.: A deep learning approach to denoise optical coherence tomography images of the optic nerve head. Sci. Rep. **9**(1), 1–13 (2019)
11. Dey, N., Messinger, J., Smith, R.T., Curcio, C.A., Gerig, G.: Robust non-negative tensor factorization, diffeomorphic motion correction, and functional statistics to understand fixation in fluorescence microscopy. In: Shen, D., et al. (eds.) Medical Image Computing and Computer Assisted Intervention – MICCAI 2019. Lecture Notes in Computer Science, vol. 11764, pp. 658–666. Springer, Cham (2019). https://doi.org/10.1007/978-3-030-32239-7_73

12. Gisbert, G., Dey, N., Ishikawa, H., Schuman, J., Fishbaugh, J., Gerig, G.: Improved denoising of optical coherence tomography via repeated acquisitions and unsupervised deep learning. Invest. Ophthalmol. Vis. Sci. **61**(9), PB0035 (2020)

13. Halupka, K.J., et al.: Retinal optical coherence tomography image enhancement via deep learning. Biomed. Opt. Exp. **9**(12), 6205–6221 (2018)

14. Hendriksen, A.A., Pelt, D.M., Batenburg, K.J.: Noise2inverse: self-supervised deep convolutional denoising for linear inverse problems in imaging. arXiv preprint arXiv:2001.11801 (2020)

15. Joshi, S., Davis, B., Jomier, M., Gerig, G.: Unbiased diffeomorphic atlas construction for computational anatomy. NeuroImage **23**, S151–S160 (2004)

16. Kafieh, R., Rabbani, H., Selesnick, I.: Three dimensional data-driven multi scale atomic representation of optical coherence tomography. IEEE Trans. Med. Imaging **34**(5), 1042–1062 (2014)

17. Kingma, D.P., Ba, J.: Adam: a method for stochastic optimization. arXiv preprint arXiv:1412.6980 (2014)

18. Kong, X., Li, K., Yang, Q., Wenyin, L., Yang, M.H.: A new image quality metric for image auto-denoising. In: Proceedings of the IEEE International Conference on Computer Vision, pp. 2888–2895 (2013)

19. Krull, A., Buchholz, T.O., Jug, F.: Noise2void-learning denoising from single noisy images. In: Proceedings of the IEEE Conference on Computer Vision and Pattern Recognition, pp. 2129–2137 (2019)

20. Laine, S., Karras, T., Lehtinen, J., Aila, T.: High-quality self-supervised deep image denoising. In: Advances in Neural Information Processing Systems, pp. 6970–6980 (2019)

21. Lehtinen, J., et al.: Noise2Noise: learning image restoration without clean data. In: ICML, pp. 2971–2980 (2018)

22. Maggioni, M., Katkovnik, V., Egiazarian, K., Foi, A.: Nonlocal transform-domain filter for volumetric data denoising and reconstruction. IEEE Trans. Image Process. **22**(1), 119–133 (2012)

23. Mittal, A., Moorthy, A.K., Bovik, A.C.: No-reference image quality assessment in the spatial domain. IEEE Trans. Image Process. **21**(12), 4695–4708 (2012)

24. Qiu, B., et al.: Noise reduction in optical coherence tomography images using a deep neural network with perceptually-sensitive loss function. Biomed. Opt. Exp. **11**(2), 817–830 (2020)

25. Ravier, M., et al.: Analysis of morphological changes of lamina cribrosa under acute intraocular pressure change. In: Frangi, A., Schnabel, J., Davatzikos, C., Alberola-López, C., Fichtinger, G. (eds.) Medical Image Computing and Computer Assisted Intervention – ICCAI 2018. Lecture Notes in Computer Science, vol. 11071, pp. 364–371. Springer, Cham (2018). https://doi.org/10.1007/978-3-030-00934-2_41

26. Romo-Bucheli, D., et al.: Reducing image variability across OCT devices with unsupervised unpaired learning for improved segmentation of retina. Biomed. Opt. Exp. **11**(1), 346–363 (2020)

27. Ronneberger, O., Fischer, P., Brox, T.: U-net: convolutional networks for biomedical image segmentation. In: Navab, N., Hornegger, J., Wells, W., Frangi, A. (eds.) International Conference on Medical Image Computing and Computer-Assisted Intervention – MICCAI 2015. Lecture Notes in Computer Science, vol. 9351, pp. 234–241. Springer, Cham (2015). https://doi.org/10.1007/978-3-319-24574-4_28

28. Wang, Z., Bovik, A.C., Sheikh, H.R., Simoncelli, E.P.: Image quality assessment: from error visibility to structural similarity. IEEE Trans. Image Process. **13**(4), 600–612 (2004)

29. Zhang, Y., et al.: A poisson-gaussian denoising dataset with real fluorescence microscopy images. In: Proceedings of the IEEE Conference on Computer Vision and Pattern Recognition, pp. 11710–11718 (2019)
30. Zhu, J.Y., Park, T., Isola, P., Efros, A.A.: Unpaired image-to-image translation using cycle-consistent adversarial networks. In: Proceedings of the IEEE International Conference on Computer Vision, pp. 2223–2232 (2017)
31. Zhu, X., Milanfar, P.: Automatic parameter selection for denoising algorithms using a no-reference measure of image content. IEEE Trans. Image Process. **19**(12), 3116–3132 (2010)

Automated Detection of Diabetic Retinopathy from Smartphone Fundus Videos

Simon Mueller[1,2], Snezhana Karpova[1], Maximilian W. M. Wintergerst[2],
Kaushik Murali[3], Mahesh P. Shanmugam[3], Robert P. Finger[2],
and Thomas Schultz[1(✉)] (iD)

[1] University of Bonn, Bonn, Germany
simue@uni-bonn.de, schultz@cs.uni-bonn.de
[2] Department of Ophthalmology, University Hospital Bonn, Bonn, Germany
[3] Sankara Eye Hospital, Bengaluru, Karnataka, India

Abstract. Even though it is important to screen patients with diabetes for signs of diabetic retinopathy (DR), doing so comprehensively remains a practical challenge in low- and middle-income countries due to limited resources and financial constraints. Supervised machine learning has shown a strong potential for automated DR detection, but has so far relied on photographs that show all relevant parts of the fundus, which require relatively costly imaging systems. We present the first approach that automatically detects DR from fundus videos that show different parts of the fundus at different times, and that can be acquired with a low-cost smartphone-based fundus imaging system. Our novel image analysis pipeline consists of three main steps: Detecting the lens with a circle Hough Transform, detecting informative frames using a Support Vector Machine, and detecting the disease itself with an attention-based multiple instance learning (MIL) CNN architecture. Our results support the feasibility of a smartphone video based approach.

1 Introduction

A system for the image-based detection of diabetic retinopathy has been certified by the U.S. Food and Drug Administration (FDA) to make a decision about further treatment completely autonomously, without consulting a doctor [1]. This illustrates the advances of deep learning methods in the last years, as well as the need for automated and therefore cheaper diagnosis for common diseases. Estimates show that over 400 million people will suffer from diabetes in the year 2030 [14]. From theses patients a third is expected to develop diabetic retinopathy which can lead to complete blindness if not diagnosed and treated early enough. A fast and reliable way to detect the early stages is necessary.

Supported by German Ophthalmic Society, German Retina Society, BONFOR GEROK Program University of Bonn (Grant No. O-137.0028), Else Kroener-Fresenius Foundation and German Scholars Organization (EKFS/GSO 16).

© Springer Nature Switzerland AG 2020
H. Fu et al. (Eds.): OMIA 2020, LNCS 12069, pp. 83–92, 2020.
https://doi.org/10.1007/978-3-030-63419-3_9

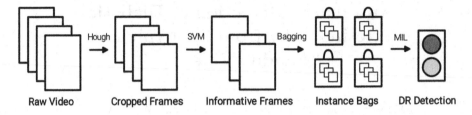

Fig. 1. Overview of our pipeline. The lens area is cropped out from raw video frames through a Hough circle transform. An SVM selects informative frames which show fundus. After bundling them into bags, a multiple instance learning (MIL) approach detects signs of referable diabetic retinopathy (DR). Results from all bags are averaged to obtain an eye-level prediction.

However, due to the cost of high-resolution ocular imaging devices required by the current FDA-approved approach, it cannot be widely used in low- and middle-income countries [4]. A solution is using low-cost adapters for smartphone-based fundus imaging like the Paxos Scope [20]. This handheld device can be combined with any recent smartphone and a fitting lens to create a simple, inexpensive ophthalmoscope. It can be used to create videos or photos of a patient's retina for further analysis. One downside is that image quality in smartphone-based fundus imaging is usually inferior to conventional digital reti- nal imaging. Models trained for traditional medical devices cannot directly be used for the Paxos image domain. The adapter, the smartphone, and the patient are in constant motion and the field of view is smaller, making it difficult to get all diagnostically relevant information in one picture.

Detecting diabetic retinopathy directly from raw, unedited video footage provides an opportunity to integrate information from many different frames, and it relieves the user from having to manually curate high quality frames. This motivates our current effort to develop an image analysis pipeline for this task. Section 2 will present our data and proposed methods, while Sect. 3 evalu- ates the achieved performance, and the importance of different building blocks. Our results establish an initial proof-of-concept, and support the feasibility of a smartphone video based approach.

2   Materials and Methods

We acquired a novel dataset, and annotated it as described in Sect. 2.1. We then developed a three-stage image analysis pipeline, illustrated in Fig. 1: A preprocessing step crops video frames to the part showing the lens of the Paxos adapter (Sect. 2.2). Second, we separate informative frames that show fundus from non-informative ones showing background (Sect. 2.3). Finally, we classify informative frames into ones showing normal fundus or signs of referable diabetic retinopathy, and we ensemble the results to arrive at a detection at the eye level (Sect. 2.4). The pipeline was implemented in Python, using packages scikit-learn, PyTorch, OpenCV, and Pandas.

2.1 Data Acquisition and Annotation

Our primary dataset has been acquired with the help of our co-authors at the cooperating Sankara Eye Hospital, Bangalore, India, in outreach eye clinics in South-India. It comprises fundus videos from 366 eyes that have been recorded with an iPod touch (6th generation, Apple Inc.) and a Paxos Scope adapter (Verana Health Inc.) for smartphone-based fundus imaging via indirect ophthalmoscopy. Manual quality assessment and rating of DR have been performed manually by trained ophthalmologists, leading to the exclusion of 58 videos (6/10/1/2 with mild/moderate/severe/proliferative DR) due to insufficient overall quality. The class distribution in the remaining 308 eyes is unbalanced, with 32/50/8/5 eyes for mild, moderate, severe, and proliferative retinopathy, respectively. The reason for this is the outreach screening setting where most participants have no or very early signs of DR. Videos have a length between 34 and 407 s and are sampled with a frame rate of 10 frames per second. They have not been edited, and thus show a mixture of informative frames, containing clear, non-blurred retina images showing vascular structures, and non-informative ones, which might show parts of the face or examination room. The videos were split into training (85% of the eyes) and test sets (15%) using stratified sampling according to the five above-mentioned classes.

To train a classifier that selects the informative frames, we annotated a subset of the frames accordingly: Since most frames are non-informative, negative examples were found by uniformly sampling all available videos, including diseased and non-diseased cases, and manually excluding informative frames. Positive examples were found by manually screening all videos for a fixed number of informative frames, in which at least 50% of the area visible through the lens of the Paxos adapter showed fundus. This led to a dataset with 534 positive and 1163 negative samples. When building and evaluating the classifier, 85% of this data was used for training, with cross validation to find the best hyperparameters. The remaining 15% were used for evaluation.

Finally, our classifier for detecting diabetic retinopathy in informative frames is trained via transfer learning. To this end, we collected data from the diabetic retinopathy detection Kaggle challenges in 2015 and 2019, which were provided by the EyePACS platform and the APTOS Symposium, respectively [2,3]. For preprocessing, all images are resized to 1024×1024 pixels and cropped to a circular size. This unifies the different resolutions stemming from a multitude of different medical devices used for capture. Also black borders are thresholded and removed. The training set contains 83126 and the validation set 9237 samples.

2.2 Cropping Frames to the Lens

As it can be seen in Fig. 2(a), only a subregion of each frame is relevant for further analysis: The circular region in the center, showing the lens of the Paxos adapter. The adapter fixes the lens at a certain distance, which results in this region having a similar size in all videos. We adapt to the remaining variation with a circle Hough Transform [8], which we use to detect a circle whose radius

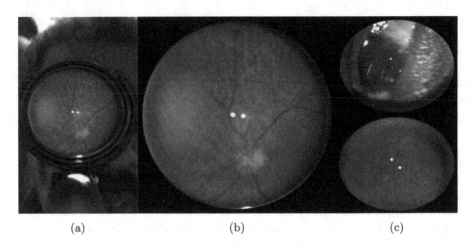

(a)   (b)   (c)

Fig. 2. Original frames (a) include a lot of irrelevant background, which we remove by cropping to the lens of the Paxos adapter (b). A second step distinguishes between non-informative (c, top) and informative frames (c, bottom) that actually show the fundus.

falls into the range of 300 to 500 pixels. This circle is then cropped out from the original input picture, as shown in Fig. 2(b). This strategy was very reliable, failing in only 30 out of 10000 frames.

2.3   Selection of Informative Frames

Substantial parts of the unedited videos are non-informative, since they only show background such as parts of the face or examination room. Figure 2(c) illustrates examples of non-informative (top) and informative frames (bottom). As it will be demonstrated in Sect. 3.2, the need to select informative frames is an important point that distinguishes our current task from the previously studied one of detecting diabetic retinopathy in smartphone based fundus photography [13]. We found that Support Vector Machine (SVM) classifiers [18] provide sufficient accuracy for this step. In particular, we apply them using feature vectors that combine two types of information: First, frames showing fundus have a characteristic color distribution, which we capture using the color histogram features introduced by Chapelle et al. [5], with exponent $a = 0.25$. Second, we use Haralick features (statistics on a co-occurrence matrix [7]) to capture differences in texture, such as ones caused by motion blurring. This choice follows Remeseiros et al. [16], who recommend Haralick features based on a comparison of different textural features for assessing retina image quality.

Since the two types of features provide complementary information, we concatenate them. To find the correct balance between the two parts of the resulting overall feature vector, we include a relative weighting factor as an additional hyperparameter. Its value is determined using cross-validation, along with the remaining hyperparameters of the SVM: Regularization parameter C, choice

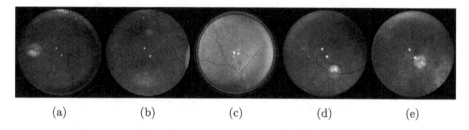

(a)   (b)   (c)   (d)   (e)

Fig. 3. Different stages of retinopathy selected from our Paxos scope dataset. (a) shows some non-diseased fundus and (b) to (e) shows the non-proliferative mild, moderate, severe stage and the proliferative stage of the disease

between linear or RBF kernel, and (if applicable) the kernel parameter γ. Cross-validation results indicated that the RBF kernel provides most accurate results.

2.4 Classification of Referable Diabetic Retinopathy

In comparison to standard frame based approaches, video based detection of diabetic retinopathy poses an important additional challenge: In the earlier stages of the disease, not all quadrants of the eye have to be affected. Therefore, even frames from a pathological eye that are selected as informative may show a field of view or have an image quality that does not reveal clear signs of the pathology. Since manual frame-wise annotations of disease biomarkers would cause an extreme effort, our system instead uses Multiple Instance Learning (MIL), a weakly supervised approach. In MIL, it is sufficient to provide a bag of frames at least one of which needs to be indicative of the disease. Specifically, we use the strategy of Ilse et al. [9], in which an attention mechanism allows the network to learn on which frames it should rely for its prediction.

Our MIL approach first uses an AlexNet [12] convolutional neural network to extract features $\mathbf{h}_k$ from each frame k within a given bag. Based on those features, a second network calculates attention weights α_k. The weighted sum $\mathbf{z} = \sum \alpha_k \mathbf{h}_k$ serves as the feature representation of the entire bag. We do not use the gating mechanism proposed by Ilse et al. [9]. Finally, $\mathbf{z}$ is fed into a fully-connected layer to obtain a binary classification between referable and non-referable retinopathy. The first category includes cases of moderate, severe non-proliferative, and proliferative retinopathy. The second one indicates no or a mild case of retinopathy. This grouping into two classes is in agreement with previous studies [6,13,15]. Examples for different stages of the disease are shown in Fig. 3. Due to the class distribution detailed in Sect. 2.1, the vast majority (50 out of 62 eyes) in the referable class correspond to mild cases, which show relatively subtle signs in the images.

To speed up the training and improve results, it is a common transfer learning technique to initialize the weights of a neural network with ones that have been obtained by training the same architecture on another data domain [19]. This assumes that the pre-trained weights are much more similar to ones that

Table 1. Results from different variants of our informative frame selection confirm that all ingredients are helpful, and good final performance is achieved.

		Performance measure				
		F1	Precision	Recall	Accuracy	ROC AUC
Original frame	Histogram	0.840	0.832	0.850	0.872	0.868
	Haralick	0.904	0.895	0.914	0.923	0.922
	Combined	0.913	0.923	0.903	0.932	0.927
Hough cropping	Histogram	0.893	0.915	0.872	0.917	0.909
	Haralick	0.918	0.901	0.936	0.940	0.939
	Combined	**0.962**	0.967	0.956	0.968	0.966

provide useful results in the new image domain compared to a random initialization. Moreover, this method can be applied successfully to small datasets on which training from scratch would overfit strongly. Therefore, we initialize the AlexNet with weights from training on the ImageNet dataset [17]. In addition, we hypothesized that refining the network based on the Kaggle Dataset (see Sect. 2.1) before training on our own video footage would improve results, since this provides us with a relatively large amount of training data for a task that is much more similar to ours than ImageNet.

The whole MIL network was trained for 70 epochs on frames from the 85% of videos marked for training, with pre-processing and frame selection as described above. Training used a cross-entropy loss, an Adam Optimizer [11] with initial learning rate 10^{-4}, learning rate reduction on plateau, batch normalization, inverse class frequency weighted sampling, weight decay 10^{-3}, and data augmentation (flipping, affine transformations, RGB-shifts, noise and cutouts). The attention weight network had 738 nodes. Labels concerning the disease status are required for each bag. To avoid an excessive variation in bag sizes, we set the maximum bag size to the median of the number of informative frames per eye. During training, we assume that at least one frame in each bag from an eye with referable retinopathy shows signs of it. We randomly shuffle the frames to reduce the risk of marker-free image sequences impacting a whole bag. Despite this, copying labels from the eye to the bag level might introduce a certain amount of label noise. During inference, we average the probabilities over all bags to obtain an estimate at the eye level.

3   Results

3.1   Evaluation of Informative Frame Selection

Table 1 shows the results of six experiments in which SVM classifiers were used to select informative frames based on different feature vectors, as well as with or without Hough based cropping. Results confirm that both color and textural

Table 2. Results from our overall disease detection pipeline demonstrate a clear benefit from selecting informative frames, and pre-training on a related dataset. ROC AUC and PR AUC are the area under the receiver operating characteristic and the precision recall curve.

	Performance measure				
	F1	Precision	Recall	ROC AUC	PR AUC
Kaggle Pre-training/Uniformly sampled	0.444	0.444	0.444	0.665	0.572
ImageNet Pre-training/SVM selection	0.429	0.600	0.333	0.740	0.515
Kaggle Pre-training (frozen)/SVM selec	0.524	0.571	0.444	0.765	0.656
Kaggle Pre-training/SVM selection	0.706	0.750	0.667	**0.841**	0.750

features are useful for selecting informative frames, that their combination provides better results than using the features in isolation, and that the selection of informative frames benefits from first cropping the frames using the circle Hough Transform. We find the results that were achieved by combining all these ingredients quite satisfactory: On a test set (217 samples), it yielded an F1-score of 0.96 for the best model, with precision and recall above 95%.

3.2 Evaluation of Disease Detection

Eye-level results from our overall pipeline are shown in the fourth row of Table 2. The other three rows show ablation studies: In the first one, we relied on the MIL attention mechanism alone instead of pre-selecting informative frames. Results cannot compete with the full pipeline. The second row shows results from pre-training only on ImageNet, illustrating that pre-training on the much more similar task from the Kaggle challenge provided a clear benefit. The domain shift between the Kaggle images and our videos can be seen from the third row, in which the AlexNet weights were frozen after the pre-training, and only the attention network and the classification layer were trained. This resulted in lower accuracy compared to refining also the feature extraction part of the network.

As it is shown in Fig. 4(a), our attention-based MIL approach was able to achieve an AUC ROC value of 0.84. Due to the imbalanced dataset, the AUC of the precision recall curve, shown in Fig. 4(b), is slightly lower (0.75).

Figure 5(a) shows the histogram of normalized (bag size corrected) attention weights. For better visualization, it has been truncated at 3.0, the last bin containing all greater weights. The histogram displays a bimodal distribution, illustrating that the network has learned to differentiate between frames that it considers to be more or less relevant for detecting the disease. Figure 5(b) shows five frames each with low and high attention weights, randomly sampled from the lower and upper tenth percentile of the weight distribution, respectively. Results confirm that the network successfully prioritized frames with a higher quality, including ones in which disease markers were present.

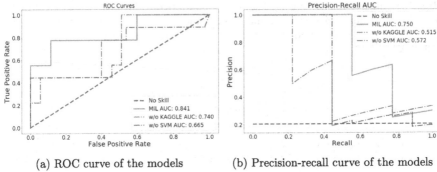

(a) ROC curve of the models   (b) Precision-recall curve of the models

Fig. 4. Varying the final probability threshold yields the receiver operator characteristics shown in (a) and the precision-recall curves in (b). Orange represents our proposed method, green and red correspond to two of our ablation studies. (Color figure online)

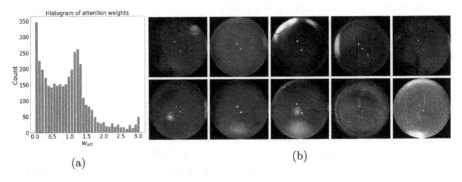

(a)   (b)

Fig. 5. A histogram of all attention weights (a) indicates separate peaks for more and less relevant frames. Example frames from the test set with small (upper row) and high attention weights (lower row) are displayed in (b). The network clearly prioritizes fundus images with a high quality.

3.3 Computational Effort

Cropping and informative frame selection are done on the CPU, the MIL approach utilizes the GPU. For a 3 min video, sampled with 10 fps, the frame extraction takes around 60 s, the cropping, preprocessing, and feature extraction 450 s and the prediction 20 s on an Intel Core i9-9940X CPU. This sums up to 8 min 50 s. On an NVIDIA GTX 2080 Ti, the Kaggle pretraining ran for 10 h 30 min. Training the MIL model took 6 h 37 min and allocated a maximum of 2.8 GB of graphics memory.

4   Discussion and Conclusion

Our work presents encouraging initial results on detecting diabetic retinopathy directly from raw, unedited smartphone videos. Even though our current dataset presents some challenges concerning size, sparse representation of more severe disease stages, as well as variations in image quality, combining traditional image analysis and machine learning techniques such as the Hough Transform and Support Vector Machines with a modern MIL classifier has allowed us to achieve promising results under realistic conditions.

In order to increase the precision and recall to a level at which they will become clinically useful, we will extend and improve our current dataset, both in terms of the overall number of samples and class balance, and in terms of image quality. In a pilot study, we found that combining the Paxos Scope with an iPhone 7 instead of an iPod touch led to noticeably improved focus, resolution, and lighting. We will also look into refining our image analysis pipeline by exploring CNN architectures that can make a more dedicated use of the temporal dimension in the videos [10].

References

1. Abràmoff, M.D., Lavin, P.T., Birch, M., Shah, N., Folk, J.C.: Pivotal trial of an autonomous AI-based diagnostic system for detection of diabetic retinopathy in primary care offices. NPJ Digit. Med. **1**(1), 39 (2018). https://doi.org/10.1038/s41746-018-0040-6
2. California Healthcare Foundation: Diabetic retinopathy detection (2015). https://www.kaggle.com/c/diabetic-retinopathy-detection
3. California Healthcare Foundation: Aptos 2019 blindness detection (2019). https://www.kaggle.com/c/aptos2019-blindness-detection/overview
4. Chang, R., Ludwig, C., Murthy, S., Pappuru, R., Jais, A., Myung, D.: A novel smartphone ophthalmic imaging adapter: user feasibility studies in Hyderabad, India. Indian J. Ophthalmol. **64**(3), 191 (2016). https://doi.org/10.4103/0301-4738.181742
5. Chapelle, O., Haffner, P., Vapnik, V.: Support vector machines for histogram-based image classification. IEEE Trans. Neural Netw. **10**(5), 1055–1064 (1999). https://doi.org/10.1109/72.788646
6. Gulshan, V., et al.: Development and validation of a deep learning algorithm for detection of diabetic retinopathy in retinal fundus photographs. JAMA **316**(22), 2402 (2016). https://doi.org/10.1001/jama.2016.17216
7. Haralick, R.: Statistical and structural approaches to texture. Proc. IEEE **67**(5), 786–804 (1979)
8. Illingworth, J., Kittler, J.: The adaptive hough transform. IEEE Trans. Pattern Anal. Mach. Intell. **9**(5), 690–698 (1987)
9. Ilse, M., Tomczak, J.M., Welling, M.: Attention-based deep multiple instance learning. In: Dy, J.G., Krause, A. (eds.) Proceedings of the International Conference on Machine Learning, PMLR (ICML), vol. 80, pp. 2132–2141 (2018)
10. Karpathy, A., Toderici, G., Shetty, S., Leung, T., Sukthankar, R., Fei-Fei, L.: Large-scale video classification with convolutional neural networks. In: IEEE Conference on Computer Vision and Pattern Recognition, pp. 1725–1732 (2014)
11. Kingma, D.P., Ba, J.: Adam: A method for stochastic optimization. In: Bengio, Y., LeCun, Y. (eds.) International Conference on Learning Representations (ICLR) (2015)

12. Krizhevsky, A., Sutskever, I., Hinton, G.E.: Imagenet classification with deep convolutional neural networks. In: Pereira, F., Burges, C.J.C., Bottou, L., Weinberger, K.Q. (eds.) Advances in Neural Information Processing Systems , vol. 25, pp. 1097–1105. Curran Associates, Inc. (2012)

13. Rajalakshmi, R., Subashini, R., Anjana, R.M., Mohan, V.: Automated diabetic retinopathy detection in smartphone-based fundus photography using artificial intelligence. Eye 32(6), 1138–1144 (2018)

14. Raman, R., Gella, L., Srinivasan, S., Sharma, T.: Diabetic retinopathy: an epidemic at home and around the world. Indian J. Ophthalmol. 64(1), 69–75 (2016). https://doi.org/10.4103/0301-4738.178150

15. Raman, R., Srinivasan, S., Virmani, S., Sivaprasad, S., Rao, C., Rajalakshmi, R.: Fundus photograph-based deep learning algorithms in detecting diabetic retinopathy. Eye 33(1), 97–109 (2018)

16. Remeseiro, B., Mendonca, A.M., Campilho, A.: Objective quality assessment of retinal images based on texture features. In: 2017 International Joint Conference on Neural Networks (IJCNN). IEEE (2017). https://doi.org/10.1109/ijcnn.2017.7966429

17. Russakovsky, O., et al.: ImageNet large scale visual recognition challenge. Int. J. Comput. Vis. (IJCV) 115(3), 211–252 (2015)

18. Schölkopf, B., Smola, A.J.: Learning with Kernels. MIT Press, Cambridge (2002)

19. Tan, C., Sun, F., Kong, T., Zhang, W., Yang, C., Liu, C.: A survey on deep transfer learning. In: Kůrková, V., Manolopoulos, Y., Hammer, B., Iliadis, L., Maglogiannis, I. (eds.) ICANN 2018. LNCS, vol. 11141, pp. 270–279. Springer, Cham (2018). https://doi.org/10.1007/978-3-030-01424-7_27

20. Wintergerst, M.W., et al.: Diabetic retinopathy screening using smartphone-based fundus imaging in india. Ophthalmology 127(11), 1529–1538 (2020)

Optic Disc, Cup and Fovea Detection from Retinal Images Using U-Net++ with EfficientNet Encoder

Ravi Kamble, Pranab Samanta, and Nitin Singhal$^{(\boxtimes)}$

AIRAMATRIX Pvt. Ltd., Mumbai, India
nitin.singhal@airamatrix.com

Abstract. The accurate detection of retinal structures like an optic disc (OD), cup, and fovea is crucial for the analysis of Age-related Macular Degeneration (AMD), Glaucoma, and other retinal conditions. Most segmentation methods rely on separate detection of these retinal structures due to which a combined analysis for computer-aided ophthalmic diagnosis and screening is challenging. To address this issue, the paper introduces an approach incorporating OD, cup, and fovea analysis together. The paper presents a novel method for the detection of OD with a cup and fovea using modified U-Net++ architecture with the EfficientNet-B4 model as a backbone. The extracted features from the EfficientNet are utilized using skip connections in U-Net++ for precise segmentation. Datasets from ADAM and REFUGE challenges are used for evaluating the performance. The proposed method achieved a success rate of 94.74% and 95.73% dice value for OD segmentation on ADAM and REFUGE data, respectively. For fovea detection, the average Euclidean distance of 26.17 pixels is achieved for the ADAM dataset. The proposed method stood first for OD detection and segmentation tasks in ISBI ADAM 2020 challenge.

Keywords: Optic disc segmentation · Fovea localization · Convolutional neural network · Age-related macular degeneration · Glaucoma

1 Introduction

Early detection and screening of retinal diseases such as glaucoma and age-related macular degeneration (AMD) play a vital role in reducing vision loss [20]. Glaucoma is a disease that damages the eye's optic nerve which can lead to permanent vision impairment [7]. AMD is the leading cause of blindness due to the presence of macular drusen in people older than 65 years. The occurrence of lesions in the macula of the eye causes loss of central vision. Hence, the optic disc (OD), optic cup (OC), and the fovea are the most important retinal landmarks in ophthalmic imaging and diagnosis [18]. OD is the yellowish vertical oval region where the nerve fibers and blood vessels merge in the retina. The optic cup

© Springer Nature Switzerland AG 2020
H. Fu et al. (Eds.): OMIA 2020, LNCS 12069, pp. 93–103, 2020.
https://doi.org/10.1007/978-3-030-63419-3_10

is the brightest area in the optic disc region shown in Fig. 1. The cup to disc ratio (CDR) is one of the important markers for the diagnosis of Glaucoma. For AMD detection, macular region analysis is important for early signs of the disease. Macula is the functional center of the retina. Accurate detection of these retinal landmarks can greatly improve diagnostic efficiency.

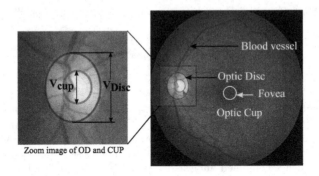

Fig. 1. Sample image from the REFUGE dataset showing retinal structures like an optic disc, cup, fovea, and blood vessels.

In recent years, several methods have been proposed for retinal structure detection. Most of the literature uses retinal features like the variation in intensities, texture and appearance for detecting OD and OC [3,8,13,16]. The past few years have seen significant progress with deep learning approaches for OD with cup segmentation. In [5], an encoder-decoder network with deep residual structure and recursive learning mechanism is proposed for robust OD localization. An end-to-end region-based CNN for joint optic disc and cup segmentation (Joint-RCNN) is proposed in [6]. For automatic glaucoma screening, a Disc-aware Ensemble Network (DENet) is reported in [4], which integrates the local disc region with global information from the whole fundus image. Also, for fovea localization, many researchers have used different CNN models for the visibility of the macular region and fovea localization [1,14]. A two-stage deep learning framework for accurate segmentation of the fovea in retinal color fundus images is presented in [14]. Recently, a simpler and more effective fovea localization algorithm based on the Faster R-CNN and physiological prior structure are presented in [21]. However, most of these methods treated either the disc with cup or the disc with fovea as two individual segmentation task.

Although many approaches have contributed work in OD, OC, and fovea segmentation, very few methods have considered all these tasks together. Since these retinal structures are spatially correlated to each other, there are advantages in combined detection and segmentation. The presence of retinal lesions in the macular region often occludes fovea, which is difficult to detect individually without using any spatial context. The fuzzy boundary of OC is often difficult to distinguish from OD and make this task quite challenging without any spatial prior.

To overcome these issues, this paper proposes a two-stage approach for segmenting retinal structures using the modified U-Net++ model with EfficientNet encoder. Our approach is free from the prior knowledge of retinal vessels. The major contributions of this work are summarized as follows:

1. We propose a two-stage approach for combined optic disc, cup, and fovea segmentation. In the first stage, a combined OD and fovea detection is performed, while in the next stage, the OD region is extracted and used for optic cup detection.
2. The proposed method uses EfficientNet-B4 encoder with modified U-Net++ architecture. The re-designed skip connection of U-Net++ and uses of concurrent channel and spatial excitation block in the decoder significantly improve the model performance. Also, the extracted features from EfficientNet show effective representations of retinal structures.
3. Our method evaluate on four different datasets including REFUGE [9], ADAM [22], IDRiD [10] and Drishti-GS [15]. Also, we have tested different variants of CNN models with extensive experimentation in comparison with state-of-the-art methods.

The rest of this paper has been organized as follows. Section 2 briefly introduces the proposed method for OD with cup and fovea segmentation. Section 3 describes the experimental results and analysis with discussion. In Sect. 4, we conclude the paper with ideas for future directions.

2   Methodology

2.1   Dataset

Four different dataset used in this paper namely, i-challenge ADAM [22] and REFUGE [9], Drishti-GS [15] and IDRiD [10]. The training, validation, and test set data comprised 400 images each in both the i-challenge dataset. The training images in ADAM and REFUGE were available in different sizes of 2124×2056, 1634×1634 and 1444×1444. In the first stage of the method, the ADAM dataset is used for OD with fovea segmentation. The REFUGE dataset is used in the second stage for OD with cup segmentation. Also, we empirically validated our approach on Drishti-GS [15] and IDRiD [10] test images for comparison with state-of-the-art methods.

Pre-processing. The main objective of the preprocessing module is to prepare the combined OD and fovea data for the segmentation. The fovea x,y center coordinates have been provided for both ADAM and REFUGE dataset. Further, we have created a fovea image with 50 pixels of the circular mask using the fovea coordinates and then combined them with OD mask images. The whole dataset images have been resized into 512×512. We utilized data augmentation including image blur, rotation, vertical and horizontal flip. Finally, with the augmentation factor of 5 on 800 images, the total 4000 images has been used for the model development. Post this, we performed data normalization on all images by using mean subtraction with dividing standard deviation. These preprocessed images are provided as input to the proposed model.

2.2 Proposed Method

In this section, we provide an overview of the proposed method for the detection of OD, OC, and fovea. The two-stage approach consisted of combined detection of OD and fovea in the first stage. After that, the disc ROI of images is obtained by cropping a sub-image with the size of 512×512 based on the center of the detected OD mask. Fine detection of OD boundaries with the optic cup is performed in the second stage. Our proposed method employs recent CNN models for the accurate detection of potential retinal structures from color fundus images. The block diagram of our approach is shown in Fig. 2.

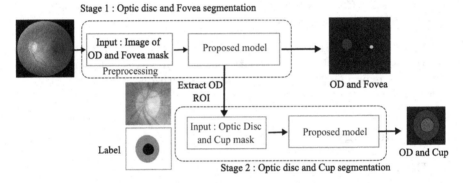

Fig. 2. Propose two-stage flow diagram for optic disc, cup, and fovea segmentation. In stage one: Combine OD and Fovea detection. In stage two: The extracted OD region of interest (ROI) given input to the model for OD with cup detection.

Model Architecture. The proposed architecture consists of two parts namely encoder and decoder. Since, the U-Net++ nested skip pathways gives corresponding semantically rich feature maps. We have utilized the U-Net++ architecture of varying depths whose decoders are connected at the same resolution via a re-designed skip pathway [24]. Using a progression of skip pathways among decoder and encoder block, U-Net++ showed great success in segmentation tasks. In the recent deep learning era, EfficientNet has perform better in the ImageNet dataset for the classification task as compared to recent state-of-the-art backbone. Hence, we have explored the use of an EfficientNet [17] as an encoder for feature extraction with U-Net++ architecture as the baseline model. Due to the availability of a dense connection in U-Net++, every node in the decoder is represented in the feature maps and is aggregated from the previous and intermediate layers from the encoder. However, the dense connection of U-Net++

creates a larger size of the feature map because of concatenating similar features from different skip pathways. Hence, the number of trainable parameters in the existing U-Net++ model is high with more computational complexity. Therefore, we redesigned the skip pathways without loss of any information in the modified U-Net++. The accumulated feature maps denoted by $s^{i,j}$ is calculated from Eq. (1).

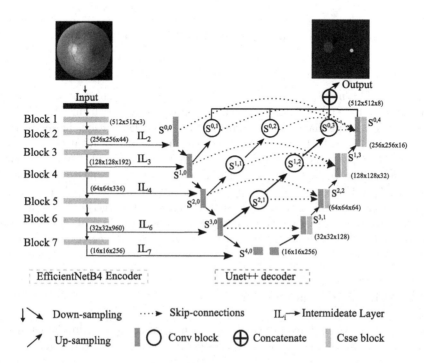

Fig. 3. Model architecture using Efficientnet-B4 as encoder with modified U-Net++ decoder.

$$s^{i,j} = \begin{cases} H\left(D(s^{i-1,j})\right), & j = 0 \\ H\left(\left[[s^{i,k}]_{j=0}^{j-1}, \ U(s^{i+1,j-1})\right]\right), & j > 0 \end{cases} \quad (1)$$

where, $H\left(\cdot\right)$ is convolution operation, $D\left(\cdot\right)$ and $U\left(\cdot\right)$ denotes a down-sampling layer and an up-sampling layer respectively. Here, $s^{i,j}$ represents the stack of feature maps which is also output from previous node $S^{i,j}$, where i and j are the downsample and convolution layer with the skip connection. The final segmented image obtained using concatenated the node output $S^{0,1}$, $S^{0,2}$, $S^{0,3}$ and $S^{0,4}$ of model which shown in Fig. 3.

The backbone of U-Net++ is the EfficientNet model, pre-trained on ImageNet, which proficiently separates various essential retinal anatomical structures. The principle block of EfficientNet is mobile reversed bottleneck convolutional (MBConv), which comprises of depthwise separable convolutional layers

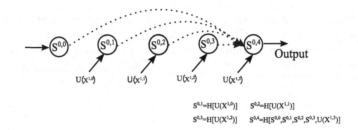

Fig. 4. The basic block of proposed model with re-designed skip connections of U-Net++.

(DWConv). The model utilizes four DWConv layers and an ordinary convolutional layer with stride 2×2 to down-sampling input size from 512×512 to 16×16. The intermediate feature maps from five blocks of EfficientNet as IL_2, IL_3, IL_4, IL_6 and IL_7 were extracted at different scales from encoder. We redesign the skip connections of U-Net++ to reduce the complexity of the baseline model as shown in Fig. 4. Also, the use of concurrent squeeze and spatial excitation (CSSE) block in decoder improves the performance [12]. At each intermediate layer level, all concatenated feature maps are merged on the ultimate node on that level. Finally, the concatenation layer combines all feature maps from transposed convolutional layers at the previous and the corresponding layer in the encoding pathway.

3 Results and Discussion

In this section, we first introduce the experimental setup and implementation details. We then provide experimental results with discussion in detail.

3.1 Experimental Set-up

All the experiments were carried on resized images of 512×512 pixels. We validated our proposed method on four datasets ADAM [22], REFUGE [9], Drishti-GS [15] and IDRiD [10]. In the experimental setup, the network was initialized with pre-trained weights on the ImageNet classification data. The model was trained using the adam optimizer with the learning rate of 0.0001, momentum was set to 0.95 and the batch size of 4 for 800 epochs. We have evaluated the hyperparameters of our method using the validation set, including learning rates, batch sizes, training epochs, and so on. The model was trained using Keras deep learning framework with an NVIDIA TITAN-RTX (24 GB) GPU.

3.2 Results and Discussion

The dice coefficients (DI) and mean intersection over union (mIoU) use to evaluate the segmentation performance of the method. For OD segmentation, the

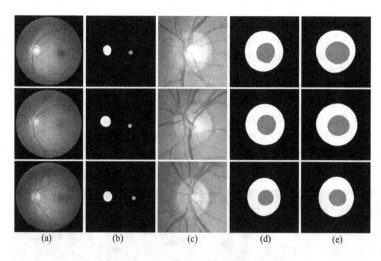

(a)   (b)   (c)   (d)   (e)

Fig. 5. Results on REFUGE validation dataset (a) Original image (b) Optic disc and fovea segmentation (c) Extracted OD patch (d) Ground truth of OD and OC (e) Predicted output of OD and cup segmentation.

obtained dice is 0.9622 and 0.9474 on validation and test set of ADAM data. For OC segmentation, the obtained dice is 0.8816 and 0.8762 on validation and test set of REFUGE data. The segmentation results on the REFUGE validation dataset are shown in Fig. 5. We have detected both OD with fovea jointly and then localize the fovea center accurately from the fovea image. In the context of fovea localization, the fovea mask was prepared from the given x, y center coordinates. Finally, the best possible fovea location was found by calculating the centroid of the segmented fovea mask. The proposed method achieved the top rank for OD detection and segmentation task on the ADAM challenge testing dataset shown in Table 1.

Table 1. Results of top five performing teams for OD segmentation and fovea localization in ISBI ADAM challenge 2020 [22].

Team Name	DI_{OD}	F1-score	ED	Semi-final	Final	Score	Rank
Aira matrix	0.9474	0.9861	26.17	5	2	2.6	1
Xxlzt	0.9485	0.9912	284.03	10	1	2.8	2
Forbitten fruit	0.9420	0.9912	19.70	4	3	3.2	3
WWW	0.9445	0.9793	36.35	8	4	4.8	4
Vuno Eye Team	0.9370	0.9893	**18.55**	2	6	5.2	5

The average Euclidean distance between the predicted and ground truth for fovea localization is 30.23 and 26.17 pixels on IDRiD and ADAM test data.

We further validate the method on a test dataset from REFUGE and Drishti-GS for OD and OC segmentation. The performance comparison with different state-of-the-art methods on the REFUGE and Drishti-GS dataset are shown in Table 2. The EfficientNet-B4 feature extractor using the proposed model can able to detect the fovea despite of lesion present in the macular region. The accurate fovea segmentation results on the retinal image with the macular lesion are shown in Fig. 6. In addition, our method does not use any prior knowledge of vessel information for the detection of these retinal structures. Therefore, reduces the computational load compared to other approaches.

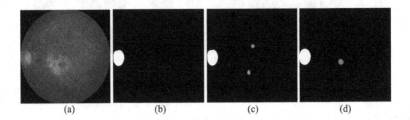

Fig. 6. Results of fovea detection in lesion image using different models on ADAM validation dataset (a) Original image (b) U-Net++ result with missing fovea detection (c) EfficientNet-U-Net++ result with false detection (d) Proposed model result with accurate fovea detection.

Table 2. The comparison of DI_{disc}, DI_{cup}, and mIoU performance with state-of-the-art methods on the REFUGE and Drishti-GS dataset. .

Method	REFUGE [9]			Drishti-GS [15]		
	DI_{disc}	DI_{cup}	mIoU	DI_{disc}	DI_{cup}	mIoU
Fu et al. [4]	0.9359	0.8648	0.8402	0.9658	0.8860	0.8588
Chen et al. [2]	0.9401	0.8674	0.8436	0.9655	0.8896	0.8594
Zhang et al. [23]	0.9529	0.8912	0.8670	0.9752	0.9314	0.8792
Wang et al. [19]	0.9460	0.8750	–	0.9740	0.9010	–
Proposed	**0.9573**	**0.8762**	**0.8725**	**0.9784**	**0.9381**	**0.8820**

Ablation Study. Recently published U-Net++ network showed the best performance over the vanilla U-Net [11]. The U-Net++ gives dense skip pathways to improve the performance [24]. However, theoretically dense skip pathways carry redundant features through the different skip connection and also increases the computational cost. Therefore, we redesigned the dense skip connections. From Table 3, the experimentation shows that the modified network outperformed over the U-Net++ and vanilla U-Net. Further, we introduce a heavy feature extractor namely EfficientNet-B4 [17] in encoder instead of vanilla encoder. We have

Table 3. The performance of different segmentation models and our proposed method for OD, OC, and fovea detection on the REFUGE test dataset. The baseline model is U-Net encoder with redesigned skip pathways.

Model	DI_{disc}	DI_{cup}	IoU_{disc}	IoU_{cup}	ED (pixels)	Parameters
U-Net [11]	0.9332	0.8537	0.8872	0.7683	46.32	7.7 M
U-Net++ [24]	0.9476	0.8537	0.8723	0.7668	43.81	21.3 M
Proposed-1	0.9479	0.8573	0.8766	0.7810	44.14	14.1M
Proposed-2	0.9535	0.8616	0.8814	0.8072	36.32	10.2 M
Proposed-3	**0.9573**	**0.8762**	**0.8847**	**0.8128**	**35.18**	**11.4 M**

Proposed-1 : U-Net encoder + skip pathways, Proposed-2 : EfficientNet + skip pathways, Proposed-3: EfficientNet + skip pathways + CSSE

trained all the models using similar hyperparameter setting. The performance of the proposed network is better than the existing models as shown in Table 3. In summary, our experiments gives the more accurate segmentation for the combined analysis of retinal structures.

4   Conclusion

In this paper, we have proposed a novel two-stage method for the detection of the optic disc with cup and fovea from fundus images. We have proposed a modified U-Net++ architecture with the EfficientNet-B4 model as a backbone for segmenting retinal structures. The redesigned skip connections of U-Net++ architecture reduces the computational requirements compared to the baseline model. We also performed extensive experiments on four public retinal fundus image datasets to demonstrate the effectiveness of our approach. We achieved the better results for the OD and OC with dice of 0.9573 and 0.8762 on REFUGE dataset. The proposed method is considered the top rank solution for optic disc detection and segmentation task in the ADAM challenge with dice of 0.9474. In the future, our approach can effectively make an impact on the retinal anatomical structure detection problem.

References

1. Alais, R., Dokládal, P., Erginay, A., Figliuzzi, B., Decencière, E.: Fast macula detection and application to retinal image quality assessment. Biomed. Signal Process. Control **55**, 101567 (2020)
2. Chen, H., Qi, X., Yu, L., Heng, P.A.: DCAN: deep contour-aware networks for accurate gland segmentation. In: Proceedings of the IEEE Conference on Computer Vision and Pattern Recognition, pp. 2487–2496 (2016)
3. Cheng, J., Yin, F., Wong, D.W.K., Tao, D., Liu, J.: Sparse dissimilarity-constrained coding for glaucoma screening. IEEE Trans. Biomed. Eng. **62**(5), 1395–1403 (2015)
4. Fu, H., et al.: Disc-aware ensemble network for glaucoma screening from fundus image. IEEE Trans. Med. Imaging **37**(11), 2493–2501 (2018)

5. Jiang, S., Chen, Z., Li, A., Wang, Y.: Robust optic disc localization by large scale learning. In: Fu, H., Garvin, M.K., MacGillivray, T., Xu, Y., Zheng, Y. (eds.) OMIA 2019. LNCS, vol. 11855, pp. 95–103. Springer, Cham (2019). https://doi.org/10.1007/978-3-030-32956-3_12

6. Jiang, Y., et al.: JointRCNN: a region-based convolutional neural network for optic disc and cup segmentation. IEEE Trans. Biomed. Eng. **67**(2), 335–343 (2020)

7. Li, L., et al.: A large-scale database and a CNN model for attention-based glaucoma detection. IEEE Trans. Med. Imaging **39**(2), 413–424 (2020)

8. Mendonça, A.M., Melo, T., Araújo, T., Campilho, A.: Optic disc and fovea detection in color eye fundus images. In: Campilho, A., Karray, F., Wang, Z. (eds.) ICIAR 2020. LNCS, vol. 12132, pp. 332–343. Springer, Cham (2020). https://doi.org/10.1007/978-3-030-50516-5_29

9. Orlando, J.I., et al.: Refuge challenge: a unified framework for evaluating automated methods for glaucoma assessment from fundus photographs. Med. Image Anal. **59**, 101570 (2020)

10. Porwal, P., et al.: Indian diabetic retinopathy image dataset (IDRiD): a database for diabetic retinopathy screening research. Data **3**(3), 25 (2018)

11. Ronneberger, O., Fischer, P., Brox, T.: U-Net: convolutional networks for biomedical image segmentation. In: Navab, N., Hornegger, J., Wells, W.M., Frangi, A.F. (eds.) MICCAI 2015. LNCS, vol. 9351, pp. 234–241. Springer, Cham (2015). https://doi.org/10.1007/978-3-319-24574-4_28

12. Roy, A.G., Navab, N., Wachinger, C.: Concurrent spatial and channel 'squeeze & excitation' in fully convolutional networks. In: Frangi, A.F., Schnabel, J.A., Davatzikos, C., Alberola-López, C., Fichtinger, G. (eds.) MICCAI 2018. LNCS, vol. 11070, pp. 421–429. Springer, Cham (2018). https://doi.org/10.1007/978-3-030-00928-1_48

13. Roychowdhury, S., Koozekanani, D.D., Kuchinka, S.N., Parhi, K.K.: Optic disc boundary and vessel origin segmentation of fundus images. IEEE J. Biomed. Health Inf. **20**(6), 1562–1574 (2016)

14. Sedai, S., Tennakoon, R., Roy, P., Cao, K., Garnavi, R.: Multi-stage segmentation of the fovea in retinal fundus images using fully convolutional neural networks. In: 2017 IEEE 14th International Symposium on Biomedical Imaging (ISBI 2017), pp. 1083–1086 (2017)

15. Sivaswamy, J., Krishnadas, S., Joshi, G.D., Jain, M., Tabish, A.U.S.: Drishti-GS: retinal image dataset for optic nerve head (onh) segmentation. In: 2014 IEEE 11th International Symposium on Biomedical Imaging (ISBI), pp. 53–56. IEEE (2014)

16. Soares, I., Castelo-Branco, M., Pinheiro, A.M.G.: Optic disc localization in retinal images based on cumulative sum fields. IEEE J. Biomed. Health Inf. **20**(2), 574–585 (2016)

17. Tan, M., Le, Q.V.: Efficientnet: rethinking model scaling for convolutional neural networks. arXiv preprint arXiv:1905.11946 (2019)

18. Ting, D.S.W., et al.: Development and validation of a deep learning system for diabetic retinopathy and related eye diseases using retinal images from multiethnic populations with diabetes. Jama **318**(22), 2211–2223 (2017)

19. Wang, S., Yu, L., Yang, X., Fu, C.W., Heng, P.A.: Patch-based output space adversarial learning for joint optic disc and cup segmentation. IEEE Trans. Med. Imaging **38**(11), 2485–2495 (2019)

20. Wong, W.L., et al.: Global prevalence of age-related macular degeneration and disease burden projection for 2020 and 2040: a systematic review and meta-analysis. Lancet Global Health **2**(2), e106–e116 (2014)

21. Wu, J., et al.: Fovea localization in fundus photographs by faster R-CNN with physiological prior. In: Fu, H., Garvin, M.K., MacGillivray, T., Xu, Y., Zheng, Y. (eds.) OMIA 2019. LNCS, vol. 11855, pp. 156–164. Springer, Cham (2019). https://doi.org/10.1007/978-3-030-32956-3_19

22. Fu, H., et al.: Adam: automatic detection challenge on age-related macular degeneration (2020). https://doi.org/10.21227/dt4f-rt59

23. Zhang, Z., Fu, H., Dai, H., Shen, J., Pang, Y., Shao, L.: ET-Net: a generic Edge-aTtention guidance network for medical image segmentation. In: Shen, D., et al. (eds.) MICCAI 2019. LNCS, vol. 11764, pp. 442–450. Springer, Cham (2019). https://doi.org/10.1007/978-3-030-32239-7_49

24. Zhou, Z., Rahman Siddiquee, M.M., Tajbakhsh, N., Liang, J.: UNet++: a nested U-Net architecture for medical image segmentation. In: Stoyanov, D., et al. (eds.) DLMIA/ML-CDS -2018. LNCS, vol. 11045, pp. 3–11. Springer, Cham (2018). https://doi.org/10.1007/978-3-030-00889-5_1

Multi-level Light U-Net and Atrous Spatial Pyramid Pooling for Optic Disc Segmentation on Fundus Image

Weixin Liu[1], Haijun Lei[1], Hai Xie[2], Benjian Zhao[1], Guanghui Yue[2], and Baiying Lei[2(✉)]

[1] Key Laboratory of Service Computing and Applications, Guangdong Province Key Laboratory of Popular High Performance Computers, College of Computer Science and Software Engineering, Shenzhen University, Shenzhen 518060, China
[2] National-Regional Key Technology Engineering Laboratory for Medical Ultrasound, Guangdong Key Laboratory for Biomedical Measurements and Ultrasound Imaging, School of Biomedical Engineering, Health Science Center, Shenzhen University, Shenzhen 518060, China
leiby@szu.edu.cn

Abstract. Optic disc (OD) is the main anatomical structures in retinal images. It is very important to conduct reliable OD segmentation in the automatic diagnosis of many fundus diseases. For OD segmentation, the previous studies with stacked convolutional layers and pooling operations often neglect the detailed spatial information. However, this information is vital to distinguish the diversity of the profile of OD and the spatial distribution of vessels. In this paper, we propose a novel OD segmentation network by designing two modules, namely, light U-Net module and atrous convolution spatial pyramid pooling module. We first extract hierarchical features by using ResNet-101 as a base network. Light U-Net module is utilized to learn the intrinsic spatial information effectively and enhance the ability of feature representation in low-level feature maps. Atrous convolution and spatial pyramid pooling module is used to incorporate global spatial information in high-level semantic features. Finally, we integrate the spatial information by feature fusion to get the segmentation results. We estimate the proposed method on two public retinal fundus image datasets (REFUGE and Drishti-GS). For the REFUGE dataset, our model achieves about 2% improvement in the mIoU and Dice over the next best method. For Drishti-GS, our method also outperforms the other state-of-the-art methods with 99.74% Dice and 93.26% mIoU.

Keywords: Optic disc segmentation · Light U-Net · Atrous convolution · Spatial pyramid pooling

1 Introduction

Optic disc (OD) is the main anatomical structure in retinal images, where abundant blood vessels are distributed. It is of great significance to conduct OD segmentation for disease monitoring and detection. For example, the location of OD can locate the

© Springer Nature Switzerland AG 2020
H. Fu et al. (Eds.): OMIA 2020, LNCS 12069, pp. 104–113, 2020.
https://doi.org/10.1007/978-3-030-63419-3_11

macular, which acts a pivotal in glaucoma detection, diabetic retinopathy detection, and age-related macular degeneration detection [1, 2]. The accurate segmentation results can be considered as an important index for blood vessel tracking, and can also be used as a marker for other retinal structures, such as fovea [3]. Therefore, it is very important to conduct reliable OD segmentation in the automatic diagnosis of many fundus diseases.

Since the OD is a bright yellow area that is approximately circular, some automatic OD segmentation methods are designed by using hand-crafted features based on clinical principles [4]. For example, the local prior knowledge is used to obtain the segmentation results by removing vessels in the region of OD [5]. Boundary detection from a monocular color fundus image is used to quantify disc representation [6]. Superpixel classification is used to estimate the performance of OD segmentation results by distinguishing every superpixel into disc and non-disc [7]. These methods use the hand-crafted local features to encode variation of the local anatomical structure base on the prior knowledge and clinical principles. However, the representation ability of these hand-crafted features is limited, which may affect the generalization performance of the model and result in poor robustness.

Deep learning techniques have been proved to produce highly distinctive representations in many computer vision tasks, such as medical image segmentation [8], detection [9], and classification [10]. The great success of convolutional neural network has guided researchers to design deep neural network structures for OD segmentation. For example, the fully convolutional network (FCN) [11] is used to segment OD by getting a classification map from the original image. Deep Retinal Image Understanding (DRIU) method [12] is used to designs task-specific layers to perform OD segmentation. MNet [13] uses the U-Net [14] as the backbone to extract a multi-level feature map to enhance the ability of subspace representation. Attention guided network (AG-Net) [15] produces attention guided filter in the upsampling layer and structural skip-connection to merge structural information and spatial information. Spatial-aware neural network (SAN) [4] considers the label prediction that depends on the context features and the spatial locations for OD and optic cup (OC) segmentation. However, these methods use frequently stacked convolutional layers and pooling operation, which neglects the detailed spatial information. This information is important for OD segmentation since the profile of the OD and the spatial distribution of the vessels has a lot of similar structural information. In this paper, we propose a light U-Net (LU-Net) to prevent losing some significant spatial information by reducing convolutional layers and pooling operations. By taking advantage of the interdependencies among feature maps, we produce an attention mechanism after the encoder of LU-Net. To incorporate global spatial information in high-level semantic features, the atrous convolution and spatial pyramid pooling (ASPP) are proposed to ensure the effective field of view of filters. Finally, we integrate the spatial information by using element-wise sum and upsampling operation to get the segmentation results.

The main contributions of this work are summarized as follows:

1) We present a novel OD segmentation network, which can adaptively capture multi-level hierarchical information using ResNet-101 as a base network and effectively integrate the spatial information via element-wise sum operation.

2) LU-Net module is utilized to prevent losing the significant spatial information by reducing convolutional layers and pooling operations. To incorporate global spatial

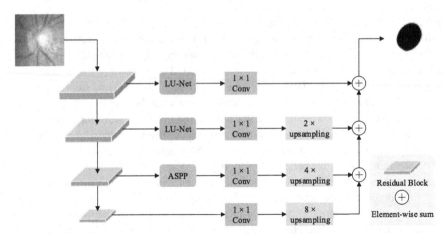

Fig. 1. Illustration of our segmentation framework. We use pretrained ResNet-101 to extract hierarchical feature maps. The LU-Net is used to extract the detailed spatial information of the shallow-level feature maps. For high-level feature maps, atrous convolution and spatial pyramid pooling (ASPP) module can extract more effective global spatial information.

information in high-level semantic features, ASPP is proposed to ensure effective field view of filters.

3) We estimate the proposed method on two public retinal fundus image datasets, REFUGE, and Drishti-GS. For REFUGE, our method achieves about 2% improvement of mean Intersection over Union (mIoU) and the Dice similarity coefficient (Dice) over the next best method. For Drishti-GS, the proposed model also outperforms the other state-of-the-art methods with 99.74% Dice and 93.26% mIoU.

2   Methodology

Figure 1 shows the architecture of our proposed method, where ResNet-101 is utilized as a base network to extract hierarchical feature maps. We extract four different feature maps from four residual blocks, respectively, which contains various dimensions and different semantic spatial information. LU-Net is used to extract significant spatial information and enhance the ability of feature representation for low-level feature maps. For high-level feature maps, we use ASPP to extract large-scale semantic features and get global context information. We use the element-wise sum operation to integrate four-stream feature maps. In the end, an upsampling operation is utilized to obtain the OD segmentation result.

2.1   Light U-Net

U-Net [14] has great success in medical image segmentation due to its specific encoding and decoding structure. However, it inevitably has a problem that the stacked convolutional layers and pooling operations neglect a lot of important detailed spatial information, for the reason that the profile of OD and the spatial distribution of vessels have much similar structural information. In this paper, we use a LU-Net, as shown in Fig. 2. Similar to the traditional U-Net method, LU-Net also consists of two main paths, the encoder path and the decoder path. The difference from U-Net is that the proposed encoder module only includes two max-pooling operations for downsampling, while the decoder is also comprised of two upsample operations, which can effectively prevent losing the significant spatial information.

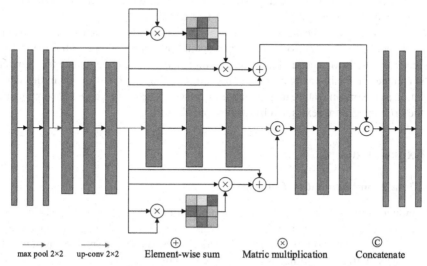

Fig. 2. The illustration of LU-Net. It only includes two max-pooling and upsampling layers. An attention mechanism is used to improve the ability of feature representation.

Moreover, we produce an attention mechanism [16] to enhance the ability of feature representation and improve the interdependence between feature maps before the pooling operation in the decoder. We reshape the original feature map and use a matrix multiplication between it and the original feature map. An attention map is obtained by applying a softmax layer. Additionally, we also utilize a matrix multiplication between the attention map and the reshaped original feature map. We further use an element-wise sum operation to integrate it with the original feature map (Fig. 3).

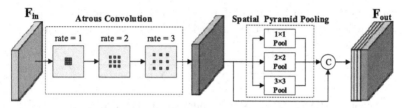

Fig. 3. The illustration of ASPP. We use atrous convolution to extract high-level semantic features and spatial pyramid pooling to encode global context information.

2.2 Atrous Convolution and Spatial Pyramid Pooling

Atrous convolution can explicitly master the size of feature maps and adjust the field-of-view of the filter to capture large-scale contextual information. Due to the low image resolution of the extracted feature map by the third residual module, it can cause a problem using conventional convolution layer. For example, the resolution and spatial information is reduced. To solve it, the atrous convolution is used to obtain more effective global information by enlarging the field-of-view of the filter. In our method, the dilatation rate of three atrous convolutions is 1, 2, and 3, respectively.

Complex objects can be detected in multiple available fields of view by using spatial pyramid pooling [17]. Therefore, we adopt a spatial pyramid pooling with three small-size receptive fields to encode global context information. Then, we reduce the number of the channel into 1 by using a 1×1 convolution and upsample it to obtain the same resolution as the origin feature map. Finally, we concatenate the upsampled feature maps and the original features extracted by atrous convolution.

3 Experiments

3.1 Dataset and Evaluation Criteria

We conduct experiments on two public retinal fundus image datasets, REFUGE [18] and Drishti-GS [19] dataset. The REFUGE dataset consists of 400 training images, 400 validation images, and 400 test images. The Drishti-GS dataset is a small dataset, which only consists of 50 training images and 51 validation images. To be consistent in setting with other methods, for the REFUGE dataset, we adopt the image from the train set as a training set and the validation set as the test set. For the Drishti-GS dataset, we maintain its original dataset distribution.

The fundus images have high resolution, but the OD is a relatively small area in contrast to the whole fundus image. Therefore, we first use the existing detection method [20] to localize the disc region and crop the size of the retinal fundus images to 448×448. For evaluation, we use the Dice similarity coefficient (Dice), which measures the similarity between two sets of data. It is defined as:

$$Dice = 2 \times \sum_{i=0}^{1} \frac{p_{ii}}{\sum_{j=0}^{1} p_{ij} + \sum_{j=0}^{1} p_{ji}}. \tag{1}$$

Mean Intersection over Union (mIoU) is a standard to measure the accuracy of the corresponding object. It is also used as an evaluation index and is defined as:

$$mIoU = \frac{1}{2} \sum_{i=0}^{1} \frac{p_{ii}}{\sum_{j=0}^{1} p_{ij} + \sum_{j=0}^{1} p_{ji} - p_{ii}}. \tag{2}$$

Pixel Accuracy (PA) is the ratio of the number of pixels correctly classified to all pixels. It is defined as:

$$PA = \frac{\sum_{i=0}^{1} p_{ii}}{\sum_{i=0}^{1} \sum_{j=0}^{1} p_{ij}}. \tag{3}$$

Frequency Weighted Intersection over Union (FWIoU) is an extension of mIoU in which weights are assigned according to the frequency of each class:

$$FWIoU = \frac{1}{\sum_{i=0}^{1} \sum_{j=0}^{1} p_{ij}} \sum \frac{p_{ii}}{\sum_{j=0}^{1} p_{ij} + \sum_{j=0}^{1} p_{ji} - p_{ii}}, \quad (4)$$

where i represent the ground truth and j represents the predicted mask. p_{ii}, p_{ij}, p_{ji} represents true positive, false positive, and false negative, respectively.

3.2 Implementation Details

Our whole framework is implemented with the PyTorch framework. For data augmentation, we only apply random horizontal flip and random vertical flip. We initialize the weights of ResNet-101 with the pre-trained model on ImageNet. During training, parameters are optimized by Adam optimizer, where momentum is set to 0.9 and weight decay is set to 0.003. Our learning rate is initially set to 0.001 and the decay rate is 0.1 every 30 epochs, where the max epoch is set to 100 for all datasets.

3.3 Comparison with State-of-the-Art

We compare our proposed method with six state-of-the-arts: FCN [11], deep contour-aware networks (DCAN) [21], U-Net [14], M-Net [13], p OSAL [22], and ET-Net [23]. The first three methods are widely used in medical segmentation. Therefore, they can used to segment OD. The latter three methods can simultaneously segment OD and OC taking into account the mutual relation between OD and OC. Our proposed method is more focused on the segmentation of OD. The OD segmentation results are shown in Table 1.

Table 1. Optic disc segmentation results on REFUGE and Drishti-GS dataset.

Method	REFUGE		Drishti-GS	
	Dice (%)	mIoU (%)	Dice (%)	mIoU (%)
FCN [11]	92.56	82.47	95.69	83.92
U-Net [14]	93.08	83.12	96.43	84.87
M-Net [13]	93.59	84.02	96.58	85.88
DCAN [21]	94.01	84.36	96.55	85.94
p OSAL [22]	94.60	–	97.40	–
ET-Net [23]	95.29	86.70	97.52	87.92
Ours	**98.22**	**88.53**	**99.74**	**93.26**

We can see that the proposed method obtains superior segmentation results than other state-of-the-art methods. For the REFUGE dataset, our method achieves about

2% improvement of Dice and mean IoU over the next best method. For Drishti-GS, we also achieve the best performance with 99.74% Dice and 93.26% mIoU. Aiming to quantitative results, we show the visualization of segmentation results, as shown in Fig. 4. We can observe that our results are closer to the ground truth.

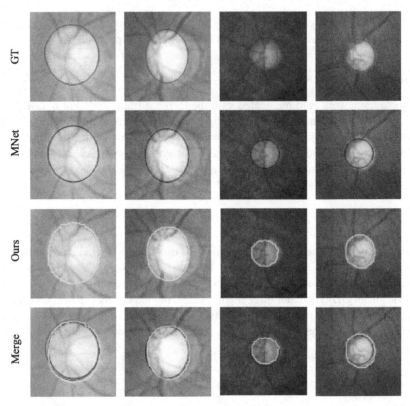

Fig. 4. Visualization of segmentation results. The first two columns rows represent images from the REFUGE dataset and the last two columns represent images from the Drishti-GS. The last row merges the result of the three segmentation boundaries. The red curve represents ground truth, the blue curve denotes the results of the MNet. The region enclosed by the yellow curve denotes the results of our proposed method. (Color figure online)

3.4   Ablation Study

To estimate the effectiveness of every module of our proposed method, we conduct experiments by adding the modules on both datasets. To avoid mutual interference of multiple modules, we only add a module at a time. To distinguish the role of different LU-Net in different level feature maps, two experiments are respectively carried out on the two modules, where LU-Net_1 and LU-Net _2 represent the modules applied for feature maps extracted by the first residual block and the second residual block, respectively. In

Table 2, the results show that adding corresponding modules to the base network, and the corresponding results are slightly improved. Since the Drishti-GS dataset only has 50 images for training and the OD in cropped image occupies a relatively small area, the global information obtained through ASPP has some interference. Therefore, the result of segmentation has a slight decrease in PA and FWIoU. In general, the experiment demonstrates that each component of our proposed method has a positive impact on the segmentation performance.

Table 2. Evaluation of the effectiveness of every module of the proposed method (%).

Method	REFUGE				Drishti-GS			
	Dice	mIoU	PA	FWIoU	Dice	mIoU	PA	FWIoU
Base	97.45	84.72	95.97	92.52	99.67	91.68	99.44	98.91
Base+LU-Net_1	97.66	85.48	96.35	93.17	99.72	92.63	99.50	99.00
Base+LU-Net_2	97.75	86.40	96.59	93.59	99.70	92.23	99.51	99.03
Base+ASPP	97.78	86.35	96.51	93.44	99.72	92.72	99.51	99.03
Base+LUNet_1+LU-Net_2	97.88	86.81	96.63	93.68	99.72	92.88	**99.55**	**99.12**
Ours	**98.22**	**88.53**	**97.22**	**94.69**	**99.74**	**93.26**	99.54	99.10

4 Conclusions

We propose a novel OD segmentation network, which can adaptively capture multi-level hierarchical information by using ResNet-101 as a base network. Light U-Net module is utilized to learn the intrinsic spatial information effectively and enhance the ability of feature representation in low-level feature maps. ASPP can incorporate global spatial information in high-level semantic feature maps. The experimental results demonstrate that our proposed method has better performance than the state-of-the-art methods on both public retinal fundus image datasets (REFUGE and Drishti-GS).

Acknowledgements. This work was supported partly by National Natural Science Foundation of China (Nos. 61871274, 61801305 and 81571758), National Natural Science Foundation of Guangdong Province (No. 2020A1515010649 and No. 2019A1515 111205), Guangdong Province Key Laboratory of Popular High Performance Computers (No. 2017B030314073), Guangdong Laboratory of Artificial-Intelligence and Cyber-Economics (SZ), Shenzhen Peacock Plan (Nos. KQTD2016053112051497 and KQTD2015033016104926), Shenzhen Key Basic Research Project (Nos. JCYJ201908 08165209410, 20190808145011259, JCYJ20180507184647636, GJHZ20190822095   414576   and   JCYJ20170302153337765,   JCYJ20170302150411789, JCYJ2017030214   2515949,   GCZX2017040715180580,   GJHZ20180418190529516, and JSGG2018050 7183215520), NTUT-SZU Joint Research Program (No. 2020003), Special Project in Key Areas of Ordinary Universities of Guangdong Province (No. 2019KZDZX1015).

References

1. Chrástek, R., et al.: Automated segmentation of the optic nerve head for diagnosis of glaucoma. Med. Image Anal. **9**, 297–314 (2005)
2. Kamble, R., Kokare, M., Deshmukh, G., Hussin, F.A., Mériaudeau, F.: Localization of optic disc and fovea in retinal images using intensity based line scanning analysis. Comput. Biol. Med. **87**, 382–396 (2017)
3. Sigut, J., Nunez, O., Fumero, F., Gonzalez, M., Arnay, R.: Contrast based circular approximation for accurate and robust optic disc segmentation in retinal images. PeerJ **5**, e3763–e3763 (2017)
4. Liu, Q., Hong, X., Li, S., Chen, Z., Zhao, G., Zou, B.: A spatial-aware joint optic disc and cup segmentation method. Neurocomputing **359**, 285–297 (2019)
5. Salazar-Gonzalez, A., Kaba, D., Li, Y., Liu, X.: Segmentation of the blood vessels and optic disk in retinal images. IEEE J. Biomed. Health Inform. **18**, 1874–1886 (2014)
6. Joshi, G.D., Sivaswamy, J., Karan, K., Prashanth, R., Krishnadas, S.R.: Vessel bend-based cup segmentation in retinal images. In: 2010 20th International Conference on Pattern Recognition, pp. 2536–2539 (2010)
7. Cheng, J., et al.: Superpixel classification based optic disc and optic cup segmentation for glaucoma screening. IEEE Trans. Med. Imaging **32**, 1019–1032 (2013)
8. Li, R., Auer, D., Wagner, C., Chen, X.: A generic ensemble based deep convolutional neural network for semi-supervised medical image segmentation. In: 2020 IEEE 17th International Symposium on Biomedical Imaging (ISBI), pp. 1168–1172 (2020)
9. Chen, Q., Sun, X., Zhang, N., Cao, Y., Liu, B.: Mini lesions detection on diabetic retinopathy images via large scale CNN features. In: 2019 IEEE 31st International Conference on Tools with Artificial Intelligence (ICTAI), vol. pp. 348–352 (2019)
10. Bajwa, M.N., et al.: Two-stage framework for optic disc localization and glaucoma classification in retinal fundus images using deep learning. BMC Med. Inform. Decis. Mak. **19**, 136 (2019)
11. Long, J., Shelhamer, E., Darrell, T.: Fully convolutional networks for semantic segmentation. In: 2015 IEEE Conference on Computer Vision and Pattern Recognition (CVPR), pp. 3431–3440 (2015)
12. Maninis, K.-K., Pont-Tuset, J., Arbeláez, P., Van Gool, L.: Deep retinal image understanding. In: Ourselin, S., Joskowicz, L., Sabuncu, M.R., Unal, G., Wells, W. (eds.) MICCAI 2016. LNCS, vol. 9901, pp. 140–148. Springer, Cham (2016). https://doi.org/10.1007/978-3-319-46723-8_17
13. Fu, H., Cheng, J., Xu, Y., Wong, D., Liu, J., Cao, X.: Joint optic disc and cup segmentation based on multi-label deep network and polar transformation. IEEE Trans. Med. Imaging (2018)
14. Ronneberger, O., Fischer, P., Brox, T.: U-Net: convolutional networks for biomedical image segmentation. In: Medical Image Computing and Computer-Assisted Intervention, pp. 234–241 (2015)
15. Zhang, S., et al.: Attention guided network for retinal image segmentation. In: International Conference on Medical Image Computing and Computer-Assisted Intervention, pp. 797–805, (2019)
16. Fu, J., et al.: Dual attention network for scene segmentation. In: 2019 IEEE/CVF Conference on Computer Vision and Pattern Recognition (CVPR), pp. 3141–3149 (2019)
17. Gu, Z., et al.: DeepDisc: optic disc segmentation based on atrous convolution and spatial pyramid pooling. In: Stoyanov, D., et al. (eds.) OMIA/COMPAY -2018. LNCS, vol. 11039, pp. 253–260. Springer, Cham (2018). https://doi.org/10.1007/978-3-030-00949-6_30

18. Orlando, J.I., Fu, H., Breda, J.B., et al.: Refuge challenge: a unified framework for evaluating automated methods for glaucoma assessment from fundus photographs. Med. Image Anal. **59**, 101570 (2020)
19. Sivaswamy, J., Krishnadas, S.R., Joshi, G.D., Jain, M., Tabish, A.U.S.: Drishti-GS: retinal image dataset for optic nerve head (ONH) segmentation. In: 2014 IEEE 11th International Symposium on Biomedical Imaging (ISBI), pp. 53–56 (2014)
20. Fu, H., et al.: Disc-aware ensemble network for glaucoma screening from fundus image. IEEE Trans. Med. Imaging **37**, 2493–2501 (2018)
21. Chen, H., Qi, X., Yu, L., P.-Heng, A.: DCAN: deep contour-aware networks for accurate gland segmentation (2016)
22. Wang, S., Yu, L., Yang, X., Fu, C., Heng, P.: Patch-based output space adversarial learning for joint optic disc and cup segmentation. IEEE Trans. Med. Imaging **38**, 2485–2495 (2019)
23. Zhang, Z., Fu, H., Dai, H., Shen, J., Pang, Y., Shao, L.: ET-Net: a generic edge-aTtention guidance network for medical image segmentation. In: Shen, D., et al. (eds.) MICCAI 2019. LNCS, vol. 11764, pp. 442–450. Springer, Cham (2019). https://doi.org/10.1007/978-3-030-32239-7_49

An Interactive Approach to Region of Interest Selection in Cytologic Analysis of Uveal Melanoma Based on Unsupervised Clustering

Haomin Chen[1(✉)], T. Y. Alvin Liu[2], Zelia Correa[2], and Mathias Unberath[1]

[1] Department of Computer Science, Johns Hopkins University, Baltimore, MD, USA
hchen135@jhu.edu

[2] Wilmer Eye Institute, School of Medicine, Johns Hopkins University, Baltimore, MD, USA

Abstract. Facilitating quantitative analysis of cytology images of fine needle aspirates of uveal melanoma is important to confirm diagnosis and inform management decisions. Extracting high-quality regions of interest (ROIs) from cytology whole slide images is a critical first step. To the best of our knowledge, we describe the first unsupervised clustering-based method for fine needle aspiration cytology (FNAC) that automatically suggests high-quality ROIs. Our method is integrated in a graphical user interface that allows for interactive refinement of ROI suggestions to tailor analysis to any specific specimen. We show that the proposed approach suggests ROIs that are in very good agreement with expert-extracted regions and demonstrate that interactive refinement results in the extraction of more high-quality regions compared to purely algorithmic extraction alone.

Keywords: Human-computer interaction · Unsupervised learning · Machine learning · Coarse to fine

1 Introduction

Clinical Background: Uveal melanoma is the most common primary intraocular malignancy in adults [21]. As standard care for uveal melanoma, Fine Needle Aspiration Biopsy (FNAB) is often performed to confirm the diagnosis and to obtain cell aspirates for both Gene Expression Profile (GEP) and Cytology of Fine Needle Aspirates (FNAC) analysis for prognostication. According to recent analysis, primary uveal melanoma clusters in two distinct subgroups according to its GEP; the first corresponding to low grade melanoma with little to no metastatic risk, and the second corresponding to high grade melanoma with high metastatic risk, which results in 6 times of 5-year probability of metastatic death [7]. While GEP analysis of fine needle aspirates has shown good accuracy for identifying patients at high risk of metastatic disease, the only commercially

© Springer Nature Switzerland AG 2020
H. Fu et al. (Eds.): OMIA 2020, LNCS 12069, pp. 114–124, 2020.
https://doi.org/10.1007/978-3-030-63419-3_12

available test is expensive, requires special storage and transportation, has a long turn around time and is only available in the US. Most importantly, despite its efficacy, the commercial GEP test still occasionally fails resulting in unpleasant clinical surprises and unexpected early metastatic death. There is increasing evidence that the underlying genetic profile affects cancer growth on multiple scales. Radiomics, for example, exploit this observation to develop imaging-derived biomarkers that are informative for prognosis [12]. We hypothesize that such multi-scale analysis will also be useful for prognosis in uveal melanoma. Specifically in addition to GEP, we would like to extract imaging-features from FNAC. In addition to complementing GEP analysis, such cytology-based test could provide a cheap and widely available alternative for prognostication of uveal melanoma [9]. However, pathologist analysis of FNAC is infeasible, as 1) it is a very time-consuming and tedious task, and 2) none of the manually defined cytopathological features proved particularly robust for predicting metastatic risk.

To reach this goal, we need to facilitate or even automate quantitative analysis of cytology whole slide images (WSIs). To this end, we develop an interactive tool that our envision will be beneficial in two ways: First, it can be deployed in pathologist-centric workflows to guide pathologist review, thereby reducing the experts workload. Second, the tool provides an opportunity for pathologists to guide algorithmic evaluation, e.g. by refining the content that is submitted for automated analysis of the slide, e.g. for GEP classification. Such an interactive design may prove beneficial in building trust, accelerating workflows, and reducing mistakes, of both automated algorithms and pathologists.

We present our first steps in this direction that consider the extraction of high-quality Region of Interests (ROIs) (areas with multiple clear cancer cells) from gigapixel-sized histological architecture, FNAC. We propose a Human-Interactive Computationally-Assisted Tool (HICAT) that supports ROI selection with a 2-step coarse-to-fine unsupervised clustering. It provides **interactivity** to allow for patient-specific refinement of ROI selection at application time. This refinement provides insight in and some control over the region selection, and results in the extraction of more informative regions compared to the purely algorithmic extraction. Such human-machine partnership may contribute to pathologists building trust in AI-assisted tools. HICAT increases Recall in ROIs from 7.44% to 42.32%, while Precision remains the same 83%. On average, 1318 ROIs per FNAC are extracted, which contains enough information for further analysis. Our AI-assisted ROI selection workflow is more than 10 times faster than manual ROI extraction by pathologists that was used previously [17].

Related Work: Histology WSI and FNAC are two main foci in pathology. Histology WSI contains an entire slice of tissue and several learning-based algorithms for ROI extraction have been proposed [3,14,15,19]. FNACs exhibit high variation in cell quality and artifact, and to our knowledge, all existing approaches for high-level FNAC analysis operate on manually identified ROIs [8,10,20]. Due to the small targets (e.g. lesions and organs) in medical imaging, coarse-to-fine concepts are widely used. Spatial coarse-to-fine segmentation is applied to target small organs and lesions [6, 16, 25–27]. Spatial coarse-to-fine clustering is also commonly used to extract ROIs from high spatial resolution WSIs and several machine-learning approaches exist for this task [3, 19]. To involve human cognition and refine algorithmic prediction, human interaction with deep learning so far has been largely limited to segmentation problems [1, 2, 11, 22, 23].

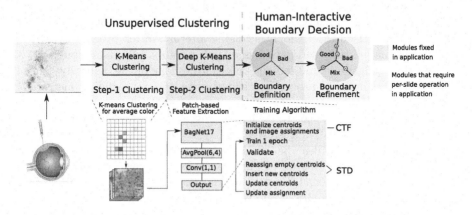

Fig. 1. Overview of the HICAT.

2   Method

Given a FNAC image, we seek to extract square-shaped ROIs, similar to those shown in Fig. 2(a), which lend themselves well for further cell-level algorithmic analysis. Our ROI extraction pipeline contains of a 2-step clustering that is followed by an interactive decision boundary definition to assign image-quality to centroids. The clustering algorithm will be discussed in Sect. 2.1 and Sect. 2.2. The first step aims to remove blank images, *i.e.* Fig. 2(g), to greatly reduce processing time for the second step, which further clusters the selected ROIs based on image content. After the 2-step clustering, a global decision boundary for all FNACs is defined by centroid-level human annotation. Interactive refinement of this decision boundary is then possible for every patient and FNAC to improve the algorithmic ROI selection based on centroid annotation (Sect. 2.3).

2.1   Step-1 Clustering

The given FNAC is first down-sampled such that each pixel in the resulting image corresponds to the average signal within one area. The size of this area is only constrained by its compatibility with the following clustering steps. We found the size 512×512 is able to perform sufficiently well. K-means clustering is then used to cluster pixel intensities into 2 centroids that intuitively correspond to regions with bright and dark average intensities. Since FNACs are acquired with the bright-field technique, pixels with low and high intensities correspond to regions with high and low tissue content, respectively. We select the darker centroid for further processing via Step-2 clustering in Sect. 2.2. Because the exact magnitude of bright and dark centroid intensities varies with cell distribution and illumination, this scheme is applied to every FNAC slide independently.

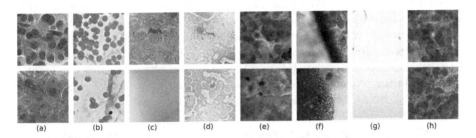

Fig. 2. Different types of ROIs in FNACs. (a) High-quality ROIs, which contain more than 3 clear cancer cells. (b) Blood cell ROIs. (c) Blurred ROIs. (d) Fluid ROIs. (e) Multi-layer cell ROIs. (f) Artifact ROIs. (g) Blank ROIs. (h) Borderline ROIs, which contain more than 3 clear cancer cells, but contains a large portion of low-quality areas.

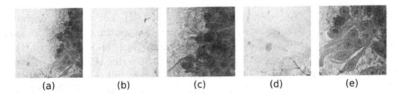

Fig. 3. An example of Step-1 clustered area and some of the corresponding Step-2 clustering ROIs. (a) Step-1 area. (b) Top-left corner. (c) Top-right corner. (d) Bottom-left corner. (e) Bottom-right corner.

2.2   Step-2 Clustering

Step-2 clustering aims to separate high-quality images with more than 3 clear cancer cells from low-quality images that either show blood cells, multiple layers of cells and fluid, are blurred or otherwise corrupted with artifact. Examples of such images are provided in Fig. 2. Since this separation is based on image content that, in cytology, can vary considerably across pixels (cf. Fig. 3), a patch-based network is applied to perform clustering on 228×228 pixel ROIs in naive resolution which is much smaller than the areas extracted from Step-1 clustering. These patches are extracted with a stride of 128 from the ROIs selected in Step-1 clustering. A previous state-of-the-art patch-based method, BagNet17 [4] is used as the backbone. The input images of size 512 × 512 pixels are first down-sampled 4 times and an average pooling layer with kernel size 6 and stride 4 is attached after the final residual block, so that each output pixel corresponds to one desired patch (if using other parameters, the receptive field's size and stride cannot be guaranteed to take on the desired value). Finally, a convolutional layer with kernel size 1 × 1 compresses the feature into a lower-dimension space with dimension d. We follow [5,24] to involve k-means clustering for the d-dimension network outputs. K-means centroids and patch assignments are initialized by the pre-trained network and are fixed in the training phase. L2 loss is applied to force patch features to be close to the assigned centroid. Centroids and patch assignments are updated during the validation phase. We reassign empty centroids during training to avoid trivial parametrization. Step-2 clustering is trained on all FNACs simultaneously.

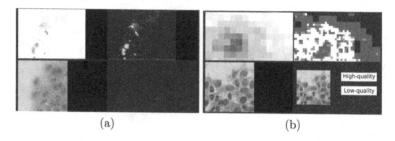

     (a)   (b)

Fig. 4. Examples for FNAC-specific ROI refinement GUI. For each screenshot, top-left image is the down-sampled WSI, top-right image shows the corresponding spatial states for all ROIs, white/light grey/grey means high-/mix-/poor-quality ROIs. Dark grey corresponds to blank images removed by Step-1 clustering. Pink pixels correspond to uncertain ROIs. Bottom left image is the corresponding full resolution ROI that the mouse hovers over. By double clicking the pixel on the down-sampled WSI or state image, a window in bottom right will pop out for annotation. (a) shows the overall behaviour of the state image. (b) shows the zoomed-in version for detail visualization.

In order to reduce the number of centroids that focus on fluid and artifact images, we introduce a centroid-based coarse-to-fine clustering strategy. Only a portion of centroids are initialized first, and new centroids are inserted during training in order to increase the probability of these centroids to account for cell images, which is referred as *CTF* in Fig. 1. We reassign/insert empty/new centroids around the centroid with the largest standard deviation of its assigned samples in feature space, instead of the centroid with the largest number of samples [5,24]. It is referred as *STD* in Fig. 1. This is because of 2 reasons: 1) A considerable number of fluid and artifact images exists and there is no use to further insert centroids for these images. 2) Fluid and artifact images are easier to separate because of the difference in complexity compared to cell images.

Consequently, centroids with cell images tend to have larger standard deviation among the assigned samples in feature space, so that inserted/re-assigned centroids are more likely to focus on cell images. The re-assignment and insertion is processed during the validation phase.

2.3 Interactive Centroid Assignment and Refinement

After Step-2 clustering, every centroid contains ROIs that exhibit similar appearance. However, at this point it is still unclear which of the ROIs in the centroids are high-/low-quality. To provide this semantic definition with minimal manual annotation requirement, we developed a Graphical User Interface (GUI) that allows for rapid centroid annotation. To this end, 10 ROIs from 10 random centroids are displayed for the user to classify. After several iterations, each centroid has more than 10 high-/poor-quality annotations. The ratio of high-quality ROIs classified to every centroid is then used to define a centroid-level boundary that separates between high- and low-quality ROIs. Because cell quality in FNACs has large variation, some ROIs cannot be clearly classified as high-/low-quality, e.g. Fig. 2(h). Therefore, we allow for some mix-quality centroids that contain roughly an equal number of high-/low-quality ROI annotations. Although there exists high-quality ROIs in mix-quality centroids, we exclude them to avoid introducing poor-quality images to influence further analysis.

During application, due to high variations in FNACs, the classifier based on the above procedure may not perform perfectly when suggesting ROIs in new FNACs. To allow for the refinement of ROI suggestions, a patient-specific refinement tool is created for pathologists to interact with, as shown in Fig. 4. Specifically, high-/low-/mix-quality assignments from boundary definition are visualized and synchronized with the corresponding FNAC image. The user can hover the mouse over the FNAC to display the underlying ROI in native resolution, and can simply click it to re-annotate if necessary. In this case, the selected ROI and all ROIs with similar features $\{x, \text{where } ||x - F||_2 < \lambda_2 L_1\}$ are all re-annotated, where F is the selected ROI's feature, L_1 is the distance to the closest centroid and λ_2 is a constant. Uncertain ROIs are also identified and displayed to users as recommended for re-annotation. Using L_1, L_2 as the distance of an ROI feature to the 2 closest centroids. The ROI is considered uncertain if the two closest centroids are high- and low-quality, respectively, and satisfies

$$\frac{||L_1 - L_2||_2}{\min\{L_1, L_2\}} < \lambda_1 \tag{1}$$

where λ_1 is a constant. The result of every click re-annotation is reflected in real time. The user has full control over when to stop the refinement.

3 Experiment

3.1 Experiment Setup

Dataset: The dataset we use includes 100 FNAC samples from 100 uveal melanoma patients. The cellular aspirates obtained from FNACs of each tumor were submitted to cytology and GEP testing. The cytology specimen was flushed on a standard pathology glass slide, smeared, and stained with hematoxylin and eosin. The specimen submitted for GEP was flushed into a tube containing extraction buffer and submitted for DecisionDx-UM testing. Whole slide scanning was performed for each cytology slide at a magnification of 40x, using the Aperio ScanScope AT machine, and the high-magnification digital image was examined using the Aperio Imagescope software.

516 areas of size 1716×926 are manually extracted and annotated from 20 slides by an expert pathologist. Every area is split into 8 small areas with equal size. Each small area is further split into 9 ROIs where the stride of ROI extraction is half of their width and height. All of these ROIs are annotated as high-/low-quality images, which results in $37, 152$ annotated ROIs. The criterion for high-quality images is the same as Fig. 2(a). All our experiments are trained on the remaining 80 slides and tested on the 20 slides with annotations.

Implementation Details: $259, 203$ areas are extracted by Step-1 clustering. In Step-2 clustering, each area corresponds to 9 ROIs with size 228×228, which results in a total of $2, 332, 827$ ROIs for training. The length d of the output feature vector is 16. Centroid-based coarse-to-fine clustering is first initialized with 32 centroids. 4 new centroids are inserted after every training epoch until a total of 100 centroids exists. We implement the model using PyTorch [18] for Step-2 clustering, and initialize them with ImageNet pre-trained weights provided by [4]. All models are optimized by Adam [13] with a learning rate of 10^{-3}. All interactive centroid assignments and specific boundary refinement were performed by an expert pathologist. During centroid definition, centroids with greater than 70% of ROIs annotated as high-quality are classified as high-quality centroids, while centroids with fewer than 30% are classified as low-quality centroids. The other centroids are mix-quality centroids. For boundary refinement, the parameters are $\lambda_1 = 0.2, \lambda_2 = 0.5$.

Table 1. Ablation study for clustering algorithm. DeepCluster (DC) is DCN [24] with BagNet17 [4] as backbone. "CTF" indicates the use of the proposed centroid-based coarse-to-fine strategy. "STD" indicates the use of the proposed mechanism of inserting/reassigning new/empty centroids to be around the centroid with the largest standard deviation of its assigned samples in feature space. (Otherwise, to be around the centroid with most samples). Numbers of high-/low-quality centroids are also reported.

Model	Recall_{gb}	Recall_{gmb}	Precision_{gmb}	Accuracy	#high-quality	#low-quality
DC [4, 24]	11.74%	7.44%	83.17%	61.43%	10	60
DC+STD	34.71%	7.89%	85.99%	63.63%	18	43
DC+STD+CTF	**51.38%**	**27.83%**	**91.56%**	**70.90%**	23	51

Evaluation Metrics: The final goal for our proposed extraction is to maximize the number of high-quality ROIs and to minimize the number of low-quality ROIs provided for further analysis. To evaluate our success, we calculate the recall, precision and accuracy on the ROIs in the 20 slides with manually extracted ROIs. Because there exist mix-quality centroids, we first report recall and precision for images only in high-/low-quality centroids, denoted as Recall_{gb}, Precision_{gb}. We also report recall, precision and accuracy for all annotated images, by treating mix-quality centroids as low-quality centroids, denoted as Recall_{gmb}, Precision_{gmb} and Accuracy. Because Precision_{gb} is the same as Precision_{gmb}, only Precision_{gmb} is recorded.

3.2 Ablation Study for Clustering Algorithm

In order to compare different clustering algorithms, human-interactive boundary definition is performed separately for all models to classify high-/mix-/low-quality centroids by the same expert pathologist. We conduct an ablation study for clustering algorithm to analyze the contributions of its novel components. The baseline is the combination of the deep clustering network, DCN [24], with Bag-Net17 [4] (referred to as *DeepCluster*) with 100 centroids. The performance by adding the two novel components: centroid-based coarse-to-fine concept (referred to as *CTF*) and the centroid insertion/reassignment algorithm (referred to as *STD*) is compared. The Step-1 clustering is kept the same across all models, which eliminates 96.5% areas as blank areas. Results are summarized in Table 1.

The effect of our proposed centroid insertion/reassignment algorithm is reflected in the comparison of *DeepCluster vs. DeepCluster+STD*. Recall_{gb} and Precision_{gmb} increase from 11.74% and 83.17% to 34.71% and 85.99% by using *STD*. Improvements are due to our observation that standard deviation of the assigned samples are efficient to tell apart centroids for high-/low-quality images. More centroids for high-quality images result in better performance.

The effect of centroid-based coarse-to-fine method is reflected in the comparison of *DeepCluster+STD vs. DeepCluster+STD+CTF*. By adding the centroid-based coarse-to-fine module to *DeepCluster+STD*, we observe substantial improvements in Recall_{gmb} and Precision_{gmb} which increase from 7.89% and 85.99% to 27.83% and 91.56%, respectively. The improvement is in line with our motivation and hypothesis that more centroids are assigned to focus on images with different cells and various visual quality. The increase in the number of high-quality centroids further supports our hypothesis.

Table 2. Ablation study for human interactive patient-specific boundary refinement.

Model	Recall_{gb}	Recall_{gmb}	Precision_{gmb}	Accuracy
Without boundary refinement	51.38%	27.83%	**91.56%**	70.90%
HICAT	**59.47%**	**42.32%**	83.09%	**74.18%**

3.3 Ablation Study for Interactive Refinement

The performance of interactive refinement of ROI suggestion is shown in Table 2. FNAC and the ROIs' labels after centroid definition is synchronously visualized as Fig. 4. An expert pathologist finished the human interactive boundary refinement for all testing FNACs. Less than 50 re-annotation clicks are performed for each slide. The pathologist stopped the process for each slide, once he determined there were adequate high-quality ROIs selected for further analysis and few low-quality ROIs exist. Comparing with/without boundary refinement shows that $Recall_{gmb}$ goes drastically up from 27.83% to 42.32%. The reduced precision from 91.56% to 83.09% may be attributed to a conservative selection of the pathologist. However, since adequate high-quality ROIs are still available for further analysis, this decrease is likely not problematic. The boost in performance is due to the variation in different FNACs. Pathologists may interact with our tool to adjust the inclusion criteria based on a specific FNAC, *e.g.* when few cells are visible, the selection criteria for high-quality ROIs can be relaxed. Finally, 1318 ROIs are extracted on average per FNAC, which contain adequate information for further analysis. The whole application process takes 15 min per FNAC, which is more than 10 times faster than manual ROI extraction. (3 min for 2-step clustering and 12 min for boundary refinement.)

4 Conclusion

In this paper, we propose an interactive and computationally-assisted tool for high-quality ROI extraction from FNACs. Our method relies on 2-step unsupervised clustering of ROI appearance and content to automatically suggest ROI of acceptable quality. These suggestions can then be refined interactively to adapt ROI selection to specific patients. We hope to contribute effective tools that support quantitative analysis of FNACs to, in the future, improve prognostication of patients suffering from uveal melanoma.

Acknowledgement. We gratefully acknowledge funding from the Emerson Collective Cancer Research Fund and internal funds provided by the Wilmer Eye Institute and the Malone Center for Engineering in Healthcare at Johns Hopkins University.

References

1. Amrehn, M., Gaube, S., Unberath, M., et al.: UI-NET: interactive artificial neural networks for iterative image segmentation based on a user model (2017)
2. Aresta, G., et al.: iW-Net: an automatic and minimalistic interactive lung nodule segmentation deep network. Sci. Rep. **9**, 11591 (2019)
3. Barker, J., Hoogi, A., Depeursinge, A., Rubin, D.L.: Automated classification of brain tumor type in whole-slide digital pathology images using local representative tiles. Med. Image Anal. **30**, 60–71 (2016)
4. Brendel, W., Bethge, M.: Approximating CNNs with bag-of-local-features models works surprisingly well on ImageNet. In: International Conference on Learning Representations (2019)

5. Caron, M., Bojanowski, P., Joulin, A., Douze, M.: Deep clustering for unsupervised learning of visual features. In: Ferrari, V., Hebert, M., Sminchisescu, C., Weiss, Y. (eds.) Computer Vision – ECCV 2018. LNCS, vol. 11218, pp. 139–156. Springer, Cham (2018). https://doi.org/10.1007/978-3-030-01264-9_9

6. Chang, L., Zhang, M., Li, W.: A coarse-to-fine approach for medical hyperspectral image classification with sparse representation. In: Yu, J., et al. (eds.) AOPC 2017: Optical Spectroscopy and Imaging, vol. 10461, pp. 136–144. International Society for Optics and Photonics, SPIE (2017)

7. Corrêa, Z., Augsburger, J.: Sufficiency of FNAB aspirates of posterior uveal melanoma for cytologic versus GEP classification in 159 patients, and relative prognostic significance of these classifications. Graefe's archive for clinical and experimental ophthalmology = Albrecht von Graefes Archiv fur klinische und experimentelle Ophthalmologie 252 (2013)

8. Dov, D., Kovalsky, S.Z., Cohen, J., Range, D.E., Henao, R., Carin, L.: A deep-learning algorithm for thyroid malignancy prediction from whole slide cytopathology images (2019)

9. Folberg, R., Augsburger, J.J., Gamel, J.W., Shields, J.A., Lang, W.R.: Fine-needle aspirates of uveal melanomas and prognosis. Am. J. Ophthalmol. 100(5), 654–657 (1985)

10. Garud, H., et al.: High-magnification multi-views based classification of breast fine needle aspiration cytology cell samples using fusion of decisions from deep convolutional networks. In: 2017 IEEE Conference on Computer Vision and Pattern Recognition Workshops (CVPRW), pp. 828–833, July 2017

11. Girard, N., Zhygallo, A., Tarabalka, Y.: ClusterNet: unsupervised generic feature learning for fast interactive satellite image segmentation. In: Image and Signal Processing for Remote Sensing XXV, vol. 11155, pp. 244–254. SPIE (2019)

12. Grossmann, P., Stringfield, O., El-Hachem, N., et al.: Defining the biological basis of radiomic phenotypes in lung cancer. In: eLife (2017)

13. Kingma, D.P., Ba, J.: Adam: a method for stochastic optimization. arXiv preprint arXiv:1412.6980 (2014)

14. Li, J., Li, W., Gertych, A., Knudsen, B.S., Speier, W., Arnold, C.W.: An attention-based multi-resolution model for prostate whole slide imageclassification and localization. CoRR abs/1905.13208 (2019)

15. Lin, H., Chen, H., Dou, Q., Wang, L., Qin, J., Heng, P.: ScanNet: a fast and dense scanning framework for metastatic breast cancer detection from whole-slide image. In: 2018 IEEE Winter Conference on Applications of Computer Vision (WACV), pp. 539–546 (2018)

16. Liu, J., Chen, F., Shi, H., Liao, H.: Single image super-resolution for MRI using a coarse-to-fine network. In: Ibrahim, F., Usman, J., Ahmad, M.Y., Hamzah, N., Teh, S.J. (eds.) ICIBEL 2017. IP, vol. 67, pp. 241–245. Springer, Singapore (2018). https://doi.org/10.1007/978-981-10-7554-4_42

17. Liu, T.A., Zhu, H., Chen, H., et al.: Gene expression profile prediction in uveal melanoma using deep learning: a pilot study for development of an alternative survival prediction tool. Ophthalmol. Retina S2468-6530, 30251–30257 (2020)

18. Paszke, A., Gross, S., Chintala, S., et al.: Automatic differentiation in PyTorch (2017)

19. Roullier, V., Lézoray, O., Ta, V.T., Elmoataz, A.: Multi-resolution graph-based analysis of histopathological whole slide images: application to mitotic cell extraction and visualization. Computer. Med. Imaging Graph. 35(7), 603–615 (2011). Whole Slide Image Process

20. Saikia, A.R., Bora, K., Mahanta, L.B., Das, A.K.: Comparative assessment of CNN architectures for classification of breast FNAC images. Tissue Cell **57**, 8–14 (2019). eM in cell and tissues
21. Singh, A.D., Turell, M.E., Topham, A.K.: Uveal melanoma: Trends in incidence, treatment, and survival. Ophthalmology **118**(9), 1881–1885 (2011)
22. Wang, G., Li, W., Zuluaga, M.A., et al.: Interactive medical image segmentation using deep learning with image-specific fine tuning. IEEE Trans. Med. Imaging **37**(7), 1562–1573 (2018)
23. Xu, N., Price, B., Cohen, S., Yang, J., Huang, T.S.: Deep interactive object selection. In: IEEE Conference on Computer Vision and Pattern Recognition, June 2016
24. Yang, B., Fu, X., Sidiropoulos, N., Hong, M.: Towards k-means-friendly spaces: simultaneous deep learning and clustering. In: 34th International Conference on Machine Learning, ICML 2017, pp. 5888–5901 (2017)
25. Yang, B., Fu, X., Sidiropoulos, N., Hong, M.: Towards k-means-friendly spaces: simultaneous deep learning and clustering. In: 34th International Conference on Machine Learning, ICML 2017, pp. 5888–5901 (2017)
26. Zhu, Z., Xia, Y., Shen, W., Fishman, E., Yuille, A.: A 3D coarse-to-fine framework for volumetric medical image segmentation. In: 2018 International Conference on 3D Vision (3DV), pp. 682–690, September 2018
27. Zhu, Z., Xia, Y., Xie, L., Fishman, E.K., Yuille, A.L.: Multi-scale coarse-to-fine segmentation for screening pancreatic ductal adenocarcinoma. CoRR abs/1807.02941 (2018)

Retinal OCT Denoising with Pseudo-Multimodal Fusion Network

Dewei Hu[1], Joseph D. Malone[2], Yigit Atay[1], Yuankai K. Tao[2],
and Ipek Oguz[1(✉)]

[1] Department of Electrical Engineering and Computer Science,
Vanderbilt University, Nashville, TN, USA
ipek.oguz@vanderbilt.edu
[2] Department of Biomedical Engineering, Vanderbilt University, Nashville, TN, USA

Abstract. Optical coherence tomography (OCT) is a prevalent imaging technique for retina. However, it is affected by multiplicative speckle noise that can degrade the visibility of essential anatomical structures, including blood vessels and tissue layers. Although averaging repeated B-scan frames can significantly improve the signal-to-noise-ratio (SNR), this requires longer acquisition time, which can introduce motion artifacts and cause discomfort to patients. In this study, we propose a learning-based method that exploits information from the single-frame noisy B-scan and a pseudo-modality that is created with the aid of the self-fusion method. The pseudo-modality provides good SNR for layers that are barely perceptible in the noisy B-scan but can over-smooth fine features such as small vessels. By using a fusion network, desired features from each modality can be combined, and the weight of their contribution is adjustable. Evaluated by intensity-based and structural metrics, the result shows that our method can effectively suppress the speckle noise and enhance the contrast between retina layers while the overall structure and small blood vessels are preserved. Compared to the single modality network, our method improves the structural similarity with low noise B-scan from 0.559 ± 0.033 to 0.576 ± 0.031.

Keywords: Optical coherence tomography · Denoising · Self-fusion

1 Introduction

Optical coherence tomography (OCT) is a powerful non-invasive ophthalmic imaging tool [9]. The limited light bandwidth of the imaging technique on which OCT is based upon, low-coherence interferometry [15], gives rise to speckle noise that can significantly degrade the image quality. In clinical practice, the thickness of the retina layers, such as the ganglion cell layer (GCL), inner plexiform layer (IPL) and retinal nerve fiber layer (RNFL), are of interest [16]. Retinal OCTs also reveal the vascular system, which is important for ocular diseases like diabetic retinopathy [12]. The speckle noise in single frame B-scans makes the

© Springer Nature Switzerland AG 2020
H. Fu et al. (Eds.): OMIA 2020, LNCS 12069, pp. 125–135, 2020.
https://doi.org/10.1007/978-3-030-63419-3_13

border of layers unclear so that it is hard to distinguish adjacent layers, such as the GCL and IPL. The noise also produces bright dots and dark holes that can hurt the homogeneity of layers and affect the visibility of the small vessels within them. A proper denoising method is thus paramount for ophthalmic diagnosis.

Acquiring multiple frames at the same anatomical location and averaging these repeated frames is the mainstream technique for OCT denoising. The more repeated frames are acquired, the closer their mean can be to the ideal ground truth. However, this increases the imaging time linearly, and can cause discomfort to patients as well as increase motion artifacts. Other hardware-based OCT denoising methods including spatial [1] and angular averaging [14] will similarly prolong the acquisition process. Ideally, an image post-processing algorithm that applies to a single frame B-scan is preferable. Throughout the paper, we denote single frame B-scan as high noise (HN) and frame-average image as low noise (LN).

The multiplicative nature of speckle noise makes it hard to be statistically modelled, as the variation of noise intensity level in different tissue increases the complexity of the problem [4]. In a recent study, Oguz et al. [11] proposed the self-fusion method for retinal OCT denoising. Inspired by multi-atlas label fusion [17], self-fusion exploits the similarity between adjacent B-scans. For each B-scan, neighboring slices within radius r are considered as 'atlases' and vote for the denoised output. As shown in Fig. 1, self-fusion works particularly well in preserving layers, and in some cases it also offers compensation in vessels. However it suffers from long computation time and loss of fine details, similar to block-matching 3D (BM3D) [5] and k singular value decomposition (K-SVD) [8].

Deep learning has become the state-of-the-art in many image processing tasks and shown great potential for image noise reduction. Although originally used for semantic segmentation, the U-Net [13] architecture enables almost all kinds of image-to-image translation [7]. Formulated as the mapping of a high noise image to its 'clean' version, the image denoising problem can easily be seen as a supervised learning algorithm. Because of the poor quality of single frame B-scan, more supplementary information and constraints are likely to be beneficial for feature preservation. For instance, observing the layered structure of the retina, Ma et al. [10] introduce an edge loss function to preserve the prevailing horizontal edges. Devalla et al. [6] investigate a variation to U-Net architecture so that the edge information is enhanced.

In this study, we propose a novel despeckling pipeline that takes advantage of both self-fusion and deep neural networks. To boost the computational efficiency, we substitute self-fusion with a network that maps HN images to self-fusion of LN, which we call a 'pseudo-modality'. From this smooth modality, we can easily extract a robust edge map to serve as a prior instead of a loss function. To combine the useful features from different modalities, we introduce a pseudo-multimodal fusion network (PMFN). It serves as a blender that can 'inpaint' [3] the fine details from HN on the canvas of clean layers from the pseudo-modality. The contributions of our work are the following:

◆ A deep network to mimic the self-fusion process, so that the self-fusion of LN image becomes accessible at test time. This further allows the processing time to be sharply reduced.

◆ A pseudo-modality that makes it possible to extract clean gradient maps from high noise B-scans and provide compensation of layers and vessels in the final denoising result.

◆ A pseudo-multimodal fusion network that combines desired features from different sources such that the contribution of each modality is adjustable.

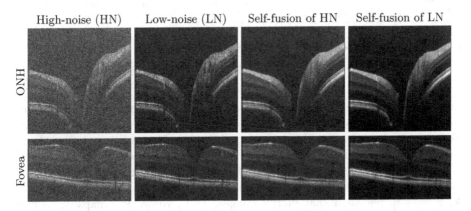

Fig. 1. Self-fusion for high-noise (HN) single B-scan and low-noise (LN) 5-average images (excess background trimmed). SNR of the HN images is 101 dB.

2   Methods

Figure 2 illustrates the overall processing pipeline.

Preprocessing. We crop every B-scan to size $[512, 500]$ to discard the massive background that is not of interest. Then we zero-pad the image to $[512, 512]$ for convenience in downsampling.

5-Frame Average. In our supervised learning problem, the ground truth is approximated by the low noise 5-frame-average B-scan (LN). The repeated frames at location i are denoted by $[\boldsymbol{X}_i^1, ..., \boldsymbol{X}_i^5]$ in Fig. 2-a. Because of eye movement during imaging, some drifting exists between both repeated frames and adjacent B-scans. We apply a rigid registration for motion correction prior to averaging.

Pseudo-Modality Creation. For self-fusion, we need deformable registration between adjacent slices. This is realized by VoxelMorph [2], a deep registration method that provides deformation field from moving image to target. This

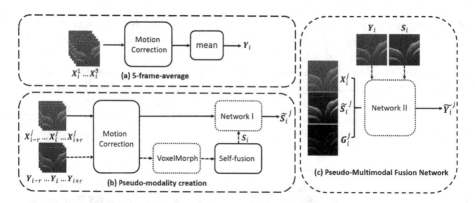

Fig. 2. Processing pipeline. Dotted box refers to a deep learning network. Process on dash arrow exists only in training. Solid arrows are for both training and testing.

provides considerable speedup compared to traditional registration algorithms. However, even without classical registration, self-fusion is still time-consuming. To further reduce the processing time, we introduce Network 1 to directly learn the self-fusion output. Time consumed by generating a self-fusion image of a B-scan drops from 7.303 ± 0.322 s to 0.253 ± 0.005 s. The idea allows us to also improve the quality of our pseudo-modality, by using S_i, the self-fusion of LN Y_i images rather than that of HN images. Thus, Network I maps a stack of consecutive HN B-scans to self-fusion of LN.

In Fig. 2-b, the noisy B-scan and its neighbors within a radius are denoted as $[X_{i-r}^j, ..., X_{i+r}^j]$, where $j = 1, 2, ..., 5$ represent the repeated frames. Their corresponding LN counterparts are named similarly, $[Y_{i-r}, ..., Y_{i+r}]$. The ground truth of Network I (i.e., the self-fusion of Y_i) and its prediction are annotated as S_i and $\tilde{S}_i^j$ respectively. Since $\tilde{S}_i^j$ contains little noise, we can use its image gradient G_i^j, computed simply via 3×3 Sobel kernels, as the edge map.

Psudo-Multimodal Fusion Network (PMFN). Figure 2-c shows the PMFN that takes a three-channel input. The noisy B-scan X_i^j has fine details including small vessels and texture, while the speckle noise is too strong to clearly reveal layer structures. The pseudo-modality $\tilde{S}_i^j$ has well-suppressed speckle noise and clean layers, but many of the subtle features are lost. So, merging the essential features from these mutually complementary modalities is our goal. To produce an output that inherit features from two sources, Network II takes feedback from the ground truth of both modalities in seeking for a balance between them. We use L1 loss for Y_i to punish loss of finer features and mean squared error (MSE) for S_i to encourage some blur effect in layers. The weight of these loss functions are determined by hyper-parameters. The overall loss function is:

$$Loss = \alpha \sum_{x,y} |\tilde{Y}_i^j(x,y) - Y_i(x,y)| + \frac{\beta}{N} \sum_{x,y} (\tilde{Y}_i^j(x,y) - S_i(x,y))^2 \quad (1)$$

N is the number of pixel in the image. Parameters α and β are the weights of the two loss functions, and they can be tuned to reach a tradeoff between layers from the pseudo-modality and the small vessels from the HN B-scan.

3 Experiments

3.1 Data Set

OCT volumes from the fovea and optic nerve head (ONH) of a single human retina were obtained. For each region, we have two volumes acquired at three different noise levels (SNR = 92 dB, 96 dB, 101 dB). Each raw volume ($[N_{Bscan}, H, W] = [500, 1024, 500]$) contains 500 B-scans of 1024×500 voxels. For every B-scan, there are 5 repeated frames taken at the same position (2500 Bscans in total) so that a 5-frame-average can be used as low-noise 'ground truth'. Since all these volumes are acquired from a single eye, to avoid information leakage, we denoise fovea volumes by training on ONH data, and vice versa.

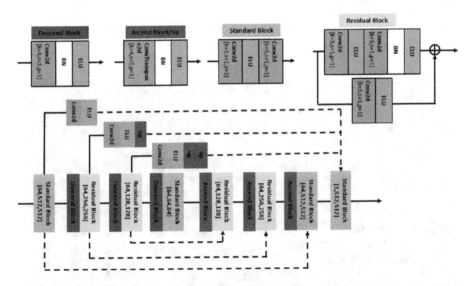

Fig. 3. Network architecture. The solid line passes the computation result of the block while the dash line refers to channel concatenation. Arrays in main trunk blocks indicate the output dimension.

3.2 Experimental Design

In this study, our goal is to show that the denoising result is improved by the processing pipeline that introduces the pseudo-modality. Thus, we will not focus on varying the network structure for better performance. Instead, we will use the Network II with single channel input X_i^j as the baseline. For this baseline, the loss function will only have feedback from Y_i. We hypothesize that the relative results between single modality and pseudo-multimodal denoising will have a similar pattern for other architectures for Network II, but exploring this is beyond the scope of the current study. Since the network architecture is not the focus of our study, we use the same multi-scale U-Net (MSUN) architecture, shown in Fig. 3 and proposed by Devalla et al. [6], for both Networks I and II.

The B-scan neighborhood radius for self-fusion was set at $r = 7$. Among the five repeated frames at each location, we only use the first one (X_i^1), except when computing the 5-average Y_i. All the models are trained on NVIDIA RTX 2080TI 11 GB GPU for 15 epochs with batch size of 1. Parameters in network are optimized by Adam optimizer with starting learning rate 10^{-4} and a decay factor of 0.3 for every epoch. In Network II, we use $\alpha = 1$ and $\beta = 1.2$.

4   Results

4.1   Visual Analysis

We first analyze the layer separation and vessel visibility in the denoised results.

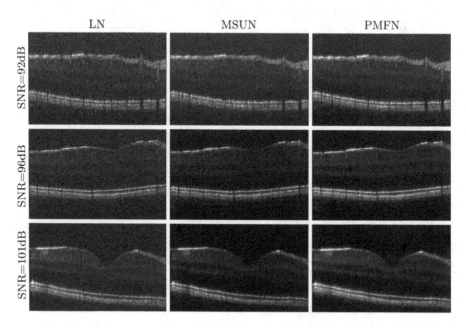

Fig. 4. Fovea denoising results for different input SNR. (Excess background trimmed.)

Figure 4 displays the denoising performance of the proposed algorithm for different input SNR levels. Compared to the baseline model, we observe that PMFN has better separation between GCL and IPL, which enables the vessels in GCL to better stand out from noise. Moreover, the improvement of smoothness and homogeneity in outer plexiform layer (OPL) makes it look more solid and its border more continuous. In addition, the retinal pigment epithelium (RPE) appears to be more crisp.

In Fig. 5, to better assess the layer separation, we focus on a B-scan with high speckle noise (SNR = 92) that severely obscures the boundary between layers. In the top row, we zoom into a region of interest (ROI) that contains 5 tissue layers (from top to bottom): GCL, IPL, inner nuclear layer (INL), OPL and outer nuclear layer (ONL). As the baseline model learns only from the high noise B-scan, layer boundaries are not clear: GCL and IPL are indistinguishable, and although the INL and OPL are preserved, they are not as homogeneous as in the PMFN result. PMFN remedies these problems.

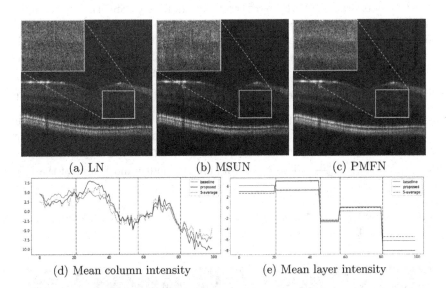

Fig. 5. Layer separation analysis. The top row shows an ROI containing 5 layers of tissue (GCL, IPL, INL, OPL, ONL) for each of (a) 5-average LN image, (b) baseline result and (c) PMFN result. (d) plots the intensity across the 5 layers within the ROI. (e) plots the mean intensity per layer. Vertical dashed lines approximate layer boundaries.

Another way of assessing the separability of layers or, in other words, the contrast between adjacent layers, is plotting the column intensity (Fig. 5-d). Since the layers within the ROI are approximately flat, we take the mean vector along the row. In order to rule out the potential difference of intensity level, we normalize the mean vector with the average intensity of ROI.

$$\bar{v} = \frac{1}{W} \sum_i^W v_i - \mu_{ROI} \tag{2}$$

where W is the width of the ROI, v_i is a column vector in the window and μ_{ROI} is a vector that has the mean of the ROI as all its elements. We plot the $\bar{v}$ for Fig. 5-a, Fig. 5-b and Fig. 5-c in Fig. 5-d. The border between layers are approximated with vertical dash lines for this visualization. In Fig. 5-d, the proposed method tends to have lower intensity in dark bands and higher intensity in bright ones. This indicates that it has better contrast between adjacent layers. Figure 5-e summarizes the mean intensity within each layer. Because of high intensity speckle noise, the baseline result completely misses the GCL-IPL distinction, whereas our method provides good separation.

4.2   Quantitative Evaluation

We report the signal-to-noise ratio (SNR), peak signal-to-noise ratio (PSNR), contrast-to-noise ratio (CNR) and structural similarity (SSIM) of our results. Normally, these metrics need an ideal ground truth without noise as a reference image. But such a ground truth is not available in our task, since the 5-frame-average LN image is far from being noiseless. Therefore, we make some adjustments to the original definitions of SNR and PSNR. We use $SNR = 10 \log_{10} \left[\frac{\sum_{x,y} [f(x,y)]^2}{\sum_{x,y} [b(x,y)]^2} \right]$ where $f(x,y)$ is the pixel intensity in foreground window and $b(x,y)$ is background pixel intensity. This assumes there is nothing but pure speckle noise in the background, and that the foreground window only contains signal. Similarly, the PSNR can be approximated by $PSNR = 10 \log_{10} \left[\frac{n_x n_y max[f(x,y)]^2}{\sum_{x,y} [b(x,y)]^2} \right]$. The n_x and n_y are the width and height of the ROI, respectively. Finally, the CNR is estimated by $CNR = \frac{|\mu_f - \mu_b|}{\sqrt{0.5(\sigma_f^2 + \sigma_b^2)}}$ where μ_f and σ_f are the mean and standard deviation of the foreground region; μ_b and σ_b are those of the background region.

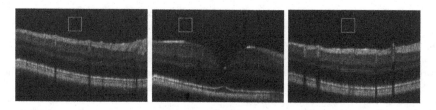

Fig. 6. Sample B-scans showing background (yellow) and foreground (red) ROIs used for SNR, CNR and PSNR estimation. 10 B-scans are chosen throughout the fovea volume to avoid bias. (Color figure online)

Every layer has a different intensity level, so we report each metric separately for RNFL, IPL, OPL and RPE. We manually picked foreground and background

ROIs from each layer, as shown in Fig. 6, for 10 B-scans. To avoid local bias, these chosen slices are far apart to be representative of the whole volume. When computing metrics for a given layer, the background ROI (yellow box) is cropped as needed to match the area of the foreground ROI (red box) for that layer. Figure 7 **(a)** to **(c)** display the evaluation result for SNR, PSNR and CNR respectively. For all layers, the proposed PMFN model gives the best SNR and CNR results, while the PSNR stays similar with the baseline multi-scale UNet model.

We also report the structural similarity index measure (SSIM) [18] of the whole B-scan. The SSIM for each input SNR level is reported in Fig. 7-d. The proposed method outperforms the baseline model for all input SNR.

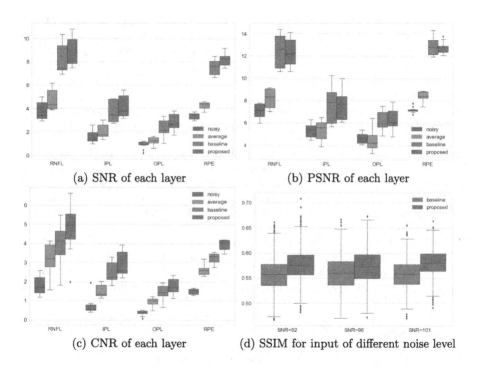

(a) SNR of each layer   (b) PSNR of each layer

(c) CNR of each layer   (d) SSIM for input of different noise level

Fig. 7. Quantitative evaluation of denoising results.

5   Conclusion and Future Work

Our study shows that the self-fusion pseudo-modality can provide major contributions to OCT denoising by emphasizing tissue layers in the retina. The fusion network allows the vessels, texture and other fine details to be preserved while enhancing the layers. Although the inherent high dimensionality of the deep network has sufficient complexity, more constraints in the form of additional information channels are able to help the model converge to a desired domain.

It is difficult to thoroughly evaluate denoising results when no ideal reference image is available. Exploring other evaluation methods remains as future work. Additionally, application of our method to other medical image modalities such as ultrasound images is also a possible future research direction.

Acknowledgements. This work is supported by Vanderbilt University Discovery Grant Program.

References

1. Avanaki, M.R., Cernat, R., Tadrous, P.J., Tatla, T., Podoleanu, A.G., Hojjatoleslami, S.A.: Spatial compounding algorithm for speckle reduction of dynamic focus OCT images. IEEE Photonics Technol. Lett. **25**(15), 1439–1442 (2013)
2. Balakrishnan, G., Zhao, A., Sabuncu, M.R., Guttag, J., Dalca, A.V.: VoxelMorph: a learning framework for deformable medical image registration. IEEE Trans. Med. Imaging **38**(8), 1788–1800 (2019)
3. Bertalmio, M., Sapiro, G., Caselles, V., Ballester, C.: Image inpainting. In: Proceedings of the 27th Annual Conference on Computer Graphics and Interactive Techniques, pp. 417–424 (2000)
4. Chen, Z., Zeng, Z., Shen, H., Zheng, X., Dai, P., Ouyang, P.: DN-GAN: denoising generative adversarial networks for speckle noise reduction in optical coherence tomography images. Biomed. Sign. Process. Control **55**, 101632 (2020)
5. Chong, B., Zhu, Y.K.: Speckle reduction in optical coherence tomography images of human finger skin by wavelet modified BM3D filter. Optics Commun. **291**, 461–469 (2013)
6. Devalla, S.K., et al.: A deep learning approach to denoise optical coherence tomography images of the optic nerve head. Sci. Rep. **9**(1), 1–13 (2019)
7. Isola, P., Zhu, J.Y., Zhou, T., Efros, A.A.: Image-to-image translation with conditional adversarial networks. In: Proceedings of the IEEE Conference on Computer Vision and Pattern Recognition, pp. 1125–1134 (2017)
8. Kafieh, R., Rabbani, H., Selesnick, I.: Three dimensional data-driven multi scale atomic representation of optical coherence tomography. IEEE Trans. Med. Imaging **34**(5), 1042–1062 (2014)
9. Li, M., Idoughi, R., Choudhury, B., Heidrich, W.: Statistical model for OCT image denoising. Biomed. Optics Express **8**(9), 3903–3917 (2017)
10. Ma, Y., Chen, X., Zhu, W., Cheng, X., Xiang, D., Shi, F.: Speckle noise reduction in optical coherence tomography images based on edge-sensitive cGAN. Biomed. Optics Express **9**(11), 5129–5146 (2018)
11. Oguz, I., Malone, J.D., Atay, Y., Tao, Y.K.: Self-fusion for OCT noise reduction. In: Medical Imaging 2020: Image Processing, vol. 11313, p. 113130C. International Society for Optics and Photonics (2020)
12. Ouyang, Yanling., Shao, Qing., Scharf, Dirk., Joussen, Antonia M., Heussen, Florian M.: Retinal vessel diameter measurements by spectral domain optical coherence tomography. Graefe's Arch. Clin. Exp. Ophthalmol. **253**(4), 499–509 (2014). https://doi.org/10.1007/s00417-014-2715-2

13. Ronneberger, Olaf., Fischer, Philipp, Brox, Thomas: U-Net: convolutional networks for biomedical image segmentation. In: Navab, Nassir, Hornegger, Joachim, Wells, William M., Frangi, Alejandro F. (eds.) MICCAI 2015. LNCS, vol. 9351, pp. 234–241. Springer, Cham (2015). https://doi.org/10.1007/978-3-319-24574-4_28

14. Schmitt, J.: Array detection for speckle reduction in optical coherence microscopy. Phys. Med. Biol. **42**(7), 1427 (1997)

15. Schmitt, J.M., Xiang, S., Yung, K.M.: Speckle in optical coherence tomography: an overview. In: Saratov Fall Meeting 1998: Light Scattering Technologies for Mechanics, Biomedicine, and Material Science, vol. 3726, pp. 450–461. International Society for Optics and Photonics (1999)

16. Tatham, A.J., Medeiros, F.A.: Detecting structural progression in glaucoma with optical coherence tomography. Ophthalmology **124**(12), S57–S65 (2017)

17. Wang, H., Suh, J.W., Das, S.R., Pluta, J.B., Craige, C., Yushkevich, P.A.: Multi-atlas segmentation with joint label fusion. IEEE Trans. Pattern Anal. Mach. Intell. **35**(3), 611–623 (2012)

18. Zhou, W.: Image quality assessment: from error measurement to structural similarity. IEEE Trans. Image Process. **13**, 600–613 (2004)

Deep-Learning-Based Estimation of 3D Optic-Nerve-Head Shape from 2D Color Fundus Photographs in Cases of Optic Disc Swelling

Mohammad Shafkat Islam[1,2], Jui-Kai Wang[1,2], Wenxiang Deng[1,2], Matthew J. Thurtell[3], Randy H. Kardon[2,3], and Mona K. Garvin[1,2(✉)]

[1] Department of Electrical and Computer Engineering, The University of Iowa, Iowa City, IA, USA
{mohammadshafkat-islam,mona-garvin}@uiowa.edu
[2] Iowa City VA Health Care System, Iowa City, IA, USA
[3] Department of Ophthalmology and Visual Sciences, The University of Iowa, Iowa City, IA, USA

Abstract. In cases of optic disc swelling, volumetric measurements and shape features are promising to evaluate the severity of the swelling and to differentiate the cause. However, previous studies have mostly focused on the use of volumetric spectral-domain optical coherence tomography (OCT), which is not always available in non-ophthalmic clinics and telemedical settings. In this work, we propose the use of a deep-learning-based approach (more specifically, an adaptation of a feature pyramid network, FPN) to obtain total-retinal-thickness (TRT) maps (as would normally be obtained from OCT) from more readily available 2D color fundus photographs. From only these thickness maps, we are able to compute both volumetric measures of swelling for quantification of the location/degree of swelling and 3D statistical shape measures for quantification of optic-nerve-head morphology. Evaluating our proposed approach (using nine-fold cross validation) on 102 paired color fundus photographs and OCT images (with the OCT acting as the ground truth) from subjects with various levels of optic disc swelling, we achieved significantly smaller errors and significantly larger linear correlations of both the volumetric measures and shape measures than that which would be obtained using a U-Net approach. The proposed method has great potential to make 3D ONH shape analysis possible even in situations where only color fundus photographs are available; these 3D shape measures can also be beneficial to help differentiate causes of optic disc swelling.

Keywords: Optic nerve head (ONH) · Shape analysis · Color fundus photographs · Optical coherence tomography (OCT) · Optic disc swelling

H. Fu et al. (Eds.): OMIA 2020, LNCS 12069, pp. 136–145, 2020.
https://doi.org/10.1007/978-3-030-63419-3_14

1   Introduction

In assessing the severity and cause of optic disc swelling, in addition to the relatively new use of quantitative volumetric measures of swelling [1], recent work has also demonstrated the promise of the use of shape features (such as measurements of the degree of deformation of Bruch's membrane towards/away from the vitreous [2–5] and changes to the 3D shape of the internal limiting membrane (ILM) [6]). While work with these new shape measures has primarily been with volumetric optical coherence tomography (OCT), an imaging modality that is commonly available in ophthalmology clinics, there is still a need to be able to assess optic disc swelling in locations where OCT is likely not available, such as in primary-care, emergency-room, and telemedical settings.

Given the more likely availability of 2D color fundus photography in such settings, it is desirable to be able to estimate 3D quantitative measures of the swelling and shape (as would normally be measured with OCT) given only 2D color fundus photographs. Early work in this area included the work of Tang et al. [7] where a multi-scale stereo matching method calculating dense correspondence between stereo-color-fundus photographs was used to estimate the optic-nerve-head (ONH) depth information; however, the requirement of good quality pairs of stereo color fundus photographs limits its applicability. Agne et al. [8] later applied a random forest classifier based on features of retinal vessels, textures, and optic disc properties extracted from monocular color fundus photographs to estimate total retinal volumes; however, a lack of location-wise depth information of the entire ONH prevented this approach from being able to compute regional volumetric measurements and shape measures. Johnson et al. [9] built upon this method to be able to output pixel-based total retinal thickness maps (between the ILM and lower bonding RPE complex); a modified version [10] using a deep neural network (U-Net [11]) was proposed later. However, while this approach [10] may be sufficient for estimation of regional swelling volumes, the authors did not extend the work for computation of shape measures where an even greater accuracy would be expected to be needed.

Thus, motivated by the need to compute 3D shape measures from fundus photographs, in this work, we first improved upon an existing method [10] to obtain a better estimation of the ONH total-retinal-thickness (TRT) map directly using color fundus photographs. From the fundus-predicted TRT maps, we evaluated the approach's ability to compute global/regional total-retinal-volumes (TRVs) as would normally be obtained from OCT. We also generated eight OCT-based ONH statistical shape models and evaluated the ability to compute shape measures from the fundus-photograph-predicted TRT thickness maps. Qualitative and quantitative results of the thickness maps and 3D shape measures were compared among the proposed method, an existing method (U-Net) [10], and the OCT truth. The proposed method has a great potential to make 3D ONH shape analysis possible even in the situations that only color fundus photographs are available; these 3D shape measures can be beneficial to help differentiate causes of optic disc swelling.

2   Methods

2.1   Overview

For the training and evaluation purposes, the ground truth of the ONH depth information was defined by the TRT map between the ILM and lower bounding surface of the retinal pigment epithelium (RPE) complex in OCT [1]. Since studies have suggested that symmetric encoder-decoders (e.g., the original U-Net) are typically less efficient than networks with an asymmetric decoder (e.g., feature pyramid network [FPN]) [11–13], we designed a neural network with a deep encoder and a lightweight decoder to achieve more accurate TRT maps from color fundus photographs (Sect. 2.2). Eight 3D shape measures were then computed for each TRT map by projection onto 3D statistical shape models previously constructed using OCT TRT maps (Sect. 2.3).

2.2   Neural Network Architecture

The proposed approach to predict TRT maps from fundus photographs was based on the feature pyramid network (FPN), and more specifically, the semantic segmentation branch of panopic FPN [13]. It was built on top of ResNeXt-50 [14] (pre-trained on ImageNet) as a feature encoder (shown in Fig. 1).

A deep ResNeXt-50 encoder and a lightweight FPN decoder resulted in an asymmetric network architecture. The network consisted of a bottom-up pathway and a top-down pathway which were connected by lateral connections. The bottom-up pathway consisted of convolution modules, each having many convolution layers. The resolution was halved each time we moved upwards along the bottom-up pathway. The output from each of these convolution modules was used by the top-down pathway through a lateral connection.

When going down along the top-down pathway, we used bilinear interpolation to upsample the previous layer by 2. We applied 1×1 convolution to the corresponding feature map from the bottom-up pathway and added it element-wise with the upsampled feature map from top-down pathway. We repeated this process and on the bottom, we had a module with 64 channels and 1/4 the resolution of the image. We applied 7×7 transposed convolution followed by batch normalization and ReLU. Finally, we applied 3×3 convolution to generate the output TRT map.

2.3   Statistical Total Retinal Shape Models in 3D

The statistical shape models needed for estimating the shape measures from TRT maps output from the network were built in advance from the OCT TRT maps. The OCT shape model started from placing 97 landmarks on each OCT TRT map. The first landmark was placed at the ONH center. Next, in a radial direction for every 30°, eight equidistant landmarks were automatically placed from $500\,\mu m$ to $2250\,\mu m$ away from the ONH center. Procrustes analysis without the scaling step was then applied to align all 102 OCT ONH shapes together; each

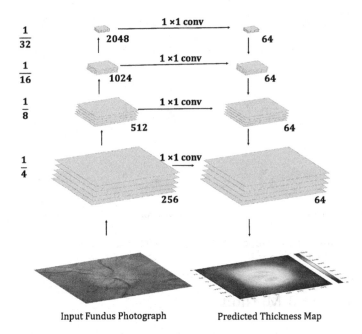

Fig. 1. Network architecture for prediction of TRT maps from fundus photographs. The downward path and lateral connection comprise the feature pyramid network. Note that the predicted thickness map is shown in pseudocolor for ease of visualization, but the actual output predicts one continuous thickness value for each pixel location.

aligned shape (s_i) and the mean shape $(\bar{s})$ were computed. Principal component analysis (PCA) was used to obtain the first k eigenvectors (i.e., the principal components: $e_1 \sim e_k$) that occupied 90% of the system energy, which is defined by the summation of the eigenvalues $(\sum \lambda_i)$. Each reconstructed shape $(\hat{s}_i)$ from the corresponding eigenvector can be described as:

$$\hat{s}_i = \bar{s} + \sum_{j=1}^{k} c_j \sqrt{\lambda_j}\, e_j, \tag{1}$$

where c_j is the shape coefficient corresponding to e_j.

Based on the input 102 OCT TRT maps, eight principal components were included to achieve 90% of the system energy $(k = 8)$. Figure 2 shows an example of the first three shape models: the overall degree of the swelling (Model 1), the location of the swelling shifting from the superior to inferior direction (Model 2), and the swelling contour change from a C-Shape to a single peak at the superior-temporal region (Model 3). Given these eight OCT shape models, the coefficient associated with each estimated TRT map from the fundus photographs was computed by projection onto each shape model.

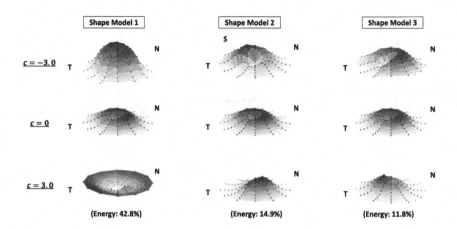

Fig. 2. An example of top three ONH shape models with varying shape coefficients based on 102 OCT TRT maps.

3   Experimental Methods

This study included 102 subjects with various degrees of optic disc swelling (from the Neuro-Ophthalmology Clinic at the University of Iowa) who had both color fundus photographs (2392 × 2048 pixels) and volumetric OCT scans (200 × 200 × 1024 voxels covering a physical space of 6 × 6 × 2 mm^3) available. The OCT scans were first segmented to compute the TRT maps. Next, these OCT TRT maps were registered with their paired color fundus photographs; then, these fundus photographs were cropped to be ONH-centered and matched with the same ONH areas as the OCTs covered. These cropped color fundus photographs were the input of the proposed method for the depth measurement. The proposed neural network was trained using Adam optimizer with an initial learning rate of $1e^{-3}$, dropping it by factor of 10 at 250 and 450 iterations with MSE loss function. The batch size was 24 and the training was performed for 2000 iterations. To prevent over-fitting due to small dataset size, we performed data augmentation by random rescaling, horizontal flipping, random rotation, random cropping, color jittering, random contrast and normalizing the images. The proposed method was evaluated by nine-fold-cross-validation, where for each fold, the model was trained on 91 images and evaluated on the remaining 11 images (except for the last fold, where the model was trained on 88 images and evaluated on 14 images). Once we had the predicted thickness map from the proposed method, we calculated the total retinal volume (TRV) [1]. We also used a central circle with 1.73 mm radius to calculate the peripapillary region volume and nasal, temporal, inferior and superior regions were defined by the four quadrants of this circle with 135° and 45° lines as boundaries. For evaluation, using the OCT volumetric measures as a ground truth, we compared the volumetric measures using our proposed deep-learning architecture to those resulting from a U-Net architecture. For each regional volume and approach, we computed the root-mean-square error (RMSE) and Pearson's correlation coefficient. Next, based on the generated eight OCT shape models, the shape measures of the estimated TRT maps from the neural networks were computed and compared. In testing for significance between our approach and the U-Net approach, to account for multiple comparisons, a conservative Benferonni-corrected p-value of $\frac{0.05}{2\times6+2\times8} = 0.0018$ was considered significant.

4 Results

The quantitative results from the proposed method and U-Net-based method are shown in Table 1 and Table 2. Example comparisons between the estimated TRT maps from the proposed method and U-Net-based approach with the OCTs (i.e, ground truths) are shown in Fig. 3. For the TRV and all of the regional volumes, the absolute differences between the proposed method and the OCT truth were significantly less than the ones between the U-Net approach and OCT truth (one-sided paired t-tests; p-values < 0.001). As shown in the table, for the total retinal volume (TRV), the root-mean-squared-error (RMSE) between the predicted volume from the proposed method and the volume measured from the OCT ground truth was $1.69\,\mathrm{mm}^3$ (vs. $2.23\,\mathrm{mm}^3$ for the U-Net-based approach) and the Pearson's correlation coefficient was $R = 0.85$ for the proposed method (vs. $R = 0.53$ for the U-Net-based approach). For regional volumes, the proposed method resulted in a RMSE of $0.24\,\mathrm{mm}^3$ (vs. $0.44\,\mathrm{mm}^3$ for U-Net), $0.22\,\mathrm{mm}^3$ (vs. $0.38\,\mathrm{mm}^3$ for U-Net), $0.25\,\mathrm{mm}^3$ (vs. $0.46\,\mathrm{mm}^3$ for U-Net), $0.25\,\mathrm{mm}^3$ (vs. $0.41\,\mathrm{mm}^3$ for U-Net) and $0.85\,\mathrm{mm}^3$ (vs. $1.48\,\mathrm{mm}^3$ for U-Net) respectively for nasal, temporal, superior, inferior and peripapillary (PP) regions. The Pearson's correlation coefficients for the proposed approach (R) of $0.86, 0.85, 0.90, 0.88$ and 0.90 for nasal, temporal, superior, inferior and peripapillary regions respectively were all significantly larger than those of the U-Net approach $(p < 0.001$ for all from the Fisher and Steiger method).

Based on the PCA of the 102 OCT TRT thickness maps, the first eight principal components (i.e., the shape models) covered 90.6% of the total system energy (Fig. 2 shows an example of the top three shape models with energy 42.8%, 14.9%, and 11.8%, respectively). For Shape Model 1 to 8, the shape measure RMSEs between the proposed method and OCT truth were $0.49, 0.60, 0.74, 0.58, 0.66, 1.03, 0.73,$ and 0.80, respectively. For all these eight models, the shape measure absolute differences between the proposed method and the OCT truth were significantly less than the ones between the U-Net and OCT truth (one-sided paired t-tests; p-values < 0.001). The shape measure Pearson's correlation coefficients between the proposed method and OCT truth were $0.88, 0.80, 0.69, 0.81, 0.76, 0.50, 0.71,$ and 0.65, respectively were all significantly larger than those of the U-Net approach $(p < 0.001$ for all).

Table 1. RMSEs and correlations between the proposed method and U-Net-based method vs. OCT for TRV and regional volumes.

	TRV	Nasal	Temporal	Superior	Inferior	Peripapillary
RMSE (mm^3)	(The lower value, the closer to the OCT volume.)					
U-Net	2.23	0.44	0.38	0.46	0.41	1.48
Proposed Method**	1.69	0.24	0.22	0.25	0.25	0.85
Correlation	(The closer the value to +1, more linearly related to OCT.)					
U-Net	0.53	0.43	0.38	0.58	0.55	0.58
Proposed Method**	0.85	0.86	0.85	0.90	0.88	0.90

** For TRV and all the regional volumes, compared to the OCT truth, the proposed method had significantly lower absolute differences than the ones from U-Net ($p < 0.001$). The Pearson's correlation coefficients (R) for the proposed approach were all significantly larger than those of the U-Net approach ($p < 0.001$).

Table 2. RMSEs and correlations between the proposed method and U-Net method vs. OCT from Shape Model 1 to 8.

	Shape Model 1	Shape Model 2	Shape Model 3	Shape Model 4	Shape Model 5	Shape Model 6	Shape Model 7	Shape Model 8
RMSE	(The lower the value, the closer to the shape measure based on OCT.)							
U-Net	0.90	1.03	1.41	1.19	1.09	1.71	1.19	1.39
Proposed Method**	0.49	0.60	0.74	0.58	0.66	1.03	0.73	0.80
Correlation	(The closer the value to +1, the more linearly related to OCT.)							
U-Net	0.53	0.37	0.01	0.07	0.30	0.06	0.17	0.25
Proposed Method**	0.88	0.80	0.69	0.81	0.76	0.50	0.71	0.65

** For all the 8 shape models, compared to the OCT truth, the shape measures from the proposed method had significantly lower absolute differences than the ones from U-Net ($p < 0.001$). The shape measure Pearson's correlation coefficients (R) for the proposed approach were all significantly larger than the U-Net approach ($p < 0.001$).

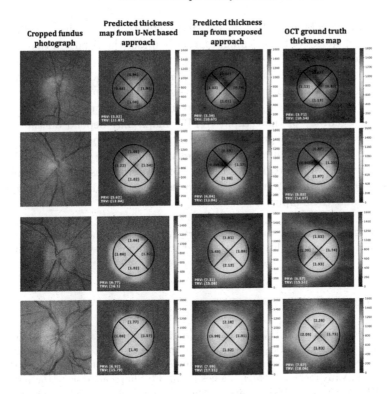

Fig. 3. Comparison of the estimated TRT map from the proposed method and U-Net-based approach with the OCT TRT map in four cases (from mild to severe swelling). The OCT-registered and cropped fundus photographs are shown in the first column. The estimated TRT maps from the U-Net based approach, proposed method and OCT ground truth are shown in the second, third and fourth column, respectively. (The units of the volumetric measurements and color bar are mm^3 and μm, respectively.) (Color figure online)

5   Discussion and Conclusion

In this study, we proposed a neural network with a deep encoder and a lightwight decoder to estimate the ONH depth information in the form of a pixel-based TRT map. Compared with the OCT truth, the proposed method estimated an excellent quality TRT map so that both the global/regional volumetric measurements and shape measures from eight different shape models had significantly less absolute errors and greater Pearson's correlations compared to a U-Net based method (p-values < 0.001 for all). In addition, the proposed 3D shape models have abilities to decompose complicated ONH morphological changes into individual, relatively straightforward shape principal components. For example, Shape Model 1 represents an overall optic disc swelling severity, Shape Model 2 represents the location of the swelling shifting, and Shape Model 3 represents the contour of the swelling change as shown in Fig. 2. These shape measures can be beneficial for future studies about evaluating treatment effects of optic disc swelling and differentiating causes of the swelling, especially under the situation that OCT is not available.

This study has a few limitations. First, there are fewer cases with extremely swollen disc comparing to mild/moderate swelling cases in our dataset, so the proposed method may have a tendency to underestimate these extreme cases. Second, the accuracy of the estimated TRT maps may depend on the quality of the color fundus photographs; for example, the unexpected blurring from bad camera focus due to operation mistakes may cause the proposed method to overestimate the swollen region. In future work, we are considering a number of options for dealing with potential camera-focus issues, including use of a sequence of acquired images as input.

Acknowledgments. This study was supported, in part, by the Department of Veterans Affairs Merit Award I01 RX001786 and the National Institutes of Health R01 EY023279.

References

1. Wang, J.K., Kardon, R.H., Kupersmith, M.J., Garvin, M.K.: Automated quantification of volumetric optic disc swelling in papilledema using spectral-domain optical coherence tomography. Invest. Ophthalmol. Vis. Sci. **53**(7), 4069–4075 (2012)
2. Sibony, P.A., Kupersmith, M.J., James Rohlf, F.: Shape analysis of the peripapillary RPE layer in papilledema and ischemic optic neuropathy. Invest. Ophthalmol. Vis. Sci. **52**(11), 7987–7995 (2011)
3. Wang, J.K., Sibony, P.A., Kardon, R.H., Kupersmith, M.J., Garvin, M.K.: Semi-automated 2D Bruch's membrane shape analysis in papilledema using spectral-domain optical coherence tomography. In: Proceedings of the SPIE 9417, Medical Imaging 2015: Biomedical Applications in Molecular, Structural, and Functional Imaging, vol. 9417, p. 941721 (2015)
4. Vuong, L.N., Hedges, T.R.: Optical coherence tomography and optic nerve edema. In: Grzybowski, A., Barboni, P. (eds.) OCT and Imaging in Central Nervous System Diseases, pp. 147–167. Springer, Cham (2020). https://doi.org/10.1007/978-3-030-26269-3_9
5. Malhotra, K., Patel, M.D., Shirazi, Z., Moss, H.E., Moss, H.E.: Association between peripapillary Bruch's membrane shape and intracranial pressure: Effect of image acquisition pattern and image analysis method, a preliminary study. Front. Neurol. **9**(December), 1137 (2018)
6. Wang, J.K., Thurtell, M.J., Kardon, R.H., Garvin, M.K.: Differentiation of papilledema from non-arteritic anterior ischemic optic neuropathy (NAION) using 3D retinal morphological features of optical coherence tomography. Invest. Ophthalmol. Vis. Sci. **61**(7), 3950 (2020). E-Abstract
7. Tang, L., Kardon, R.H., Wang, J.K., Garvin, M.K., Lee, K., Abràmoff, M.D.: Quantitative evaluation of papilledema from stereoscopic color fundus photographs. Invest. Ophthalmol. Vis. Sci. **53**(8), 4490–4497 (2012)
8. Agne, J., Wang, J.K., Kardon, R.H., Garvin, M.K.: Determining degree of optic nerve edema from color fundus photography. In: Proceedings of the SPIE 9414, Medical Imaging 2015: Computer-Aided Diagnosis, p. 94140F (2015)

9. Johnson, S.S., Wang, J.-K., Islam, M.S., Thurtell, M.J., Kardon, R.H., Garvin, M.K.: Local estimation of the degree of optic disc swelling from color fundus photography. In: Stoyanov, D., et al. (eds.) OMIA/COMPAY -2018. LNCS, vol. 11039, pp. 277–284. Springer, Cham (2018). https://doi.org/10.1007/978-3-030-00949-6_33

10. Johnson, S.J., Islam, M.S., Wang, J.K., Matthew, T.J., Kardon, R.H., Garvin, M.K.: Deep-learning-based estimation of regional volumetric information from 2D fundus photography in cases of optic disc swelling. Invest. Ophthalmol. Vis. Sci. **60**(9), 3597 (2019). E-Abstract

11. Ronneberger, O., Fischer, P., Brox, T.: U-Net: convolutional networks for biomedical image segmentation. In: Navab, N., Hornegger, J., Wells, W.M., Frangi, A.F. (eds.) MICCAI 2015. LNCS, vol. 9351, pp. 234–241. Springer, Cham (2015). https://doi.org/10.1007/978-3-319-24574-4_28

12. Lin, T.Y., Dollár, P., Girshick, R., He, K., Hariharan, B., Belongie, S.: Feature pyramid networks for object detection. In: Proceedings of the IEEE Conference on Computer Vision and Pattern Recognition, 2117–2125 (2017)

13. Kirillov, A., Girshick, R., He, K., Dollár, P.: Panoptic feature pyramid networks. In: Proceedings of the IEEE Conference on Computer Vision and Pattern Recognition, pp. 6399–6408 (2019)

14. Xie, S., Girshick, R., Dollár, P., Tu, Z., He, K.: Aggregated residual transformations for deep neural networks. In: Proceedings of the IEEE Conference on Computer Vision and Pattern Recognition, pp. 1492–1500 (2017)

Weakly Supervised Retinal Detachment Segmentation Using Deep Feature Propagation Learning in SD-OCT Images

Tieqiao Wang, Sijie Niu[✉], Jiwen Dong, and Yuehui Chen

Shandong Provincial Key Laboratory of Network Based Intelligent Computing,
School of Information Science and Engineering,
University of Jinan, Jinan 250022, China
sjniu@hotmail.com

Abstract. Most automated segmentation approaches for quantitative assessment of sub-retinal fluid regions rely heavily on retinal anatomy knowledge (e.g. layer segmentation) and pixel-level annotation, which requires excessive manual intervention and huge learning costs. In this paper, we propose a weakly supervised learning method for the quantitative analysis of lesion regions in spectral domain optical coherence tomography (SD-OCT) images. Specifically, we first obtain more accurate positioning through improved class activation mapping; second, in the feature propagation learning network, the multi-scale features learned by the slice-level classification are employed to expand its activation area and generate soft labels; finally, we use generated soft labels to train a fully supervised network for more robust results. The proposed method is evaluated on subjects from a dataset with 23 volumes for cross-validation experiments. The experimental results demonstrate that the proposed method can achieve encouraging segmentation accuracy comparable to strong supervision methods only utilizing image-level labels.

Keywords: SD-OCT images · Medical image segmentation · Weakly supervision learning · Convolutional neural network

1 Introduction

Central serous chorioretinopathy (CSC) is one of the most common retinopathies, which is common among middle-aged men [2]. Neurosensory retinal detachment (NRD) and pigment epithelial detachment (PED) are the main manifestations of CSC. With the development of retinal imaging techniques, SD-OCT becomes an increasingly popular method for diagnosing ophthalmic diseases with the ability to provide high-resolution, cross-sectional and three-dimensional representations. Therefore, measuring the quantity of CSC and monitoring its change over time is

This work was supported by the National Natural Science Foundation of China under Grant No. 61701192, 61671242, 61872419, 61873324.

of significant importance in clinical assessment. However, manual delineation is laborious even for experienced experts and often suffers from inter-variability.

Currently, to address the above problem, many methods have been proposed to quantify and analyze the CSC in SD-OCT images. Mathematical based methods (e.g. level sets) [7,13], graph search model [14], enface fundus driven method [15] have been proposed to segment the subretinal fluid. Later, semi-supervised approaches [3,16,17] have been presented to address the problem of low contrast and speckle noise in SD-OCT image. The supervised learning methods, including random forest [5], K nearest neighbor [8], kernel regression [11], and deep learning [12], have been introduced to extracting the fluid regions in SD-OCT image. With the drastic advance of deep learning, recent deep learning networks have demonstrated successful performance of image segmentation tasks. A RelayNet proposed by Roy et al. [10] is employed to obtain the retinal layers and fluid regions. Gao et al. [4] proposed a novel image-to-image double-branched and area-constraint fully convolutional networks (DA-FCN). Hrvoje Bogunovic et al. [1] introduced a benchmark and reported the analysis of the challenge RETOUCH. Although deep-learning methods have achieved existing results for segmenting CSC in SD-OCT images, they all rely heavily on manual pixel-level annotations [4] and some forms of complicated data preparations [16] like layer segmentation. These problems greatly increase labor costs and limit related applications.

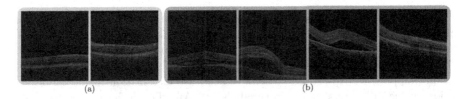

Fig. 1. The picture-level annotations used in our proposed method, normal (Fig. 1(a)) and abnormal slices (Fig. 1(b)) are labeled as 0 and 1, respectively.

To tackle the above challenging problems, weakly supervised learning methods are widely studied recently. Among various forms of weak annotations, image-level labels are the most user-friendly, which is convenient and cheap to collect. Unlike pixel-level labels and scribble annotations, which require more or less accurate outlines and locations of target areas, image-level labels only need to give a general category judgment for a specific slice. Thus, the image-level annotation method not only greatly improves the labeling efficiency of professional clinicians, but also makes labeling by the enthusiastic citizens possible. In our task, as the slices are shown in Fig. 1, the images with subretinal fluid regions are considered as abnormal and annotated 1, while the images without such lesion regions are taken as normal and labeled 0. To our best knowledge, there are no weakly supervised methods utilizing image-level labels to achieve CSC segmentation in OCT images. Therefore, to develop a weakly supervised learning method using these available weakly labeled data is becoming significantly important.

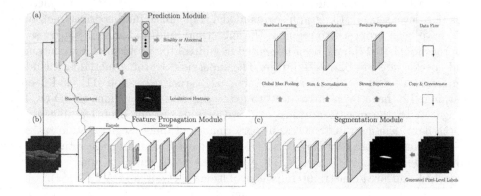

Fig. 2. The proposed weakly supervised network has three parts: (a) Prediction Module obtains a more pure activation region; (b) Feature Propagation Module benefits from features of different sizes of the network to expand the influence of the activation region; and (c) Segmentation Module uses feature propagation result to train and obtain more robust segmentation.

In this paper, we propose a weakly supervised deep feature propagation learning for retinal detachment segmentation in SD-OCT images using subjects with image-level annotations. The schematic diagram of our method is shown in Fig. 2. The proposed method has the following three contributions: (1) The class activation mapping was improved to achieve accurate localization inside the lesion regions using only the slice category labels. (2) An efficient feature propagation model was proposed, which utilizes deep to shallow features learned by the classification network to expand the impact of the active area. (3) The most efficient labeling in the medical field is the 0–1 binary judgment of health or abnormality. The propagation learning method employs only slice categories and achieves a segmentation effect comparable to strong pixel-level supervision, which is of far-reaching significance in the field of computer-assisted medical image analysis by reducing annotation costs and improving learning efficiency.

2   Methodology

The proposed feature propagation learning method consists of three modules, as the architecture overview shown in Fig. 2. The prediction module uses a fully convolutional network similar to the class activation mapping (CAM) [18], which learns to predict the saliency map of the lesion region from the input image. The feature propagation module propagates, constrains, and refines the salient features of the prediction module by propagating this feature among multi-scale feature maps to generate pixel-level soft labels. The fully supervised module trains end-to-end strong supervised segmentation networks using soft labels generated by feature propagation learning.

In the following sections, we first describe the prediction module in Sect. 2.1, then the operating mechanism of our newly designed feature propagation learning module in Sect. 2.2. The fully supervised module is described in Sect. 2.3.

2.1 Saliency Map Generation Based on Improved CAM

Inspired by the CAM method [18], we utilize global pooling to activate salient lesion regions, since this strategy is able to capture general location information of lesion regions only using image-level labels. To make the positioning of the prediction module more accurate and located inside the target area, we use global maximum pooling (GMP) instead of global average pooling (GAP) to process the features generated by the last layer of convolution.

In the proposed class activation mapping module, we keep the input convolution layer and the first three stages of ResNet-50 except for the pooling operation after the input convolution. Then, we use global maximum pooling to output the spatial maximum of the feature map of each unit in the last convolution layer to train a binary classifier.

Specifically, let donate $\mathcal{F} \in \mathbb{R}^{C \times \frac{h}{8} \times \frac{w}{8}}$ as the feature maps of in the last convolution, where C, h, w represent channel, height, width. The maximum response obtained by using global maximum pooling is defined as:

$$f_c = \max \mathcal{F}_c, c \in \{1, 2, ..., C\}, \mathcal{F}_c \in \mathbb{R}^{\frac{h}{8} \times \frac{w}{8}} \tag{1}$$

In this task, slice identification (i.e., normal or abnormal) is taken as a binary classification and BCE loss is the most widely used loss in such tasks. So we use it as the loss function, which is defined as:

$$\mathcal{L}_{bce} = -\sum_{1}^{N} [g_n \log r_n + (1 - g_n) \log(1 - r_n)] \tag{2}$$

where N is the total number of training slices; for a specific slice, $g_n \in \{0, 1\}$ donates the ground truth label and $r_n \in (0, 1)$ represents the binary classification result of the prediction module, which is defined as:

$$r_n = \frac{1}{1 + \exp(-\sum_1^C f_c)} \tag{3}$$

As previously explained, f_c represents the global maximum of the feature map, reflecting the most significant part of the feature map in each of the C channels. We use the sum of these maximum values to generate 0 (normal) or 1 (abnormal) category results, which significantly enhances the network's ability to accurately obtain the location of the lesion. Because generating the network output in this way is helpful for activating (learning to form larger feature values) feature maps containing significant abnormal features, while suppressing (learning to form smaller feature values) containing normal tissues or background. Next, we also employ the same strategy to obtain the salient activation map $\mathcal{M} \in \mathbb{R}^{\frac{h}{8} \times \frac{w}{8}}$:

$$\mathcal{M}(x, y) = \sum_{i=1}^{c} \mathcal{F}_i \tag{4}$$

Generally, both global maximum pooling and global average pooling can highlight the distinguishable regions beneficial for classification. The latter is more widely used since it can provide larger distinguishable regions. However, in our task, the global average pooling (Fig. 3(a)) mainly focuses on the retinal layer structure information rather than the lesion regions. Fortunately, the global maximum pooling (Fig. 3(b)) identifies the most distinguishable regions, which are the part of regions we want to segment. Therefore we utilize the global maximum pooling to determine the positioning of the lesion. This is of great significance for segmenting lesion regions with evenly distributed textures. Thanks to this characteristic, the classification network can obtain the accurate location information and the feature distribution of lesion regions simultaneously.

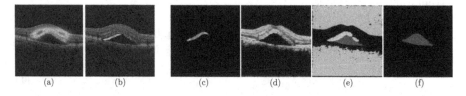

Fig. 3. The first two images show the comparison results using different pooling methods, where (a) and (b) respectively represent the global average pooling and the global maximum pooling; the last four images demonstrate the mechanism and results of feature propagation module, where figure (c), (d), (e), and (f) respectively represent the saliency map, reference map, intersection regions, and results obtained by feature propagation learning.

2.2   Soft Label Using Feature Propagation Learning

The feature propagation module (Fig. 2(b)) is a U-Net-like Encoder-Decoder network [9]. However, different from the decoder in strong supervised networks, we utilize multi-scale features generated by the classification network as guide information to propose a feature propagation learning module, thus this module involves no extra parameters.

In the encoder part, the architecture retains all the structures of ResNet-50 consisted of 5 residual block groups, where the input convolution layer shares weights with the prediction module. This part learns from the category information to generate multi-scale feature maps and then we propose a feature propagation module without learning. During the training process, the encoder part will generate five saliency maps, which will be propagated in reverse order to the decoder as reference maps represented by $\mathcal{R}_i(i \in \{1,2,3,4,5\})$ (Fig. 2(b)).

The goal of the decoder part is to highlight the lesion regions using the proposed two feature propagation strategies, thereby generating optimized soft labels. Specifically, based on the characteristic that the prediction probability of the lesion regions is identical to that of the background, the mechanism of feature propagation in the decoder is defined as:

$$\mathcal{S}_{i-1} = \mathcal{R}_i \cap (\uplus \mathcal{S}_i), i \in \{4,3,2,1\}, \mathcal{S}_4 = \mathcal{M} \tag{5}$$

where $\cap$ and $\uplus$ represent the saliency region intersection and the expansion operation. $\mathcal{S}_i$ represents the saliency map obtained at the i-th stage, where the initial localization heatmap is $\mathcal{M}$ generated by the prediction module, and $\mathcal{S}_0$ is the final segmentation result of feature propagation module.

During feature propagation learning (Fig. 3(c–f)), we first expand the saliency region obtained in the previous step, and then perform threshold segmentation on the saliency map and the reference map respectively. After the two images are superimposed, several different connectivity areas are generated, where the green part in Fig. 3(e) indicates the intersection of the two images. In the extended part, red regions in Fig. 3(e) indicates that the predicted probability value is similar to the intersection part, and yellow regions in Fig. 3(e) indicates the remaining part. In this way, the region similar to the intersection is preserved, and the segmentation results are iteratively updated and optimized after repeated feature propagations.

2.3   Lesion Segmentation with Strong Supervised Network

The soft labels generated by the feature propagation learning network train the fully supervised network (e.g., Deeplab V3, U-net) to obtain a more robust segmentation result. The problem solved here is that during the training process, a small sample of the localization network does not make correct classification, but it will have a more severe impact on the feature propagation learning. Therefore, we masked this problem with category information and trained a fully supervised segmentation network with correct generate labels.

3   Experiments

3.1   Datasets and Evaluation Metrics

Our analysis is based on one challenging dataset with NRD-fluid from [15,16], including 15 patients comprised of 23 vol (one patient may include more than one volume); each volume contains 128 images of 512×1024 pixels. This work was approved by the Institutional Review Board (IRB) of the First Affiliated Hospital of Nanjing Medical University with informed consent. Ground truth segmentation outlines were obtained by two experienced retinal experts.

The performance of segmentation accuracy is evaluated by the following metrics: 1) dice similarity coefficient (DSC), 2) true positive volume fraction (TPVF), and 3) positive predicative value (PPV). We denote R, TP, FP, and G as result of the method, true positive set, false positive set, and ground truth, respectively. These evaluation metrics are defined as: $DSC = \frac{2 \times TP}{R+G}$, $TPVF = \frac{TP}{G}$, $PPV = \frac{TP}{TP+FP}$.

Table 1. The segmentation accuracy results obtained by different methods, two experts annotated the ground-truth labels (only for evaluation); where SoftGT (soft label ground truth) donates the segmentation results obtained from feature propagation module, Ours+U and Ours+D respectively represent the experimental results utilizing the fully supervised network U-net and Deeplab V3 with soft labels.

Method	Expert 1			Expert 2		
	DSC (%)	TPVF (%)	PPV (%)	DSC (%)	TPVF (%)	PPV (%)
LPHC [14]	65.7 ± 10.5	81.2 ± 9.3	55.8 ± 12.8	65.3 ± 10.4	81.3 ± 9.4	55.6 ± 13.3
FLSCV [13]	79.4 ± 20.2	84.4 ± 15.1	63.4 ± 7.3	78.9 ± 21.7	84.4 ± 16.0	86.2 ± 7.3
U-Net [9]	83.7 ± 6.2	90.3 ± 0.35	91.5 ± 6.8	84.3 ± 7.9	91.4 ± 5.2	92.8 ± 5.6
SS-KNN [8]	85.9 ± 4.1	80.3 ± 6.5	91.8 ± 3.8	86.1 ± 4.1	80.9 ± 6.6	92.3 ± 3.8
FCN [6]	87.0 ± 15.5	82.4 ± 19.9	95.9 ± 5.1	86.6 ± 15.6	82.6 ± 20.0	94.9 ± 5.1
RF [5]	88.9 ± 4.2	92.5 ± 4.3	91.9 ± 2.2	87.1 ± 4.3	92.6 ± 4.4	92.4 ± 2.0
CMF [16]	94.3 ± 2.6	92.0 ± 3.9	94.0 ± 3.5	93.9 ± 2.5	92.1 ± 4.1	93.0 ± 3.4
EFD [15]	94.6 ± 4.1	94.3 ± 5.1	94.1 ± 5.3	93.7 ± 4.0	94.2 ± 5.2	93.0 ± 4.8
DA-FCN [4]	**95.6 ± 1.6**	**94.4 ± 3.2**	**97.0 ± 1.1**	**95.0 ± 1.8**	**94.3 ± 1.8**	**95.8 ± 1.4**
SoftGT	86.9 ± 6.7	85.1 ± 11.5	90.0 ± 4.6	86.3 ± 6.7	84.9 ± 11.7	89.0 ± 4.7
Ours+U	91.2 ± 1.3	91.8 ± 2.1	90.7 ± 3.3	90.5 ± 1.2	91.5 ± 1.9	89.7 ± 3.0
Ours+D	92.4 ± 1.8	91.9 ± 2.3	93.0 ± 3.2	92.0 ± 2.0	91.8 ± 2.2	92.3 ± 3.4

3.2   Comparison Experiments

We compare our proposed model with nine state-of-the-art segmentation methods in SD-OCT images, including **(1) traditional segmentation methods:** label propagation and higher-order constraint (LPHC) [14], fuzzy level set with cross-sectional voting (FLSCV) [13], stratified sampling k-nearest neighbor classifier based algorithm (SS-KNN) [8], enface fundus-driven method (EFD) [15]; and **(2) strong supervised machine learning methods:** random forest classifier based method (RF) [5], continuous max-flow approach (CMF) [16], fully convolutional networks (FCN) [6], U-Net [9], and double-branched and area-constraint network (DA-FCN) [4].

Table 1 shows the mean DSC, TPVF, and PPV of all comparison methods for segmenting CSC. It can be seen that the performance of our proposed method is close to strong supervised methods. We illustrate the performance of different methods in several challenging and representative slices in Fig. 4. It can be seen that feature propagation learning has excellent segmentation potential to achieve excellent lesion boundary segmentation.

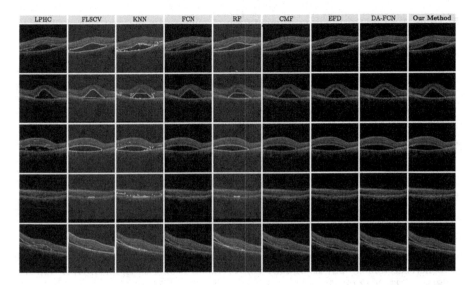

Fig. 4. Qualitative comparison of the proposed feature propagation learning method with other methods, where the yellow line represents the segmentation results of a certain method, and the red line represents the ground truth given by an ophthalmologist. (Color figure online)

4   Conclusion

In this paper, we present a weakly supervised method for segmenting CSC, in which only image-level annotation data collected is available for model training. To accurately locate the saliency region of the lesions, we improved the CAM to further focus on the targets. And also, we proposed an efficient feature propagation methods to generate the soft label for training segmentation model. Experiments demonstrate that our proposed method achieves a comparable effect to that of full-supervision and traditional techniques. Moreover, our proposed method is more straightforward and has cheaper implementation costs, which is a good inspiration for clinical research of retinal-related lesion segmentation in SD-OCT images.

References

1. Bogunović, H., et al.: RETOUCH: the retinal oct fluid detection and segmentation benchmark and challenge. IEEE Trans. Med. Imaging **38**(8), 1858–1874 (2019)
2. Dansingani, K.K., et al.: Annular lesions and catenary forms in chronic central serous chorioretinopathy. Am. J. Ophthalmol. **166**, 60–67 (2016)
3. Fernandez, D.C.: Delineating fluid-filled region boundaries in optical coherence tomography images of the retina. IEEE Trans. Med. Imaging **24**(8), 929–945 (2005)
4. Gao, K., et al.: Double-branched and area-constraint fully convolutional networks for automated serous retinal detachment segmentation in sd-oct images. Comput. Methods Programs Biomed. **176**, 69–80 (2019)

5. Lang, A., et al.: Automatic segmentation of microcystic macular edema in OCT. Biomed. Opt. Express 6(1), 155–169 (2015)
6. Long, J., Shelhamer, E., Darrell, T.: Fully convolutional networks for semantic segmentation. In: Proceedings of the IEEE Conference on Computer Vision and Pattern Recognition, pp. 3431–3440 (2015)
7. Novosel, J., Wang, Z., de Jong, H., Van Velthoven, M., Vermeer, K.A., van Vliet, L.J.: Locally-adaptive loosely-coupled level sets for retinal layer and fluid segmentation in subjects with central serous retinopathy. In: 2016 IEEE 13th International Symposium on Biomedical Imaging (ISBI), pp. 702–705. IEEE (2016)
8. Quellec, G., Lee, K., Dolejsi, M., Garvin, M.K., Abramoff, M.D., Sonka, M.: Three-dimensional analysis of retinal layer texture: identification of fluid-filled regions in SD-OCT of the macula. IEEE Trans. Med. Imaging 29(6), 1321–1330 (2010)
9. Ronneberger, O., Fischer, P., Brox, T.: U-Net: convolutional networks for biomedical image segmentation. In: Navab, N., Hornegger, J., Wells, W.M., Frangi, A.F. (eds.) MICCAI 2015. LNCS, vol. 9351, pp. 234–241. Springer, Cham (2015). https://doi.org/10.1007/978-3-319-24574-4_28
10. Roy, A.G., et al.: ReLayNet: retinal layer and fluid segmentation of macular optical coherence tomography using fully convolutional networks. Biomed. Opt. Express 8(8), 3627–3642 (2017)
11. Schaap, M., et al.: Coronary lumen segmentation using graph cuts and robust kernel regression. In: Prince, J.L., Pham, D.L., Myers, K.J. (eds.) IPMI 2009. LNCS, vol. 5636, pp. 528–539. Springer, Heidelberg (2009). https://doi.org/10.1007/978-3-642-02498-6_44
12. Venhuizen, F.G., et al.: Deep learning approach for the detection and quantification of intraretinal cystoid fluid in multivendor optical coherence tomography. Biomed. Opt. Express 9(4), 1545–1569 (2018)
13. Wang, J., et al.: Automated volumetric segmentation of retinal fluid on optical coherence tomography. Biomed. Opt. Express 7(4), 1577–1589 (2016)
14. Wang, T., et al.: Label propagation and higher-order constraint-based segmentation of fluid-associated regions in retinal SD-OCT images. Inf. Sci. 358, 92–111 (2016)
15. Wu, M., et al.: Automatic subretinal fluid segmentation of retinal SD-OCT images with neurosensory retinal detachment guided by enface fundus imaging. IEEE Trans. Biomed. Eng. 65(1), 87–95 (2017)
16. Wu, M., et al.: Three-dimensional continuous max flow optimization-based serous retinal detachment segmentation in SD-OCT for central serous chorioretinopathy. Biomed. Opt. Express 8(9), 4257–4274 (2017)
17. Zheng, Y., Sahni, J., Campa, C., Stangos, A.N., Raj, A., Harding, S.P.: Computerized assessment of intraretinal and subretinal fluid regions in spectral-domain optical coherence tomography images of the retina. Am. J. Ophthalmol. 155(2), 277–286 (2013)
18. Zhou, B., Khosla, A., Lapedriza, A., Oliva, A., Torralba, A.: Learning deep features for discriminative localization. In: Proceedings of the IEEE Conference on Computer Vision and Pattern Recognition, pp. 2921–2929 (2016)

A Framework for the Discovery of Retinal Biomarkers in Optical Coherence Tomography Angiography (OCTA)

Ylenia Giarratano[1]([✉]), Alisa Pavel[2,3,5], Jie Lian[4,5], Rayna Andreeva[5], Alessandro Fontanella[5], Rik Sarkar[5], Laura J. Reid[6], Shareen Forbes[6], Dan Pugh[6], Tariq E. Farrah[6], Neeraj Dhaun[6], Baljean Dhillon[7,8], Tom MacGillivray[8], and Miguel O. Bernabeu[1]

[1] Centre for Medical Informatics, Usher Institute, University of Edinburgh, Edinburgh, UK
ylenia.giarratano@ed.ac.uk
[2] Faculty of Medicine and Health Technology, Tampere University, Tampere, Finland
[3] BioMediTech Institute, Tampere University, Tampere, Finland
[4] Institute of Computer Science, University of St. Gallen, St. Gallen, Switzerland
[5] School of Informatics, University of Edinburgh, Edinburgh, UK
[6] Queen's Medical Research Institute, University of Edinburgh, Edinburgh, UK
[7] School of Clinical Sciences, University of Edinburgh, Edinburgh, UK
[8] Centre for Clinical Brain Sciences, University of Edinburgh, Edinburgh, UK

Abstract. Recent studies have demonstrated the potential of OCTA retinal imaging for the discovery of biomarkers of vascular disease of the eye and other organs. Furthermore, advances in deep learning have made it possible to train algorithms for the automated detection of such biomarkers. However, two key limitations of this approach are the need for large numbers of labeled images to train the algorithms, which are often not met by the typical single-centre prospective studies in the literature, and the lack of interpretability of the features learned during training. In the current study, we developed a network analysis framework to characterise retinal vasculature where geometric and topological information are exploited to increase the performance of classifiers trained on tens of OCTA images. We demonstrate our approach in two different diseases with a retinal vascular footprint: diabetic retinopathy (DR) and chronic kidney disease (CKD). Our approach enables the discovery of previously unreported retinal vascular morphological differences in DR and CKD, and demonstrate the potential of OCTA for automated disease assessment.

Keywords: Optical coherence tomography angiography · Vascular network · Graph analysis · Retinal biomarkers

1 Introduction

Optical coherence tomography angiography (OCTA) is a fast and efficient imaging modality that allows the visualisation of retinal vasculature at the capillary

© Springer Nature Switzerland AG 2020
H. Fu et al. (Eds.): OMIA 2020, LNCS 12069, pp. 155–164, 2020.
https://doi.org/10.1007/978-3-030-63419-3_16

level. This technology offers the advantage of visualising *in vivo* the microvasculature without any invasive procedure, emerging as a promising modality to investigate microvascular disease. However, the usefulness of OCTA as a diagnostic tool depends on the availability of accurate and reproducible image quantification metrics to identify retinal microvascular changes. Machine learning (ML), and in particular deep learning (DL) in recent years, has emerged as a promising approach for automated image analysis. Despite the popularity of DL in medical applications, these techniques typically require large amounts of labeled data for training, and a straight forward clinical interpretation of the features learned during training might not be possible. Hence, several existing approaches in the literature for the analysis of OCTA scans have focused on a small set of interpretable candidate biomarkers based on accumulated clinical knowledge. In diabetic retinopathy, metrics related to the morphology of the foveal avascular zone (FAZ), the central part of the retina responsible for the sharpest vision, and vascular-based metrics such as vessel density and capillary nonperfusion have been used as biomarkers to investigate disease progression [6,8,10,15]. In addition, vessel density has been considered in Alzheimer's disease [18,21] and chronic kidney disease [17], highlighting the potential of retinal OCTA imaging to investigate disease of other organs, an area of increasing interest [19]. Albeit promising, these phenotypes are not representative of the full spectrum of retinal vascular morphometric characteristics that could be exploited for diagnosis. Hence, novel approaches to biomarker discovery are urgently needed. Furthermore, automated classification of diabetic retinopathy severity has been recently explored and support vector machine classification models, based on vessel density, vessel caliber, and FAZ measurements, have been proposed in [1,11]. Transfer learning was recently used to reduce the volume of data required to train DL models for the prediction of diabetic retinopathy patient status from OCTA images [7] without the need of feature engineering. However, such approach has not been able to provide to date interpretability of results.

In the current study, we propose a fully automated approach to the classification of OCTA images according to disease status based on interpretable retinal vascular features (i.e., quantifications of vascular characteristics). Our framework enables: hypothesis-free discovery of new retinal biomarkers of disease; development of ML classifiers based on modestly sized image datasets without compromising features interpretability. We propose new microvascular metrics based on geometrical and topological properties of the graph representation of the vasculature and we show applications in two case studies: diabetic retinopathy (DR) and chronic kidney disease (CKD). In the DR substudy, we replicate previous findings of changes in vessel morphology and vessel density [4,6] and discover new discriminative topological features. In the CKD substudy, we discover previously unreported structural and functional changes, and we are the first to report automated classification of CKD patient status based on OCTA retinal imaging. Finally, we show our DR and CKD classifiers outperform or achieve comparable performances of state-of-the-art DL approaches even when considering transfer learning, with the added advantage of features interpretability.

2   Methods

2.1   Vascular Graph Construction

Images of the left and right eye of the study participants are obtained using a commercial OCTA device (RTVue XR Avanti; Optovue). Only the superficial layer (from the internal limiting membrane layer (ILM) to the inner plexiform layer (IPL)), are considered for all metrics. Superficial and deep layers (from the IPL to the bottom of the outer plexiform layer) with 3×3 mm field of view are used to compute FAZ metrics (Fig. 1A). Input of our approach is the binary mask of the retinal plexus of interest (Fig. 1B). Firstly, we apply automated segmentation by using a U-Net architecture as described in [2]. Morphological thinning is then performed on the binary image to obtain a one pixelwise wide skeleton of the vasculature. In order to construct the graph and preserve the morphological structure of the network, we use a map that, considering the skeletonized image, S, of $n \times n$ pixels, for each row i and column j, the element $s_{ij} \in \{0, 1\}$ is associated to the coordinates (i, j). Vertices of our graph are then found as coordinates of the white pixel of the binary mask. To construct edges, we analyse the neighborhood of size 2×2, drawing firstly vertical and horizontal connections, and in absence of links, we explore connections along the diagonals. This procedure allows us to find edges that preserve the morphological structure of the network avoiding over connectivity. Finally, to each node, we assign two attributes: coordinates and radius. The latter is used to compute edge attribute thickness as the average radius of its end points, and keep track of vessel width. Radii are calculated starting from the original image, by computing vessel boundaries and their Euclidean distance from the pixel centre-line representing our vertex. The final network is rescaled according to the original pixel size (Fig. 1C). Considering the anatomy of the vasculature, we assume small disconnected components as segmentation artifacts, and only the largest connected component is used in our analysis.

2.2   Graph Simplification

Due to the size of the images, the final vascular network is highly dense in the number of nodes and edges. To compute morphological metrics that require to explore all the nodes in the network, which can be a very time-consuming procedure, we adopted a simplified version of the graph that preserves the vasculature structure. Briefly, let $G = (V, E)$ be our initial graph and $e_A, e_B \in E$ two adjacent edges of starting and end points (u, v) and (v, w), respectively. If e_A and e_B lay on the same line then remove e_A and e_B, and create a new edge, $e_{AB} = (u, w)$. This simplification is used, for example, to speed up the process of finding the intercapillary space, since it reduces computational time, without affecting the morphology of the network (see Fig. 1C, E).

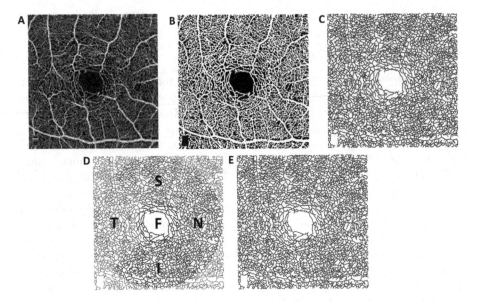

Fig. 1. (A) Original image (Superficial+Deep layers). (B) Binary image obtained using U-Net. (C) Graph representation of the vascular network. (D) Regions of interest in the network: foveal (**F**), superior (**S**), nasal (**N**), inferior (**I**), temporal (**T**). (E) Simplified graph (nodes in red, edges in black). (Color figure online)

2.3   Feature Extraction

Our graph representation of the vascular network allows us to exploit many vascular interpretable features that have never been used to investigate OCTA images before. We compute the following features for each of the regions of interest in the retinal plexus (foveal, superior, nasal, inferior, and temporal, Fig. 1D). In the case of distributions, mean, median, variance, skewness, and kurtosis are reported.

Graph-Based Features. An overview of the vascular network is obtained by computing basic graph metrics. Graph density measures the sparseness of the network, average clustering coefficient is used to measure how closely connected the nodes in the network are. Graph diameter describing the maximum eccentricity, i.e. the maximum distance between any two nodes in the network and the graph radius, describing its minimum, are calculated to understand the span of the network. Finally, edges thickness is used to investigate vessels widening and thinning possibly associated with diseases.

Coordinate-Based Features. These metrics are related to the position of each node in the network. They mainly capture the morphology and size of portions of the graph. Among these metrics, we find common retinal measures related to the foveal avascular zone (FAZ), a crucial part in the retina that has been observed widening in people with diabetic conditions [15]. We are interested in FAZ area, perimeter, and shape. FAZ area (A) and perimeter (P) are computed by considering all the points making up its boundary as vertices of a polygon. Based on this measurement FAZ circularity is defined as $C = 4\pi A/P^2$. To characterise FAZ shape we use the acircularity index, computed as $P/(2\pi R)$, where R is the radius of a circle of size equal to the FAZ area, and the axis ratio, calculated by fitting an ellipse in the FAZ and then computing major and minor axis. Supposing FAZ boundary, B, describing a path on which an object is moving, and each node of coordinate (x_i, y_i) in B as an observation of the object taken in constant time intervals, we can then compute the speed of the object, its curvature (the deviation of a curve from a straight line as $k = |x'y'' - y'x''|/(x'^2 + y'^2)^{3/2}$), and the number of turning points to estimate boundary smoothness.

Finally, vessel tortuosity has been previously associated with diabetes. We define the tortuosity as the ratio of the length of the path between two branching points against the Euclidean distance between its end points.

Flow-Based Features. Characterisation of the resistance to blood flow of a given vessel can be done by using Poiseuille's law defined as $R(l, r) = \Delta P/Q = 8\eta l/\pi r^4$, where ΔP is the pressure difference between the two ends of the vascular segment and Q is the flow rate. Given the length (l) and radius (r) of the vessel and assuming constant viscosity of blood ($\eta = 2.084 \times 10^{-3} Pa \cdot s$), we can compute the resistance at each vessel segment.

Another measurement that we extract is the area to flow capacity ratio. Tissue is supplied by oxygen and nutrients carried in the vessels, considering the size of the intercapillary space (a face in the graph), the radius, and length of the vessels that enclose it, we can estimate the ratio between tissue area and flow capacity (under the assumption of vessels cylindrical in shape).

Topology-Based Features. The retinal microvasculature is a complex and intertwined network, the investigation of changes underlying its loopy structure can reveal valuable insight into disease detection and progression. As suggested in [3] and [9] biological networks can be mapped into binary tree structures. The mapping implementation is based on the algorithm described in [9]: starting from the retinal loopy graph (containing only loops and therefore free of nodes of degree one), we find the area enclosed by edges, called *faces*, representing the leaves of the tree. At each step, we remove the shortest edge in the face boundary so that small loops are merged into bigger loops. To find the initial faces, we use the doubly connected edge list (DCEL) and the algorithm described in [12]. To ensure a binary tree root a pseudo loop surrounding the initial network is created. The binary tree mapping allows us to exploit new metrics, such as tree depth, indicating how homogeneous the loops are distributed over the network structure, tree leaves, showing the number of loops, tree asymmetry, how much the structure deviates from a perfect binary tree. To characterise the shape, we can use the number of exterior and interior edges, where an external edge has a bifurcation at its upstream end, tree altitude and total exterior path length [20]. Strahler-branching ratio is calculated by assigning a hierarchical ordering to the edges of the binary tree. We can then, classify each external edge as external-external or external-internal based on the Strahler order of the sibling edge [14].

Topological pattern comparison can be done by introducing graphlets up to size 4: small subgraphs whose distribution can elucidate repeated motives in the network. To reduce computational time, graphlets distribution is estimated based on a sample distribution. Finally we use random walks to characterise the average path length in the network. We select 1000 walks of length 300, where all the walks start from a randomly selected node, and compare it to the euclidean distance between start and end node.

2.4 Demographics and Statistical Analysis

We considered three groups of participants: 26 diabetic subjects with and without diabetic retinopathy (12 DR and 14 NoDR, respectively), 25 subjects that suffer from chronic kidney disease (CKD), and 25 age- and gender-matched healthy subjects (Controls). For each participant, only one eye was considered for our analysis. All the included images were free from major observable artifacts such as vertical and horizontal line distortions. Each patient scan was used by our framework to extract meaningful morphological and topological metrics. Statistical analysis was then performed to investigate features that are significantly different across groups and possibly associated with disease status. Shapiro-Wilk test was used to assess features normally distributed. In three groups comparison (DR, NoDR, and Controls) we performed one-way analysis of variance (ANOVA), in the case of variables normally distributed, and nonparametric Kruskal-Wallis test otherwise. For one versus one comparisons, we used t-tests for the normally distributed features, and Mann–Whitney test in the failure of Shapiro-Wilk test. In the case of multiple comparison, Bonferroni correction was applied.

After removing highly correlated metrics, we performed feature selection within a ten-fold cross-validation. In DR study, 30 features with the highest mutual information were selected before using Random Forest as classification model. In the CKD study, only the features that are statistically significant in each fold were used before applying support vector machines (SVM). Finally, we provided comparisons of our models with state-of-the-art DL approaches to patient classification. A VGG16 architecture with transfer learning was used as described in [7] to classify the same OCTA images. Ten-fold cross-validation and data augmentation was used in both sub-studies. Sensitivity, specificity, accuracy, and area under the curve (AUC) were reported for performance evaluation.

3   Results

Diabetic Cohort. Among the 189 statistically significant features, 79 were graph-based, 28 coordinate-based, 67 topology-based, and 15 flow-based. From these features, vessel skeleton density and the enlargement of the intercapillary spaces have been already reported [5, 16]. Figure 2A–C displays three features of interest: a) number of nodes, which is equivalent to the previously reported vessel skeleton density metric (since nodes represent pixels in the skeleton); b) mean size of the intercapillary spaces, a candidate for simple clinical inspection; and c) the median circularity of the intercapillary space in the nasal segment, which could distinguish between Controls and DR, and between Controls and NoDR, highlighting the importance of shape analysis. Interestingly, these three features showed a monotonic decrease/increase going from Controls to NoDR and finally DR, highlighting that the network properties of NoDR appear as an intermediate stage between Controls and DR. Random Forest provided the highest AUC (0.84) in the classification of the three groups, outperforming VGG16 with transfer learning and data augmentation (AUC = 0.79) (Table 1).

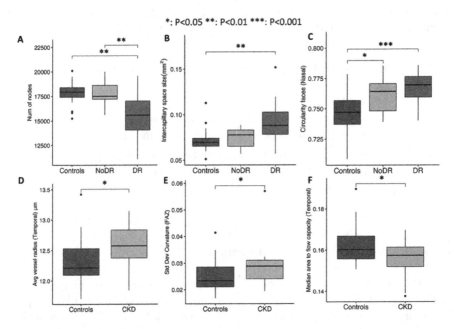

Fig. 2. Statistical significant features in diabetic (DR, NoDR) and CKD groups compared with Controls.

CKD Cohort. We found 43 statistically significant features, including 10 graph-based metrics, 20 coordinate-based metrics, 10 topology-based metrics, and 3 flow-based metrics. Our results showed differences in previously unreported morphological and flow metrics. The CKD group shows larger values of

Table 1. Table of classification performances in DR study

	Controls		NoDR		DR	
	Our approach	VGG16	Our approach	VGG16	Our approach	VGG16
ACC (mean ± SE)	**0.80 ± 0.07**	0.78 ± 0.05	**0.75 ± 0.08**	0.72 ± 0.04	**0.82 ± 0.06**	0.77 ± 0.04
SEN (mean ± SE)	0.79 ± 0.08	**0.90 ± 0.05**	**0.30 ± 0.10**	0.20 ± 0.13	**0.55 ± 0.19**	0.55 ± 0.11
SPE (mean ± SE)	**0.77 ± 0.08**	0.67 ± 0.11	**0.88 ± 0.05**	0.88 ± 0.05	0.88 ± 0.05	0.86 ± 0.05
AUC (mean ± SD)	**0.90 ± 0.11**	0.90 ± 0.15	**0.67 ± 0.37**	0.67± 0.28	**0.81 ± 0.12**	0.75 ± 0.22

vessel radius in the temporal region of the retina, as well as a high imbalance in the curvature measurements of the FAZ, indicating high variability of this parameter in the disease group. Moreover, the newly introduced area to flow capacity has been found lower in the temporal area of the CKD group underlining the strong connection between structural and functional changes (2D–F). In contrast with our diabetic cohort (and previous DR studies), common measurements such as vessel density and size of intercapillary spaces did not differ between CKD and controls, highlighting that the retinal vascular changes in CKD could be perceived clinically as much more subtle. This is also confirmed by classification performances. Both SVM and VGG16 performed poorly in the classification task (Table 2), achieving the same AUC equals to 0.62.

Table 2. Table of classification performances in CKD study

	Controls		CKD	
	Our approach	VGG16	Our approach	VGG16
ACC	**0.52 ± 0.09**	0.48 ± 0.08	**0.52 ± 0.09**	0.48 ± 0.08
SEN	0.58 ± 0.14	**0.61 ± 0.09**	**0.47 ± 0.15**	0.38 ± 0.12
SPE	**0.47 ± 0.15**	0.38 ± 0.12	0.58 ± 0.14	**0.61 ± 0.09**
AUC	0.62 ± 0.29	0.62 ± 0.37	0.62 ± 0.29	0.62 ± 0.37

4   Discussion and Conclusions

With the increasing interest in mining the retinal landscape for biomarkers of both eye and systemic disease, which some authors have termed oculomics [19], OCTA has become a key modality for the study of the retinal microvascular system *in vivo*. Previous studies have shown associations between changes in the retinal microvascular structure and conditions as diverse as diabetic retinopathy, Alzheimer's disease, and chronic kidney disease. Early identification of these alterations can contribute to timely target patients at risk and effectively monitor disease progression. Quantifying these changes by matching selected vascular features may provide a non-invasive alternative to characterise vascular dysfunctions and gain valuable insights for clinical practice. In this study, we propose a novel network analysis framework for hypothesis-free discovery of new retinal biomarkers of disease and the development of machine learning classifiers based on modestly sized image datasets without compromising on the interpretability of the classification features. These geometric and topological features may elucidate vascular alterations and unravel clinically relevant measurements. We demonstrate our approach in two different diseases with a retinal vascular footprint: diabetic retinopathy and chronic kidney disease. In the diabetic cohort, we are capable of replicating previous findings of structural alterations associated with disease. In both sub-studies, we uncover a large number of previously unreported biomarkers. Furthermore, our automated image classification approach outperforms or achieves comparable results of state-of-the-art deep learning approaches with the added advantage of feature interpretability. Our results confirm that automated classification of chronic kidney disease status based on OCTA imaging is a more challenging task. Future work should investigate the development of more advanced feature selection approaches for model construction that can leverage the large number of biomarkers discovered without suffering from what is known as peaking phenomenon (too large set of features leads to poorer performances than a small set of selected features [13]), and validate our results on larger cohorts to support statistical analysis. Our methodology lays the foundation of a novel prospective approach for retinal microvascular analysis that can realise the full diagnostic potential of OCTA imaging.

References

1. Alam, M., Zhang, Y., Lim, J.I., Chan, R.V., Yang, M., Yao, X.: Quantitative optical coherence tomography angiography features for objective classification and staging of diabetic retinopathy. Retina (Philadelphia, Pa.) 40(2), 322–332 (2020)
2. Giarratano, Y., et al.: Automated segmentation of optical coherence tomography angiography images: benchmark data and clinically relevant metrics. arXiv:1912.09978v2 (2020)
3. Katifori, E., Magnasco, M.O.: Quantifying loopy network architectures. PLoS ONE 7(6), e37994 (2012)
4. Khadamy, J., Aghdam, K., Falavarjani, K.: An update on optical coherence tomography angiography in diabetic retinopathy. J. Ophthalmic Vis. Res. 13, 487 (2018)
5. Kim, A.Y., Chu, Z., Shahidzadeh, A., Wang, R.K., Puliafito, C.A., Kashani, A.H.: Quantifying microvascular density and morphology in diabetic retinopathy using spectral-domain optical coherence tomography angiography. Investig. Ophthalmol. Vis. Sci. 57(9), OCT362–OCT370 (2016)
6. Krawitz, B.D., et al.: Acircularity index and axis ratio of the foveal avascular zone in diabetic eyes and healthy controls measured by optical coherence tomography angiography. Vis. Res. 139, 177–186 (2017)
7. Le, D., Alam, M.N., Lim, J.I., Chan, R.V.P., Yao, X.: Deep learning for objective OCTA detection of diabetic retinopathy. In: Manns, F., Ho, A.,Söderberg, P.G. (eds.) Ophthalmic Technologies XXX. vol. 11218, pp. 98 –103. International Society for Optics and Photonics, SPIE (2020)
8. Mastropasqua, R., et al.: Foveal avascular zone area and parafoveal vessel density measurements in different stages of diabetic retinopathy by optical coherence tomography angiography. Int. J. Ophthalmol. 10(10), 1545–1551 (2017)

9. Modes, C.D., Magnasco, M.O., Katifori, E.: Extracting hidden hierarchies in 3D distribution networks. Phys. Rev. X **6**(3), 1–12 (2016)

10. Nesper, P.L., et al.: Quantifying microvascular abnormalities with increasing severity of diabetic retinopathy using optical coherence tomography angiography. Investig. Ophthalmol. Vis. Sci. **58**(6), BIO307–BIO315 (2017)

11. Sandhu, H.S., et al.: Automated diabetic retinopathy detection using optical coherence tomography angiography: a pilot study. Br. J. Ophthalmol. **102**(11), 1564–1569 (2018)

12. Schneider, S., Sbalzarini, I.F.: Finding faces in a planar embedding of a graph. Technical report, MOSAIC Group, MPI-CBG (2015)

13. Sima, C., Dougherty, E.R.: The peaking phenomenon in the presence of feature-selection. Pattern Recognit. Lett. **29**(11), 1667–1674 (2008)

14. Smart, J.S.: The analysis of drainage network composition. Earth Surf. Process. **3**(2), 129–170 (1978)

15. Takase, N., Nozaki, M., Kato, A., Ozeki, H., Yoshida, M., Ogura, Y.: Enlargement of foveal avascular zone in diabetic eyes evaluated by en face optical coherence tomography angiography. Retina **35**(11), 2377–2383 (2015)

16. Tang, F.Y., et al.: Determinants of quantitative optical coherence tomography angiography metrics in patients with diabetes. Sci. Rep. **7**(1), 1–10 (2017)

17. Vadalà, M., Castellucci, M., Guarrasi, G., Terrasi, M., La Blasca, T., Mulè, G.: Retinal and choroidal vasculature changes associated with chronic kidney disease. Graefe's Arch. Clin. Exp. Ophthalmol. **257**(8), 1687–1698 (2019). https://doi.org/10.1007/s00417-019-04358-3

18. Van De Kreeke, J.A., et al.: Optical coherence tomography angiography in preclinical Alzheimer's disease. Br. J. Ophthalmol. **104**, 157–161 (2019)

19. Wagner, S.K., et al.: Insights into systemic disease through retinal imaging-based oculomics. Transl. Vis. Sci. Technol. **9**(2), 6 (2020)

20. Werner, C., Smart, J.S.: Some new methods of topologic classification of channel networks. Geogr. Anal. **5**(4), 271–295 (1973)

21. Yoon, S.P., et al.: Retinal microvascular and neurodegenerative changes in Alzheimer's disease and mild cognitive impairment compared with control participants. Ophthalmol. Retin. **3**(6), 489–499 (2019)

An Automated Aggressive Posterior Retinopathy of Prematurity Diagnosis System by Squeeze and Excitation Hierarchical Bilinear Pooling Network

Rugang Zhang[1], Jinfeng Zhao[2], Guozhen Chen[1], Hai Xie[1], Guanghui Yue[1], Tianfu Wang[1], Guoming Zhang[2(✉)], and Baiying Lei[1(✉)]

[1] National-Regional Key Technology Engineering Laboratory for Medical Ultrasound, Guangdong Key Laboratory for Biomedical Measurements and Ultrasound Imaging, School of Biomedical Engineering, Health Science Center, Shenzhen University, Shenzhen, China
leiby@szu.edu.cn
[2] Shenzhen Eye Hospital, Shenzhen Key Ophthalmic Laboratory, The Second Affiliated Hospital of Jinan University, Shenzhen, China

Abstract. Aggressive Posterior Retinopathy of Prematurity (AP-ROP) is a special type of Retinopathy of Prematurity (ROP), which is one of the most common childhood blindness that occurs in premature infants. AP-ROP is uncommon, atypical, progresses rapidly and prone to misdiagnosis. If it is not detected and treated timely, it will rapidly progress to the fifth stage of ROP that causes easily retinal detachment and blindness. Early diagnosis of AP-ROP is the key to reduce the blindness rate of the disease. In this paper, we apply computer-aided methods for early AP-ROP diagnosis. The proposed method utilizes a Squeeze and Excitation Hierarchical Bilinear Pooling (SE-HBP) network to complete early diagnosis of AP-ROP. Specifically, the SE module can automatically obtain the important information of the channel, where the useless features are suppressed and the useful features are emphasized to enhance the feature extraction capability of the network. The HBP module can complement the information of the feature layers to capture the feature relationship between the layers so that the representation ability of the model can be enhanced. Finally, in order to solve the imbalance problem of AP-ROP fundus image data, we use a focal loss function, which can effectively alleviate the accuracy reduction that caused by the data imbalance. The experimental results show that our system can effectively distinguish AP-ROP with the fundus images, which has a potential application in assisting the ophthalmologists to determine the AP-ROP.

Keywords: Retinopathy of Prematurity · Hierarchical Bilinear Pooling · Squeeze and Excitation · Focal loss

1 Introduction

Retinopathy of Prematurity (ROP) is a retinal vascular proliferative blindness disease that occurs in premature infants and low-weight newborns, even about 19% of the cases

© Springer Nature Switzerland AG 2020
H. Fu et al. (Eds.): OMIA 2020, LNCS 12069, pp. 165–174, 2020.
https://doi.org/10.1007/978-3-030-63419-3_17

evolved into blindness in children worldwide. Studies have found that the reason is that the undergrown retina is associated with large amounts of oxygen exposure. The development of ROP is rapid, and if treatment is not timely, patients may be blind [1]. According to statistics, approximately 187,400 infants worldwide suffered from varying degrees of ROP in 2010, and as many as 20,000 of them had severe visual impairment or blindness. With the advanced care for newborns, the incidence of ROP is gradually increasing in low and middle income countries [2]. Early diagnosis is the key to reduce ROP blindness.

Aggressive Posterior Retinopathy of Prematurity (AP-ROP) is a special type of ROP. Unlike regular ROP, AP-ROP may present plus disease, retinal hemorrhages, flat neovascularization (FNV) or ischemic capillary nonperfusion regions [3]. AP-ROP develops much faster than regular ROP. If it is not detected and treated in time, the disease will rapidly progress to the fifth stage of ROP, which means that the retina will be completely detached so that the blindness occurs [4]. The early intervention can significantly reduce the incidence of AP-ROP blindness, so early diagnosis is particularly important [5].

There are several differences between regular ROP and AP-ROP from the fundus images, according to the International Classification of ROP (ICROP) guideline:

1) Regular ROP is characterized by a slight boundary ridge or demarcation line between the vascularized and no vascularized retina. As shown in Fig. 1(b), a slight boundary ridge appears on the right side of the Regular ROP image.
2) As shown in Fig. 1(c), AP-ROP may also present a slight boundary ridge or demarcation line on the image, but some typical features will appear, such as vessels dilation and tortuosity and retinal hemorrhages [6].

Clinical diagnosis of AP-ROP is still problematic due to the following reasons. First, the development and condition of AP-ROP are not routine, which is different from that of Regular ROP [7]. Due to the low incidence rate of AP-ROP and its atypical condition, many ophthalmologists have insufficient experience in diagnosing the symptom, thus easily misdiagnosed as Regular ROP so that the patients miss the optimal treatment period. Second, there is a lack of prevalence ophthalmologists. Although some clinics have advanced inspection machines, the professional prematurity ophthalmologists are deficient to diagnose AP-ROP using fundus images. Third, the classification guidelines

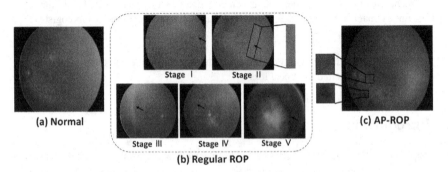

Fig. 1. Fundus images of Normal (a), Regular ROP (b) and AR-ROP (c).

provide only qualitative signs [8], however, the diagnosis of AP-ROP usually depends on the visual inspection of the image by a major ophthalmologist, which is subjective [9]. The previous studies have reported that different ophthalmologists may have different diagnosis results for the same fundus image [10]. Computer-assisted diagnosis tools have showed remarkable performance in detecting Regular ROP from the fundus images, which may help ophthalmologists detect AP-ROP as well. It can speed up the examination and reduce the rate of misdiagnosis, which is significant for reducing the blindness rate of AP-ROP.

Studies have shown that deep learning (DL) has excellent performance in the field of image analysis [11]. It has been successfully used in the automatic diagnosis of many retinopathy, such as glaucoma [12], diabetes retinopathy [13], macular degeneration [14] and cataract [15]. There are also studies using deep learning to automatically identify ROP fundus images [16]. But few studies use deep learning to automatically realize the diagnosis of AP-ROP. In this paper, we propose an automatic AP-ROP diagnosis system using convolutional neural network. The implementation of the system faces the following challenges:

1) The boundary ridge or demarcation line of AP-ROP is blurry and the contrast is low. The tortuosity of the blood vessels in some AP-ROP cases is similar to the ones in normal fundus image, which will be easily confused for the diagnosis network.
2) In practice, prevalence ophthalmologists capture multiple fields of view of the retina when acquiring fundus images, so that the features of the disease will appear at different locations in the fundus images.
3) The quality of the AP-ROP fundus images is various and many of them are poor in quality due to equipment imaging and operators.
4) The incidence rate of AP-ROP is very low, the number of cases is far below ROP, and the training data have serious data imbalance among categories, which will affect the training of network.

In order to solve the challenge one and two, we use the Hierarchical Bilinear Pooling (HBP) module, which can make use of the interaction between layers to complement the characteristics of the layers and reduce the loss of useful information between the layers. This is helpful to reduce the impact caused by the different image fields and solve the problem of similar features between different classes. To solve challenge three, we use the Squeeze and Excitation module to help the network emphasize useful information and suppress useless information to improve the feature extraction ability of the proposed network. Finally, we utilize the Focal-Loss to solve the problem of the challenge four, which can solve the problem of unbalanced data distribution by assigning different weights to the data of different labels. The contributions of this paper are summarized as follows.

1) This study adopts a HBP method to automatically diagnose AP-ROP, and uses SE method to improve the feature extraction ability of the proposed framework.
2) For the problem of data imbalance, we utilize the Focal-Loss to solve it, which can assign different weights to different amounts of data to balance the impact of different sizes of data in the stage of training.

3) Finally, we conduct multiple sets of comparative experiments to prove the effectiveness of our method.

2 Methodology

Our method is based on ResNet50, which use the residual module in the network. The addition of the residual module allows the ResNet to solve the problem of gradient disappearance. Therefore, the network does not need to learn the output of the entire network layer, it only needs to learn the residual value of the output between the layers. The addition of the residual module does not add additional computing resources, and greatly improves the training speed of the network model and enhances the final result. On this basis, we use the HBP method, SE method, and Focal-Loss in the proposed framework according to the purpose of this study (Fig. 2).

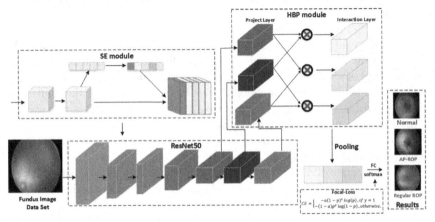

Fig. 2. Structure of SE-HBP network. The SE-HBP network is based on ResNet50. We add the SE module at the end of each residual module to strengthen the feature extraction ability. At the same time, we interacts the features of the high-dimensional space between layers and compress the integrated high-dimensional features into compact features to improve the performance of the network.

2.1 Hierarchical Bilinear Pooling Module

The HBP module itself is used for fine-grained visual recognition and shows good results [17]. The subclasses of fine-grained identification often have high similarity and can only be identified with some local parts. At the same time, the image varies as backgrounds for fine-grained identification. This is similar to the difficulty of AP-ROP fundus image classification. Considering the classification of AP-ROP, different images have different fields of view, and some AP-ROP fundus images have a high similarity to Normal fundus images and Regular ROP fundus images.

The HBP method realizes the interaction between layers by integrating the features of different convolutional layers in high-dimensional space through the element-wise multiplication. Then the high-dimensional features are compressed through summation to obtain the interactive features of the HBP model, which enhances the feature representation capabilities of the network. The formula expression is as follows:

$$Z_{HBP} = HBP(x, y, z, \cdots) = P^T z_{int}$$
$$= P^T concat\left(U^T x \cdot V^T y, U^T x \cdot S^T z, V^T y \cdot S^T z, \cdots\right) \tag{1}$$

2.2 Squeeze and Excitation Module

The SE module is a channel-based attention mechanism [18]. It models the important information of each feature channel, and then enhances or suppresses the relevant channels according to the task.

First, the squeeze operation compresses the features and turns the two-dimensional feature channel into a real number with a global receptive field, which represents the global distribution of responses on the feature channel. Second, the excitation operation uses the parameter w to generate weights for each feature channel, which is used to explicitly model the correlation between feature channels. Finally, the operation of reweight weights the output weight of excitation to the previous features channel by channel through multiplication to complete the recalibration of the features.

2.3 Focal-Loss

In order to solve the problem of data imbalance, we use Focal-Loss [19]. When we calculate the classification loss, the commonly used loss function is the cross entropy function:

$$CE = \begin{cases} -\log(p), & if\, y = 1 \\ -\log(1 - p), & otherwise. \end{cases} \tag{2}$$

by adding parameters α and γ to Eq. (2), the formula becomes:

$$CE = \begin{cases} -a(1 - p)^\gamma \log(p), & if\, y = 1 \\ -(1 - a)p^\gamma \log(1 - p), & otherwise. \end{cases} \tag{3}$$

Equation (3) indicates Focal-Loss, usually the values of α and γ are fixed. When the data is wrongly divided by the network, the p will be small, and the adjustment factor of Focal-Loss has little effect on the loss function. But if the data is easier to judge for the network, the p will be large and the loss function will be greatly reduced. By adjusting the loss function by α and γ, we solve the data imbalance problem of AP-ROP.

3   Experiments

3.1   Data

The data of this paper were collected in local eye hospital. The collection was performed by professional ophthalmologists, and the collection device is RetCam3. The diagnosis of AP-ROP comes from the visual inspection of ophthalmologist. In order to obtain the image information of the entire eyeball in all directions, it is necessary to capture fundus images in multiple directions when collecting data. Therefore, multiple fundus images are captured at different angles in one acquisition. The characteristics of retinopathy are shown in Fig. 1, only one fundus image can detect the characteristics of disease, the eye can be judged to retinopathy. According to the requirements of clinical diagnosis, we use a single picture as a unit to incorporate multiple images from different angles into the fundus image data set.

Dataset annotation is performed by senior ophthalmologists. We send the same dataset to three professional ophthalmologists to accomplish the annotation. Similar to the flowchart of the network, they annotate the fundus images in the dataset with or without ROP, and then distinguish the fundus images with ROP as AP-ROP or regular ROP. After that, we pick out the fundus images with different opinions and discuss them. Finally, we utilize voting operation to determine the results of this image. If the image is poor quality, it will be discarded.

Table 1 lists the details of the dataset. Among them, the data of Regular ROP includes 1, 2, 3 stages of ROP. In the dataset, the fundus images at various stages are randomly distributed. To save computing resources, we adjusted the original fundus image size to 224×224.

Table 1. Dataset distribution in this study.

Dataset	AP-ROP	Regular-ROP	Normal	Total
Training set	1367	3101	5219	9687
Testing set	331	797	1280	2408
Total	1698	3898	6499	12095

This study divides the data into two parts: training set and test set. The training set is only used to train the network, and the test set is completely independent of the training set. The test set is used to evaluate the performance of the network. The angle of view of the fundus image data will be randomly disturbed, which can simulate the fundus examination situation in the hospital to a certain extent. We use several of the most commonly used evaluation criteria to evaluate our model, including accuracy, sensitivity, specificity, precision, and F1 score.

3.2   Results

In this study, we conduct multiple sets of comparative experiments, including comparing the modules introduced in this study with the original network, and compare them on the

ResNet50 and 101 networks. The experimental results are shown in Table 2. We can see that compared with the basic network, each module shows an increasing performance for our proposed network. The proposed network obtains the best performance, which demonstrates that our method is effective.

Table 2. The performance of the different networks.

Module	Accuracy	Sensitivity	Specificity	Precision	F1-score
VGG16	93.81%	85.34%	96.61%	91.81%	88.43%
ResNet50	94.81%	87.09%	96.97%	93.71%	90.21%
ResNet101	91.69%	80.83%	94.92%	90.22%	84.99%
ResNet50+Focal-Loss	95.93%	89.92%	97.84%	94.50%	92.13%
ResNet101+Focal-Loss	92.28%	83.70%	96.29%	89.20%	86.31%
ResNet50+SE Block	95.93%	89.85%	97.81%	95.01%	92.29%
ResNet101+SE Block	92.98%	80.99%	95.79%	94.05%	85.77%
ResNet50+HBP Block	96.01%	89.96%	97.80%	94.82%	92.30%
ResNet101+HBP Block	94.02%	85.60%	96.98%	92.95%	88.73%
SE-HP 50	**96.59%**	**90.62%**	**97.92%**	**96.59%**	**93.39%**
SE-HP 101	**95.43%**	**87.30%**	**97.25%**	**95.75%**	**90.96%**

The t-SNE visualization of the ResNet-50, ResNet-101 and the proposed network is shown in Fig. 3. We can see that our proposed network is more differentiated for the classification of AP-ROP, Regular ROP, and Normal fundus images, which indicates that our network is more expressive.

In order to better evaluate the SE-HP Network in this study, we invite three prevalence ophthalmologists to participate in the evaluation of network performance. We use a new comparison data set. The comparative dataset has a total of 100 fundus images, including 50 normal fundus images, 30 Regular ROP fundus images, and 20 AP-ROP fundus images.

We send the comparative dataset to three prevalence ophthalmologists for diagnosis and statistical results. We also use this dataset to evaluate the SE-HP 50. The final results are shown in Table 3. From Table 3, we can see that our network has a certain advantage over ophthalmologists in the diagnosis of AP-ROP, and the classification of ordinary fundus images and conventional ROP fundus images is close to the diagnosis of ophthalmologist. At the same time, we can observe that the ophthalmologists are easy to misdiagnose AP-ROP due to the atypical AP-ROP condition. Our system can effectively help ophthalmologists to determine on AP-ROP during diagnosis. During the evaluation, we find that the diagnosis speed of the automatic diagnosis system for AP-ROP is much faster than that of ophthalmologists, which shows that the study system has certain help in relieving medical pressure.

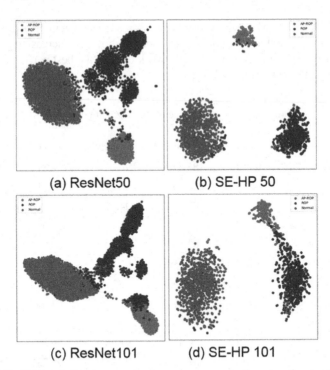

(a) ResNet50   (b) SE-HP 50

(c) ResNet101   (d) SE-HP 101

Fig. 3. T-SNE of Network. The improvements we propose make the network more discriminative recognition of classification results.

Table 3. Evaluation Results.

	Normal Acc	Regular ROP Acc	AP-ROP Acc
Ophthalmologist 1	100%	93.30%	70.00%
Ophthalmologist 2	100%	100%	85.00%
Ophthalmologist 3	100%	100%	90.00%
SE-HP 50	100%	96.67%	100%

4   Conclusions

In this paper, we propose a new CNN structure based on ResNet50 and ResNet101 to automatically identify AP-ROP. Specifically, we use the HBP module to obtain the information between CNN convolutional layers and complement each other to enhance the performance of the network. At the same time, we utilize the SE module to enhance the feature extraction capabilities of CNN. Finally, for the problem of data imbalance, we use Focal-Loss to solve it. The experimental results show that our method achieves a promising performance on detecting AP-ROP. The optimal result is 96.59% of SE-HP 50. It can be seen from the t-SNE visualization that our proposed modules enforce the network to extract more discriminative features so that the classification performance is improved. Hence, this study can effectively prompt ophthalmologists to assist ophthalmologists in diagnosing AP-ROP, thereby reducing the misdiagnosis rate of ophthalmologists and the blindness rate of the disease.

Acknowledgements. This work was supported partly by National Natural Science Foundation of China (Nos. 61871274, 61801305 and 81571758), National Natural Science Foundation of Guangdong Province (No. 2020A1515010649 and No. 2019A1515111205), Guangdong Province Key Laboratory of Popular High Performance Computers (No. 2017B030314073), Guangdong Laboratory of Artificial-Intelligence and Cyber-Economics (SZ), Shenzhen Peacock Plan (Nos. KQTD2016053112051497 and KQTD2015033016104926), Shenzhen Key Basic Research Project (Nos. JCYJ20190808165209410, 20190808145011259, JCYJ20180507184647636, GJHZ20190822095414576 and JCYJ20170302153337765, JCYJ20170302150411789, JCYJ201703 0214 2515949, GCZX2017040715180580, GJHZ 20180418190529516, and JSGG 20180507183215520), NTUT-SZU Joint Research Program (No. 2020003).

References

1. Aggarwal, R., Agarwal, R., Deorari, A.K., Paul, V.K.: Retinopathy of prematurity. Indian J. Pediatr. **69**(1), 83–86 (2002). https://doi.org/10.1007/BF02723783
2. Blencowe, H., Lawn, J.E., Vazquez, T., et al.: Preterm-associated visual impairment and estimates of retinopathy of prematurity at regional and global levels for 2010. Pediatr. Res. **74**(S1), 35–49 (2013)
3. Vinekar, A., Chidambara, L., Jayadev, C., et al.: Monitoring neovascularization in aggressive posterior retinopathy of prematurity using optical coherence tomography angiography. J. Am. Assoc. Pediatr. Ophthalmol. Strabismus **20**(3), 271–274 (2016)
4. Rajashekar, D., Srinivasa, G., Vinekar, A.: Comprehensive retinal image analysis for aggressive posterior retinopathy of prematurity. PLoS ONE **11**(10), e0163923 (2016)
5. Taylor, S., Brown, J.M., Gupta, K., et al.: Monitoring disease progression with a quantitative severity scale for retinopathy of prematurity using deep learning. JAMA Ophthalmol. **137**(9), 1022–1028 (2019)
6. Woo R, Chan R V P, Vinekar A, et al.: Aggressive posterior retinopathy of prematurity: a pilot study of quantitative analysis of vascular features. Graefe's Arch. Clin. Exp. Ophthalmol. **253**(2), 181–187 (2015)
7. Kim, S.J., Campbell, J.P., Kalpathy-Cramer, J., et al.: Accuracy and reliability of eye-based vs quadrant-based diagnosis of plus disease in retinopathy of prematurity. JAMA Ophthalmol. **136**(6), 648–655 (2018)
8. Prematurity ICftCoRo: The international classification of retinopathy of prematurity revisited. Arch. Ophthalmol. **123**(7), 991 (2005)
9. American Academy of Pediatrics Section on Ophthalmology: Screening examination of premature infants for retinopathy of prematurity. Pediatrics **131**(1), 189–195 (2013)
10. Chiang, M.F., Jiang, L., Gelman, R., et al.: Interexpert agreement of plus disease diagnosis in retinopathy of prematurity. Arch. Ophthalmol. **125**(7), 875–880 (2007)
11. Brown, J.M., Campbell, J.P., Beers, A., et al.: Automated diagnosis of plus disease in retinopathy of prematurity using deep convolutional neural networks. JAMA Ophthalmol. **136**(7), 803–810 (2018)
12. Diaz-Pinto, A., Colomer, A., Naranjo, V., et al.: Retinal image synthesis and semi-supervised learning for glaucoma assessment. IEEE Trans. Med. Imaging **38**(9), 2211–2218 (2019)

13. Gulshan, V., Peng, L., Coram, M., et al.: Development and validation of a deep learning algorithm for detection of diabetic retinopathy in retinal fundus photographs. JAMA **316**(22), 2402–2410 (2016)
14. Russakoff, D.B., Lamin, A., Oakley, J.D., et al.: Deep learning for prediction of AMD progression: a pilot study. Investig. Ophthalmol. Vis. Sci. **60**(2), 712–722 (2019)
15. Long, E., Lin, H., Liu, Z., et al.: An artificial intelligence platform for the multihospital collaborative management of congenital cataracts. Nat. Biomed. Eng. **1**(2), 1–8 (2017)
16. Zhao, J., Lei, B., Wu, Z., et al.: A deep learning framework for identifying zone I in RetCam images. IEEE Access **7**, 103530–103537 (2019)
17. Yu, C., Zhao, X., Zheng, Q., Zhang, P., You, X.: Hierarchical bilinear pooling for fine-grained visual recognition. In: Ferrari, V., Hebert, M., Sminchisescu, C., Weiss, Y. (eds.) ECCV 2018. LNCS, vol. 11220, pp. 595–610. Springer, Cham (2018). https://doi.org/10.1007/978-3-030-01270-0_35
18. Hu, J., Shen, L., Sun, G.: Squeeze-and-excitation networks. In: Proceedings of the IEEE Conference on Computer Vision and Pattern Recognition, pp. 7132–7141 (2018)
19. Lin, T.Y., Goyal, P., Girshick, R., et al.: Focal loss for dense object detection. In: Proceedings of the IEEE International Conference on Computer Vision, pp. 2980–2988 (2017)

Weakly-Supervised Lesion-Aware and Consistency Regularization for Retinitis Pigmentosa Detection from Ultra-Widefield Images

Benjian Zhao[1], Haijun Lei[1], Xianlu Zeng[2], Jiuwen Cao[3], Hai Xie[4], Guanghui Yue[4], Jiantao Wang[2], Guoming Zhang[2], and Baiying Lei[4(✉)]

[1] Guangdong Province Key Laboratory of Popular High-Performance Computers, College of Computer Science and Software Engineering, Shenzhen University, Shenzhen, China
[2] Shenzhen Eye Hospital, Shenzhen Key Ophthalmic Laboratory, The Second Affiliated Hospital of Jinan University, Shenzhen, China
[3] Artificial Intelligence Institute, Hangzhou Dianzi University, Zhejiang, China
[4] National-Regional Key Technology Engineering Laboratory for Medical Ultrasound, Guangdong Key Laboratory for Biomedical Measurements and Ultrasound Imaging, School of Biomedical Engineering, Health Science Center, Shenzhen University, Shenzhen, China
leiby@szu.edu.cn

Abstract. Retinitis pigmentosa (RP) is one of the most common retinal diseases caused by gene defects, which can lead to night blindness or complete blindness. Accurate diagnosis and lesion identification are significant tasks for clinicians to assess fundus images. However, due to some limitations, it is still challenging to design a method that can simultaneously diagnose and accomplish lesion identification so that the accurate lesion identification can promote the accuracy of diagnosis. In this paper, we propose a method based on weakly-supervised lesion-aware and consistency regularization to detect RP and generate lesion attention map (LAM). Specifically, we extend global average pooling to multiple scales, and use multi-scale features to offset the gap between semantic information and spatial information to generate a more refined LAM. At the same time, we regularize LAMs with different affine transforms for the same sample, and force them to produce more accurate predictions and reduce the overconfidence of the network, which can enhance LAM to cover lesions. We use two central datasets to verify the effectiveness of the proposed model. We train the proposed model in one dataset and test it in the other dataset to verify the generalization performance. Experimental results show that our method achieves promising performance.

Keywords: Retinitis pigmentosa · Deep learning · Lesion attention map · Consistency regularization

1 Introduction

Retinitis pigmentosa (RP) is one of the most common genetic heterogeneous retinal disease which belongs to inherited retinal dystrophies (IRD) [1]. In clinical diagnosis,

© Springer Nature Switzerland AG 2020
H. Fu et al. (Eds.): OMIA 2020, LNCS 12069, pp. 175–184, 2020.
https://doi.org/10.1007/978-3-030-63419-3_18

due to ultra-widefield (UWF) images can contain peripheral lesions of the retina, thus it is a useful tool to detect IRD diseases such as RP, as shown in Fig. 1(a) [2]. Accurate diagnosis and lesion identification are significant tasks for clinicians to assess fundus images [3]. Although the convolutional neural network (CNN) has achieved success in the field of medical image [4], it is still challenging to design a method that can diagnose and generate lesion attention map (LAM) simultaneously due to some limitations. (1) The training data only has binary diagnostic labels and lacks pixel-wise annotation of lesion information. (2) The size difference of RP lesions is various, and the distribution is inhomogeneous. Also, UWF images are disturbed by eyelids, eyelashes, and artifacts [5]; (3) The small amount of data sample is easy to occurs overfitting for CNN network, which results in poor generalization performance and identification of the wrong area [6].

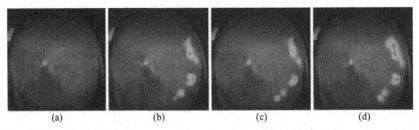

(a)   (b)   (c)   (d)

Fig. 1. An example of RP and LAMs generated by different methods. (a) original image, (b) and (c) are the LAM generated by using color distortion and rescale, respectively, (d) is generated by our method, which shows more lesions covered.

The weakly-supervised learning can learn from the weak-label data to identify the lesions and further improve the reliability of diagnosis. Recently, CNN trained with diagnostic labels has achieved some progress in the localization of lesions [7, 8]. For example, Zhao *et al.* [9] proposed a multi-task learning framework, which used weakly-supervised learning to perform lesion identification, optic disc segmentation, and glaucoma diagnosis simultaneously, and built a pyramid integrated structure to identify lesions using multi-scale features. In these models, the global average pooling (GAP) [10] preserves the spatial structure of the feature maps, which can be used to generate discriminative LAM. However, these LAMs usually only cover the most discriminative area, which cannot solve the problem of the wide distribution of RP lesions.

Ideally, LAM should cover all lesion areas, but it is difficult to produce accurate identification due to the supervision gap between weakly-supervision and full supervision with pixel-wise lesion annotation. Furthermore, different transformed images will produce different LAMs, as shown in Fig. 1 (b) and (c). To improve the ability of weakly-supervised learning in object identification, many researches focus on integrating regularization factors and improving the ability of object identification by constraining the prediction distribution of the network. For example, Tang *et al.* [11] directly integrated the regularizers into the loss function of weakly-supervised learning and proved that it can simplify the training and improve the quality and efficiency of training. Wang *et al.* [12] proposed a self-supervised equivariant attention mechanism by using an implicit equivalence constraint, where the transformed images are consistently regularized to shrink the supervised gap between fully supervised and weakly-supervised learning.

In this paper, we propose a method based on weakly-supervised lesion-aware and consistency regularization for UWF images to diagnose and identify the lesions of RP. Specifically, we use ResNet50 [13] as the backbone network and expand the GAP to multiple scales, so that we can use multi-scale information to offset the gap between semantic information and spatial information and generate a more refined LAM. At the same time, inspired by [12], we constrain the LAM of the same sample with different affine transforms to produce more accurate predictions, which can reduce the overconfidence of the network and enhance the ability of the LAM to cover the lesions. Besides, our regularization is based on the LAM, which can avoid the interference of other parts of the image, such as eyelids and eyelashes.

2 Methodology

Figure 2 summarizes our network architecture. We use ResNet50 as the backbone network, where the original fully connection layer is replaced by GAP, further extend it to multiple convolutional layers, to generate more refined LAM by aggregating multi-scale features. At the same time, we use a set of random affine transforms, where we input the original image and the transformed image into the model and generate the corresponding LAMs. Then we use the consistency regularization constraint to force them to produce more consistent and accurate predictions.

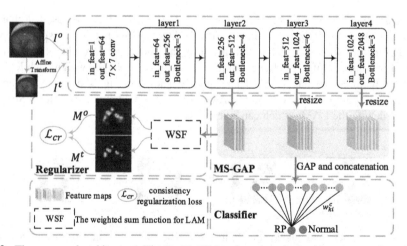

Fig. 2. The proposed architecture. The ResNet50 is selected as the backbone network, and the GAP is extended to extract multi-scale features to offset the gap between deep semantic information and spatial information. Then the consistency regularization is applied for different transforms for the same sample to force them to produce more consistent predictions.

2.1 Multi-scale Global Average Pooling

GAP can not only reduce the parameters of the fully connection layer, but also make full use of the spatial information. Due to the various distribution and size of lesions in RP, the size of discriminative feature is reduced to a point where it is difficult to produce a LAM with accurate spatial information. Therefore, we introduce a multi-scale global average pooling (MS-GAP) to effectively aggregate the multi-scale global features of lesions. In our implementation, we aggregate three scale feature maps to obtain more accurate features representation for fundus image, as shown in Fig. 2.

To aggregate the multi-scale features, we first resize all features to the same size and then use GAP to generate feature vectors of three scales and concatenate them. For a given feature map, let $f_{ki}(x, y)$ denote the activation of the i-th scale feature unit k at the spatial position (x, y). Then, for the feature unit k of scale i, the result of using GAP is $F_{ki} = \sum_{x,y} f_{ki}(x, y)$. Therefore, for a given class c, the classification score that is input into the softmax layer can be expressed as $S^c = \sum_{k,i} w_{ki}^c F_{ki}$, where w_{ki}^c is the weight of feature unit k corresponding to class c in the i-th scale. Thus, we can obtain

$$S^c = \sum_i \sum_k w_{ki}^c \sum_{x,y} f_{ki}(x, y), \tag{1}$$

Let S_I denote the score vector of sample I from a dataset $\mathcal{D}$, and l is the corresponding one-hot label. Therefore, the classification objective can be represented by the following standard classification loss function:

$$\mathcal{L}_{cls} = -\sum_{\mathcal{D}} l \cdot logS_I, \tag{2}$$

Class activation mapping (CAM) is a method of lesion identification based on channel attention, which is realized by projection from binary classification to spatial LAM. Through the classification weight optimized by the above standard classification loss, the feature units helpful for RP classification are given a larger weight, while other unrelated feature units have a smaller weight. As shown in Fig. 3, the feature maps of all units are aggregated into a single LAM by the weighted sum function (WSF). Let $M(x, y)$ denote the LAM, which can be expressed as:

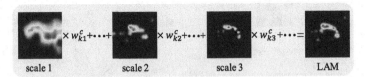

Fig. 3. The weighted sum function (WSF) for LAM. The three scale unit has been resized to the same size, and the weight is trained by the classifier.

$$M(x, y) = \sum_i \sum_k w_{ki}^c f_{ki}(x, y), \tag{3}$$

three features with different semantic information and spatial information are aggregated to generate a more accurate LAM.

2.2 Consistency Regularization

An ideal LAM should cover all lesions, although MS-GAP is used to offset the gap between deep semantic information and spatial location, LAM is difficult to cover all lesions due to the gap between weakly-supervision and fully-supervision. To solve this problem, inspired by [12], we use consistency regularization to constrain the LAMs of the same sample with different affine transforms. By forcing them to produce consistent predictions, we can improve the feature learning ability. Besides, since the lesion area is located in the retina, the regularization of LAM can avoid the interference of eyelids and eyelashes for UWF images, which is conducive to network learning.

For given sample I, let I^o denote original image, and I^t denote transformed image. We use a set of random affine transforms to augment feature learning, these transforms including rescale, color distortion, flip, and erase. Note that, for the transform that will change the spatial position information, we will reverse the LAM to the original spatial position. We input a set of I^o and I^t into the network, and we use M^o and M^t to represent the LAM of the I^o and I^t, respectively. Then we calculate the distance between M^o and M^t to optimize the network. This regularization objective function is expressed as follows:

$$\mathcal{L}_{cr} = \sum MSE(M^o, M^t), \tag{4}$$

where MSE is defined as mean square error. Through this regularization loss, the learned features can cover more lesion areas and reduce the prediction of overconfidence so that more meaningful features can be learned.

Finally, combining the classification loss and the consistency regularization objective function, the whole network objective function can be expressed as follows:

$$\mathcal{L} = \mathcal{L}_{cls}^o + \mathcal{L}_{cls}^t + \mathcal{L}_{cr}, \tag{5}$$

where $\mathcal{L}_{cls}^o$ and $\mathcal{L}_{cls}^t$ denotes original image and transformed image classification loss respectively. The classification loss is used to learn discriminative targets, while the regularization loss is used to constrain the network to learn more lesions, which can improve the accuracy of LAM and generalization performance of the network.

3 Experiments

3.1 Dataset and Implementation

We use two center UWF data in our experiments. The first one was collected from a local hospital, including 473 RP images and 948 normal images which were captured via Optos. The original images are 2600×2048 high-resolution, which were captured from different patients registered with the hospital from 2016 to 2019. Two experts were engaged to label these images as normal and RP. We call it UWF-1 for short. The second one is a public dataset Masumoto [14, 15], which was collected from a Japanese hospital. It contains 150 RP images and 223 normal images. The original images are 3900×3072 high-resolution, where the images were collected between 2011 and 2017. We call it UWF-2 for shot.

To verify the generalization performance of the model, we divide UWF-1 dataset 50% for training and 50% for testing randomly, and the smaller dataset UWF-2 only used for test. We employ accuracy (Acc), precision (Pre), recall (Rec) and F1-score (F1) to evaluate the performance of the model on the test sets.

3.2 Lesion Attention Map Visualization

In this section, we display some visual LAMs. In CNN, the shallow features contain more geometric features and spatial information, while the deep features contain more semantic features and discriminant information. Figure 4 shows different levels of LAM and a multi-scale aggregated LAM. The first column in this figure is the lesion area roughly outlined by us, the second to fourth columns are the LAM generate by using the feature maps of layer 2, layer 3 and layer 4 respectively in the backbone network, and the last column is the multi-scale aggregated LAM.

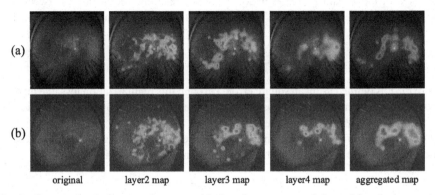

Fig. 4. Comparative lesion attention map with three layers map and the multi-scale aggregated map. (a) from UWF-1 test set and (b) from UWF-2.

It can be seen that due to the shallowness of layer 2, the output LAM does not focus on the lesion area well, but covers a large area of retina, which indicates that the characteristics of this layer have a lot of spatial structure information, while the LAMs of layer 3 and layer 4 have focused on the lesion area, but all focus on a part of the lesion area with discrimination. Therefore, the deeper the layer, the more focused the LAM is. In contrast, the multi-scale aggregated LAM covers more lesion areas and reduces the gap between deep semantic information and shallow spatial information, which is more accurate. Note that although the LAM of layer 2 does not focus on the lesion areas well, the aggregation of features at this level can fuse more spatial information and improve the robustness of the network, the quantitative experiments will be shown in the next section.

Due to the gap between weakly-supervision and full supervision with pixel-wise lesion mask, it is difficult to produce a very accurate LAM. Figure 5 shows the LAM generated by our consistent regularization and non-regularization. The first column is the lesion area we roughly outlined, the second column is the LAM generated without regularization, and the third column is the result with consistent regularization. It can be seen that the regularized LAM has a more uniform distribution and wider coverage in the lesion area, which indicates that the regularization can enforce the network to learn more lesion information and reduces the overconfidence prediction, so that more accurate lesion recognition can be produced.

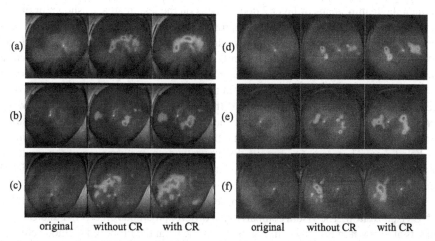

Fig. 5. Comparative LAM with and without used consistency regularization. (a)–(c) from UWF-1 test set and (d)–(f) from UWF-2.

3.3 Classification Performance

The classification performance of different methods is reported in Table 1. In this paper, we chose three basic models, ResNet50 [13], VGG16 [16] and InceptionV3 [17], as the comparison methods. These models contain the characteristics of deep networks, hence they are suitable for the research benchmark.

Table 1. Classification performance of different methods (%).

Method	UWF-1				UWF-2			
	Acc	Pre	Rec	F1	Acc	Pre	Rec	F1
VGG16	95.21	99.70	86.10	92.24	89.54	98.26	75.33	85.28
InceptionV3	95.92	99.52	88.14	93.48	90.35	98.80	77.20	86.36
ResNet50	95.63	99.80	86.86	92.97	92.23	89.54	91.33	90.43
Ours (3GAP)	96.34	92.68	96.61	94.61	92.49	87.65	94.64	91.03
Ours (2GAP+CR)	98.31	99.56	95.34	97.40	94.64	93.92	92.67	93.29
Ours (3GAP+CR)	98.73	99.56	96.61	98.06	95.17	95.21	92.67	93.92

To quantitatively evaluate the performance of the model, we compare the effects of regularization and MS-GAP on the classification performance of the model. 3GAP and 2GAP in Table 1 represent feature aggregation of three and two scales respectively, and CR represents consistent regularization. It can be seen from the last two rows in Table 1 that the performance of feature aggregation using three scales is close to that of two scales, but the former is a little better than the latter in UWF-2. We think that although the feature maps of layer 2 do not focus on the lesion area, as shown in Fig. 4, but the robustness of the model can be improved by fusing its spatial information. From the comparison between the last two rows in Table 1 and the previous methods, it can be seen that the classification accuracy in UWF-1 is improved by 2–3%, while that in UWF-2 is improved by 2–5%. It shows that regularization has a great positive impact on the performance of the model, especially in improving the generalization performance. Because the two datasets come from two different regions, and the differences between them, i.e. image resolution, illumination conditions and so on, hinder the generalization performance of the model. However, traditional supervised learning needs a large number of labeled data. Therefore, to improve the generalization performance of the model in the training with a small amount of data, it is very important to integrate additional regularization.

To evaluate the superiority of the proposed method more intuitively, we conduct the t-SNE visualization. The visual comparison of different methods on UWF-1 and UWF-2 datasets are shown in Fig. 6. From Fig. 6, we can see that the proposed method achieves quite good detection performance on the two datasets, the RP and normal images can be split well.

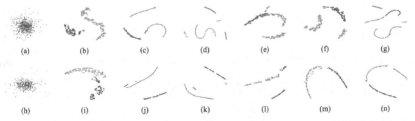

Fig. 6. The t-SNE visualization of different methods on UWF-1 test set and UWF-2. (a) and (h) indicates the original distribution of the UWF-1 and UWF-2 dataset, respectively. (b)–(g) and (i)–(n) represent the results of Table 1 six methods in two datasets, respectively.

4   Conclusion

We propose a method based on weakly-supervised lesion-aware and consistent regularization for the diagnosis of RP and generating LAM. We extend the global average pooling to multiple scales and use multi-scale feature aggregation to offset the gap between deep semantic information and spatial information, so that more detailed LAM can be generated. At the same time, we conduct consistency regularization constraints on different affine transforms of the same sample to force them to learn more lesion information, so as to reduce the prediction of overconfidence. The experimental results demonstrate that our method has better classification performance and better generation ability of the LAM.

Acknowledgements. This work was supported partly by National Natural Science Foundation of China (Nos. 61871274, 61801305 and 81571758), National Natural Science Foundation of Guangdong Province (No. 2020A1515010649 and No. 2019A1515 111205), Guangdong Province Key Laboratory of Popular High Performance Computers (No. 2017B030314073), Guangdong Laboratory of Artificial-Intelligence and Cyber-Economics (SZ), Shenzhen Peacock Plan (Nos. KQTD2016053112051497 and KQTD2015033016104926), Shenzhen Key Basic Research Project (Nos. JCYJ201908 08165209410, 20190808145011259, JCYJ20180507184647636, GJHZ20190822095 414576 and JCYJ20170302153337765, JCYJ20170302150411789, JCYJ2017030214 2515949, GCZX2017040715180580, GJHZ20180418190529516, and JSGG2018050 7183215520), NTUT-SZU Joint Research Program (No. 2020003), Special Project in Key Areas of Ordinary Universities of Guangdong Province (No. 2019KZDZX1015).

References

1. Hartong, D.T., Berson, E.L., Dryja, T.P.: Retinitis pigmentosa. Lancet **368**, 1795–1809 (2006)
2. Cicinelli, M.V., Marchese, A., Bordato, A., Manitto, M.P., Bandello, F., Parodi, M.B.: Reviewing the role of ultra-widefield imaging in inherited retinal dystrophies. Ophthalmol. Ther. 1–15 (2020)
3. Olthoff, C.M., Schouten, J.S., van de Borne, B.W., Webers, C.A.: Noncompliance with ocular hypotensive treatment in patients with glaucoma or ocular hypertension: an evidence-based review. Ophthalmology **112**, 953–961, e957 (2005)
4. Nagasato, D., et al.: Hayashi: deep neural network-based method for detecting central retinal vein occlusion using ultrawide-field fundus ophthalmoscopy. J. Ophthalmol. **2018** (2018)
5. Masumoto, H., et al.: Accuracy of a deep convolutional neural network in detection of retinitis pigmentosa on ultrawide-field images. PeerJ **7**, e6900 (2019)
6. Litjens, G., et al.: A survey on deep learning in medical image analysis. Med. Image Anal. **42**, 60–88 (2017)
7. Liao, W., Zou, B., Zhao, R., Chen, Y., He, Z., Zhou, M.: Clinical interpretable deep learning model for glaucoma diagnosis. IEEE J. Biomed. Health Inform. **24**, 1405–1412 (2019)
8. Wang, Z., Yin, Y., Shi, J., Fang, W., Li, H., Wang, X.: Zoom-in-net: deep mining lesions for diabetic retinopathy detection. In: Descoteaux, M., Maier-Hein, L., Franz, A., Jannin, P., Collins, D.L., Duchesne, S. (eds.) MICCAI 2017. LNCS, vol. 10435, pp. 267–275. Springer, Cham (2017). https://doi.org/10.1007/978-3-319-66179-7_31
9. Zhao, R., Liao, W., Zou, B., Chen, Z., Li, S.: Weakly-supervised simultaneous evidence identification and segmentation for automated glaucoma diagnosis. In: AAAI, pp. 809–816 (2019)
10. Zhou, B., Khosla, A., Lapedriza, A., Oliva, A., Torralba, A.: Learning deep features for discriminative localization. In: CVPR, pp. 2921–2929 (2016)
11. Tang, M., Perazzi, F., Djelouah, A., Ayed, I.B., Schroers, C., Boykov, Y.: On Regularized losses for weakly-supervised CNN segmentation. In: Ferrari, V., Hebert, M., Sminchisescu, C., Weiss, Y. (eds.) ECCV 2018. LNCS, vol. 11220, pp. 524–540. Springer, Cham (2018). https://doi.org/10.1007/978-3-030-01270-0_31
12. Wang, Y., Zhang, J., Kan, M., Shan, S., Chen, X.: Self-supervised equivariant attention mechanism for weakly supervised semantic segmentation. In: CVPR, pp. 12275–12284 (2020)

13. He, K., Zhang, X., Ren, S., Sun, J.: Deep residual learning for image recognition. In: CVPR, pp. 770–778 (2016)
14. Masahiro, K.: masumoto RP data normal optos (2018). https://figshare.com/articles/mas umoto_RP_data_normal_optos/7403825
15. Masahiro, K.: masumoto RP data RP optos (2018). https://figshare.com/articles/masumoto_ RP_data_RP_optos/7403831
16. Simonyan, K., Zisserman, A.: Very deep convolutional networks for large-scale image recognition. In: ICLR (2015)
17. Szegedy, C., Vanhoucke, V., Ioffe, S., Shlens, J., Wojna, Z.: Rethinking the inception architecture for computer vision. In: CVPR, pp. 2818–2826 (2016)

A Conditional Generative Adversarial Network-Based Method for Eye Fundus Image Quality Enhancement

Andrés D. Pérez[1]([✉]) [iD], Oscar Perdomo[2] [iD], Hernán Rios[3] [iD],
Francisco Rodríguez[3] [iD], and Fabio A. González[1] [iD]

[1] MindLab Research Group, Universidad Nacional de Colombia, Bogotá, Colombia
{anperezpe,fagonzalezo}@unal.edu.co
[2] Universidad del Rosario, Bogotá, Colombia
oscarj.perdomo@urosario.edu.co
[3] Fundación Oftalmológica Nacional, Bogotá, Colombia
hernanandresrios@gmail.com, fjrodriguez@fon.org.co

Abstract. Eye fundus image quality represents a significant factor involved in ophthalmic screening. Usually, eye fundus image quality is affected by artefacts, brightness, and contrast hindering ophthalmic diagnosis. This paper presents a conditional generative adversarial network-based method to enhance eye fundus image quality, which is trained using automatically generated synthetic bad-quality/good-quality image pairs. The method was evaluated in a public eye fundus dataset with three classes: good, usable and bad quality according to specialist annotations with 0.64 Kappa. The proposed method enhanced the image quality from usable to good class in 72.33% of images. Likewise, the image quality was improved from the bad category to usable class, and from bad to good class in 56.21% and 29.49% respectively.

Keywords: Image quality enhancement · Synthetic quality degradation · Eye fundus image · Conditional generative adversarial network

1 Introduction

Deep learning models used for eye screening based on eye fundus images have obtained outstanding results in the classification of retinal diseases, such as Diabetic Retinopathy (DR), Diabetic Macular Edema (DME) and Age-Related Macular Degeneration (AMD) among others [1].

These models have improved the prognosis of ocular diseases, increasing the number of early and proper treatments positively impacting in people's life quality [2]. For that reason, the need to ensure optimal working conditions in the screening facilities, and medical devices is mandatory. However, acquisition devices often are affected by external factors such as found noise, blurring, missed focus, illumination, and contrast issues hindering the detection by experts.

© Springer Nature Switzerland AG 2020
H. Fu et al. (Eds.): OMIA 2020, LNCS 12069, pp. 185–194, 2020.
https://doi.org/10.1007/978-3-030-63419-3_19

The mishandling of these factors affects the ability of experts and deep learning models performance [3,4]. Some works have been previously addressed these issues offering enhancement or adjustment methods in order to improve the available data to guarantee the specialist diagnosis. Sahu et al. [3] proposed a noise removal and contrast enhancement method based on contrast limited adaptative histogram equalization (CLAHE). Singh et al. [5] described the use of median filters with Histogram Equalization (HE) and CLAHE use with curvelet transform for image enhancement in segmentation tasks. Bandara et al. [6] presented an enhancement technique based in a Coye [7] algorithm variant improved with a Hough line transform that is based on vessel reconstruction. Raja et al. [8] explains the use of multi-directional local histogram equalization. Wahid et al. [9] explained the combination of fuzzy logic and histogram-based enhancement algorithm with CLAHE for eye fundus visual quality enhancement. Finally, Zhou et al. [4] detailed a two steps method for eye fundus quality enhancement based on a color gain matrix with gamma correction factor adjustment and an L channel CLAHE implementation.

Recently, different deep learning techniques for quality enhancement of natural images have been proposed. In particular, Yang et al. [10] developed a Multi-Frame Convolutional Neural Network (MF-CNN) to enhance the quality of the compressed video. Vu et al. [11] exposes a convolutional neural network for image quality enhancement which also can be trained for super-resolution imaging. One of the most popular networks for image reconstruction and image generation, due to its versatility and adaptability to different tasks, is the Pix2Pix model proposed by Isola et al. [12]. This method consists of a Conditional Generative Adversarial Network (cGAN) that generates new samples from a pre-establish (conditional) condition provided during its training. With regards to eye fundus quality enhancement, one of the newest and relevant work is the proposed by Yoo et al. [13]. This method is based on cycleGANs that provides a solution for quality enhancement without the need of paired images (good and bad quality) which is difficult to find in a common medical environment.

This article presents a method called Pix2Pix-Fundus Oculi Quality Enhancer (P2P-FOQE) for eye fundus image quality enhancement. Our method combines a Pix2Pix model [12] with a pre-enhancement [4] and a post-enhancement stage [14]. The method achieves a generalized fundus oculi enhancement without altering implicit image characteristics that could be interpreted as artifacts. This provides the possibility for practical usage in a real clinical setting.

The method was evaluated over a public eye fundus dataset with quality annotations from an ophthalmology specialist, enhancing the image quality, according to an automatic quality classifier, from usable to good class in 72.33% of the cases. Likewise, the image quality was improved from bad to usable class, and from bad to good class in 56.21% and 29.49%, respectively.

The remainder of the article is organized as follows: Sect. 2 explains in detail the proposed method. Section 3 shows the experimental evaluation of the method including the evaluation dataset, the experimental setup, the results and discussion. Finally, Sect. 4 reports the main conclusions and future works.

2   Pix2Pix-Fundus Oculi Quality Enhancer (P2P-FOQE)

Figure 1 shows the overall pipeline of the proposed method for eye fundus image quality enhancement. P2P-FOQE has three sequential stages. The first stage deals with the image resizing and luminosity-contrast adjustment. The second stage handles the core image enhancement. Finally, the third stage applies a CLAHE transformation for limited contrast adjustment. The following subsections discuss the details of the three stages.

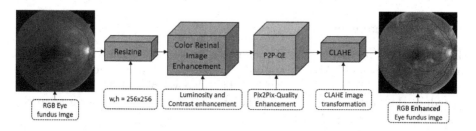

Fig. 1. Box diagram for our proposed P2P-FOQE. Stage 1) Pre-enhancement; Stage 2) Pix2Pix Enhancement; Stage 3) Post-enhancement

2.1   Pre-enhancement

This stage receives a resized color fundus image to a resolution of $256 \times 256 \times 3$ keeping its aspect ratio. Then, the image pre-enhancement is performed using our implementation from the color retinal image enhancement method presented by Zhou et al. [4]. First, the method focuses in luminosity enhancement, working over the value channel from the HSV color space representation together with a gamma correction to ensure the luminosity-channel independence generating a luminance gain matrix. In specific, that is applied over the original $R(x, y)$, $G(x, y)$ & $B(x, y)$ image components, obtaining the $r'(x, y)$, $g'(x, y)$ & $b'(x, y)$ luminosity enhanced. Then, the second step enhance the contrast, by applying a CLAHE transformation over the L channel from a LAB color space by obtaining a new splitted channel representation designated as follows: $r''(x, y)$, $g''(x, y)$ & $b''(x, y)$. Finally, these arrays are stacked into one single array obtaining a final pre-enhanced image shape of $256 \times 256 \times 3$. This pre-enhanced image is used as input for the P2P-FOQE model which consists of a Pix2Pix architecture.

2.2   Pix2Pix Enhancement

Pix2Pix is one of the most widely used deep learning models in the last years. It has been used for synthesizing photos from label maps, colorizing images and reconstructing objects from diverse representations, among others. The Pix2Pix model was used for eye-fundus image enhancement by mapping good quality features from good quality images to bad quality images. In this process, a quality enhanced representation is transferred from one image to a bad quality image. The architecture is summarized in two blocks: the conditional GAN Generator (G) is constituted by a modified U-Net following skip connections, helping the generator to avoid the information bottleneck. Then, the conditional GAN Discriminator (D) is a GAN termed as Patch-GAN which is based on patches scale, similar to obtain local styling. This Patch-GAN forces low-frequency correctness by the use of an L1 term to avoid noise such as blurring over the enhancement. At last, a discriminator output patch size of $30 \times 30 \times 1$ is obtained to classify a $70 \times 70 \times 1$ image portion aiming to produce the enhanced eye fundus image.

2.3   Post-enhancement

This final stage receives a partial enhanced fundus image with a $256 \times 256 \times 3$ resolution, where a CLAHE is applied through the RGB channels to limit its contrast amplification by a factor of 1.5 (this value was obtained in a grid search) to reduce the problem of noise-amplification commonly noticeable in adaptive histogram equalization (AHE).

2.4   Training the P2P-FOQE Model

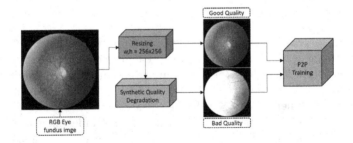

Fig. 2. Box diagram for training our proposed P2P-FOQE method

The training of P2P-FOQE model requires as input two eye fundus images from the patient's eye with good and bad quality as shown in Fig. 2. However, a free public data-sets of eye fundus images with these requirements is not available. Due to this limitation, it was devised a synthetic-quality-degradation strategy that generates bad quality versions of good quality images. The P2P-FOQE applies a set of transformations such as blurring and brightness at random levels to obtain a noisy/degraded versions of the original good quality images. Besides, random areas were cropped for fovea-decentering and an outer light halo was added to create synthetical bad quality images. Then, the Pix2Pix enhancement model is trained using the pair of images: the original image and the synthetically degraded image. One of the main advantages of this approach is the possible use of both private and public datasets from previous studies. In the same manner, the generation of a synthetic controlled representation helps to minimize the risk of overfitting caused by the imbalance between the generator and discriminator during training.

3 Experimental Evaluation

3.1 Dataset for Eye Fundus Image Quality Enhancement

Kaggle dataset[1] provides a set of 88702 real-world eye fundus images with diverse resolutions and pathologies. In particular, the Kaggle dataset contains varied image quality features (such as luminance, contrast, and artifacts, among others). Fu et al. [15] defined three classes to evaluate the quality in this dataset (good, usable and bad). However, for this study the image quality is defined according to the compliance of specific characteristics with a more stringent criterion using the same three categories explained in details as follows:

- Good: Optimal quality, focus on the foveal region and optic nerve, regular illumination of the entire field, with full presence of the optic nerve and macula, with the presence of the entire route the temporal arches at the macular level. Without the presence of artifacts.
- Usable: Non-optimal quality, focus on the foveal region and optic nerve, irregular illumination of the entire field, with full presence of the optic nerve and macula, with the presence of at least 3/4 parts of the route the temporal arches at the macular level. It may have few artifacts that are not or confused with real injuries.
- Bad: Poor quality, there is no focus on the foveal or optic nerve regions, irregular illumination, with the incomplete presence of the optic nerve or macula, with the presence of less than 3/4 parts of the temporal arches at the macular level. The significant presence of artifacts that avoid to evaluate the macular region or optic nerve, or artifacts that simulate retinal lesions.

From the Kaggle dataset with Fu et al. criterion, were randomly selected 1876 images per quality category which were reviewed and re-classified (according to our classification criterion) as follows: 927-good, 1890-usable and 2811-bad by an ophthalmology specialist. When comparing the new labels to the ones provided by Fu et al. the level of coincidence obtained, using Kappa measure, was 0.64.

The color fundus images are resized to a resolution of 256×256 pixels keeping its aspect ratio both to feed the Pix2Pix model and speed-up the training process. Images were transformed applying different quality degradation transformations: blurring, brightness, fovea-centering (randomly applied during the training), light halo and a mixture of these previous transformations as presented in Fig. 3. This process produced a synthetic dataset of paired good-bad quality images with 927 images per category which was randomly subsampled and divided into training and validation sets in a 80-20%-near ratio.

---

[1] https://www.kaggle.com/c/diabetic-retinopathy-detection.

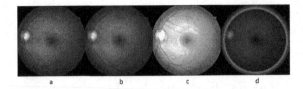

Fig. 3. Synthetic quality degradation samples comparison. a) Original image. b) Blurring degradation. c) Brightness degradation. d) Mixing of blurring, brightness and halo light

3.2 Experimental Setup

The Pix2Pix model was trained during 250 epochs using an Adam optimizer for generator and discriminator with a learning rate of $2e^{-4}$ and with a momentum of 0.5 and 0.999 for $beta_1$ and $beta_2$ respectively. This training was done using a Nvidia GeForce RTX 2070 Super with a runtime of approximately of 9.02 h.

The quality of enhanced images was assessed using two quality evaluation/classification baselines. The first one, is a quality classifier method termed MFQ-Net by Pérez et al. [16] which was trained with images labeled with the new ophthalmology specialist criteria, to estimate the quality of an input eye fundus image. This model classifies an image into three categories: bad, usable and good. Besides, the quality of generated images was evaluated using the Automatic Quality Evaluation (AQE) method proposed by Bartling et al. [17] which focuses in sharpness and illuminance classifying the quality in four categories: very good, good, acceptable and not-acceptable.

3.3 Results and Discussion

The whole dataset reported in Sect. 3 was enhanced using our proposed method (P2P-FOQE) and six enhancement state-of-the-art methods such as CLAHE with 1.5 clip limit [14], color gain matrix with gamma correction factor adjustment and an L channel-CLAHE (L-CLAHE) by Zhou et al. [4], Pix2Pix enhancement by Isola et al. [12], cycleGANs enhancement by Yoo et al. [13], and combinations of channel-CLAHE plus Pix2Pix, and Pix2Pix plus CLAHE. Then, seven new data sets of images were generated with the application of the previous enhancement methods. The illustration over a sample image for these enhancements is shown in Fig. 4.

The generated seven data sets were evaluated using the MFQ-Net trained according to ophthalmologist criteria and, the AQE method that classifies according to sharpness and illuminance criteria as explained in detail in Sect. 3.

The quality classification results obtained using the MFQ-Net on the seven enhanced data sets and the image dataset without enhancement (Non-enhance) are summarized in Table 1. This table contains the percentage of samples for each original category: Original-Good (OG), Original-Usable (OU), and Original-Bad (OB), and the classification into three subcategories according to

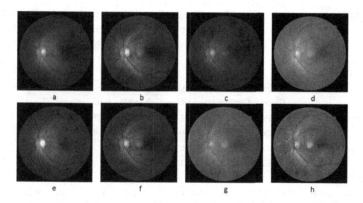

Fig. 4. Illustration of different enhancement methods over the same image. a) Original color fundus image; b) CLAHE; c) color gain matrix with gamma correction and CLAHE; d) Pix2Pix; e) cycleGANs; f) Channel-CLAHE with Pix2Pix; g) Pix2Pix with CLAHE; and h) P2P-FOQE proposed method.

the re-classification given by the classifier. The first row corresponding to the no-enhance method, where the OG images were reclassified by the MFQ-Net classifier in 84.79%, 14.89%, and 0.32% for good, usable, and bad categories respectively. The OU images were reclassified in 14.18%, 75.03%, and 10.79%, for good, usable, and bad categories respectively. Finally, the OB images were reclassified in 0.85%, 11.99%, and 87.13%, for good, usable, and bad categories respectively. The enhancement obtained with the P2P-FOQE method was the highest for Good label into the three main categories as reported in Table 1. Moreover, the P2P-FOQE method outperforms the quality classification results of non-enhance and state-of-the-art methods in OU and OB categories with percentages of 72.33% and 29.49% respectively, compared to the non-enhance method with 14.18% and 0.85% for OU and OB categories respectively, Pix2Pix + CLAHE method for OU category of 66.77% and, cycleGANs method [13] in OB category of 23.94% as reported in Table 1.

The classification results obtained using the AQE method on the seven enhanced data sets and the image dataset without enhancement are presented in Table 2. Unlike the Table 1, the Table 2 contains four sub-categories: Very Good (VG), Good (G), Acceptable (A), and Not-Acceptable (NA), for each category according to AQE criteria as presented in the Subsect. 3.2. The first row corresponding to the non-enhance method, where the OG images were reclassified by the AQE classifier in 0.22%, 9.06%, 85.87%, and 0.00% for VG, G, A and NA categories respectively. The OU images were reclassified in 0.00%, 3.28%, 74.02%, and 22.70% for VG, G, A and NA categories respectively. Finally, the OB images were reclassified in 0.00%, 0.39%, 35.75%, and 63.86% for VG, G, A and NA categories respectively.

The P2P-FOQE method had an outstanding performance in the quality classification of VG and G classes compared to non-enhance and state-of-the-art

Table 1. MFQ-Net evaluation results and enhancement methods comparison. OG, OU and OB refers to the original Good, Usable and Bad categories respectively. Each original category is subdivided into new classification. In bold, the two highest percentages for each good subcategory.

Method	OG			OU			OB		
	Good	Usable	Bad	Good	Usable	Bad	Good	Usable	Bad
Non-enhance	84.79	14.89	0.32	14.18	75.03	10.79	0.85	11.99	87.16
CLAHE [14]	**98.06**	1.94	0.00	64.44	33.92	1.64	12.20	32.23	55.57
L-CLAHE [4]	89.97	10.03	0.00	25.61	69.15	5.24	4.41	31.95	63.96
Pix2Pix [12]	77.02	22.22	0.76	13.97	74.13	11.90	0.92	18.43	80.65
L-CLAHE + Pix2Pix	85.44	14.56	0.00	24.60	70.95	4.44	3.91	41.66	54.43
Pix2Pix + CLAHE	97.95	2.05	0.00	**66.77**	32.17	1.06	18.25	40.66	41.09
cycleGANs [13]	88.46	11.43	0.11	47.78	50.79	1.43	**23.94**	61.86	14.19
P2P-FOQE	**98.06**	1.94	0.00	**72.33**	27.41	0.26	**29.49**	56.21	14.30

methods in OU and OB categories. Besides, the proposed method presented the best results in VG and G classes in OB category and, the lowest percentages of NA class in the three categories as presented in Table 2.

Table 2. AQE evaluation results and enhancement methods comparison. OG, OU and OB refers to the original Good, Usable and Bad categories respectively. Each original category is subdivided into new classification. In bold, the two highest percentages for VG and G subcategories.

Method	OG				OU				OB			
	VG	G	A	NA	VG	G	A	NA	VG	G	A	NA
Non-enhance	0.22	9.06	85.87	4.85	0.00	3.28	74.02	22.70	0.00	0.39	35.75	63.86
CLAHE [14]	**48.87**	48.65	2.48	0.00	**26.83**	57.25	15.71	0.21	2.13	**25.86**	51.01	20.99
L-CLAHE [4]	0.11	25.03	74.33	0.54	0.00	9.79	77.30	12.91	0.18	3.45	59.84	36.54
Pix2Pix [12]	0.00	0.76	80.04	19.20	0.00	0.26	54.97	44.76	0.00	0.07	17.47	82.46
L-CLAHE + Pix2Pix	0.00	2.59	91.80	5.61	0.00	0.69	74.50	24.81	0.07	0.28	45.89	53.75
Pix2Pix + CLAHE	19.96	**70.77**	9.28	0.00	8.15	**63.97**	27.62	0.26	0.39	20.38	65.07	14.16
cycleGANs [13]	7.01	16.40	73.79	2.80	8.15	32.38	56.40	3.07	**3.59**	21.10	55.96	19.35
P2P-FOQE	**37.65**	**60.52**	1.83	0.00	**21.06**	**72.22**	6.67	0.05	**6.30**	**68.23**	25.15	0.32

The whole enhanced image data set obtained with our P2P-FOQE method was qualitatively evaluated by expert. The expert found that the proposed method enhanced some features in the color fundus images as depicted in Fig. 5. In particular, (a-b center) images generated patterns that looks like intraretinal hemorrhages and the vessels have irregular walls with interrupted paths. However, our proposed method (a-b right) presented hypopigmented findings accentuated and the neuroretinal ring is better preserved. Moreover, the fundus image (c-center) produced a notorious black spot that could be diagnosed as melanoma-like lesion (cancer of the choroid) in comparison with the enhanced image obtained by our method that attenuates the black spot (c-right).

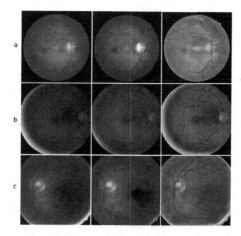

Fig. 5. [Left] Color fundus images; [Center] enhanced images using cycleGANs [13] and, [Right] enhanced images using P2P-FOQE proposed method.

4 Conclusions

This paper presented a deep learning method-based on a Pix2Pix model, termed P2P-FOQE, for enhancing the quality of eye fundus images. The obtained Kappa coefficient in conjunction with the results obtained, presents a more stringent evaluation criterion by the specialist (compared against the Fu et al. quality criterion) which helps both the study and the model to produce a higher performance and robustness. The comparison review reveals that while L-CLAHE + Pix2Pix is close to producing a detailed image, noise-controlling provided by CLAHE at near-constant regions of the image is required. Also, the complexity of the problem is so great due to the great amount of factors involved in such a way that to solve this problem a joint solution is required that is capable of attacking each one of these factors. Even though the cycleGANs method does not require paired images (good-bad quality), it is clear that our proposed method is superior, minimizing the negative impact of the images and preserving their important qualities for proper diagnosis. The future work includes the exploration of newer generative models, deep super-resolution methods and different strategies to integrate them in the current model.

References

1. Perdomo, O., González, F.A.: A systematic review of deep learning methods applied to ocular images. Cienc. Ing. Neogranad **30**(1) (2016). https://doi.org/10.18359/rcin.4242
2. Gharaibeh, N., Al-Hazaimeh, O.M., Al-Naami, B., Nahar, K.M.: An effective image processing method for detection of diabetic retinopathy diseases from retinal fundus images. IJSISE **11**(4), 206–216. (2018). IEL. https://doi.org/10.1504/IJSISE.2018.093825

3. Sahu, S., Singh, A.K., Ghrera, S.P., Elhoseny, M.: An approach for de-noising and contrast enhancement of retinal fundus image using CLAHE. Opt. Laser Technol. **110**, 87–98 (2019). https://doi.org/10.1016/j.optlastec.2018.06.061

4. Zhou, M., Jin, K., Wang, S., Ye, J., Qian, D.: Color retinal image enhancement based on luminosity and contrast adjustment. IEEE Trans. Biomed. Eng. **65**(3), 521–527 (2017). https://doi.org/10.1109/TBME.2017.2700627

5. Singh, B., Jayasree, K.: Implementation of diabetic retinopathy detection system for enhance digital fundus images. IJATIR **7**(6), 874–876 (2015)

6. Bandara, A.M.R.R., Giragama, P.W.G.R.M.P.B.: A retinal image enhancement technique for blood vessel segmentation algorithm. ICIIS 1–5 (2017). https://doi.org/10.1109/ICIINFS.2017.8300426

7. Coye, T.: A novel retinal blood vessel segmentation algorithm for fundus images. In: MATLAB Central File Exchange, January 2017 (2015)

8. Raja, S.S., Vasuki, S.: Screening diabetic retinopathy in developing countries using retinal images. Appl. Med. Inform. **36**(1), 13–22 (2015)

9. Wahid, F.F., Sugandhi, K., Raju, G.: Two stage histogram enhancement schemes to improve visual quality of fundus images. In: Singh, M., Gupta, P.K., Tyagi, V., Flusser, J., Ören, T. (eds.) ICACDS 2018. CCIS, vol. 905, pp. 1–11. Springer, Singapore (2018). https://doi.org/10.1007/978-981-13-1810-8_1

10. Yang, R., Xu, M., Wang, Z., Li, T.: Multi-frame quality enhancement for compressed video. In: Proceedings of the IEEE Conference on Computer Vision and Pattern Recognition (CVPR), Salt Lake City, UT, USA, pp. 6664–6673 (2018). https://doi.org/10.1109/CVPR.2018.00697

11. Vu, T., Nguyen, C.V., Pham, T.X., Luu, T.M., Yoo, C.D.: Fast and efficient image quality enhancement via desubpixel convolutional neural networks. In: Leal-Taixé, L., Roth, S. (eds.) ECCV 2018. LNCS, vol. 11133, pp. 243–259. Springer, Cham (2019). https://doi.org/10.1007/978-3-030-11021-5_16

12. Isola, P., Zhu, J.Y., Zhou, T., Efros, A.A.: Image-to-image translation with conditional adversarial networks. In: Proceedings of the IEEE Conference on Computer Vision and Pattern Recognition, pp. 1125–1134 (2017). https://doi.org/10.1109/CVPR.2017.632

13. Yoo, T.K., Choi, J.Y., Kim, H.K.: CycleGAN-based deep learning technique for artifact reduction in fundus photography. Graefes Arch. Clin. Exp. Ophthalmol. **258**(8), 1631–1637 (2020). https://doi.org/10.1007/s00417-020-04709-5

14. Zuiderveld, K.: Contrast limited adaptive histogram equalization. In: Graphics Gems, pp. 474–485, Academic Press (1994)

15. Fu, H., et al.: Evaluation of retinal image quality assessment networks in different color-spaces. In: Shen, D., et al. (eds.) MICCAI 2019. LNCS, vol. 11764, pp. 48–56. Springer, Cham (2019). https://doi.org/10.1007/978-3-030-32239-7_6

16. Pérez, A.D., Perdomo, O., González, F.A.: A lightweight deep learning model for mobile eye fundus image quality assessment. In: Proceedings of SPIE 11330, 15th International Symposium on Medical Information Processing and Analysis (SIPAIM) (2020). https://doi.org/10.1117/12.2547126

17. Bartling, H., Wanger, P., Martin, L.: Automated quality evaluation of digital fundus photographs. Acta Ophthalmol. **87**(6), 643–647 (2009). https://doi.org/10.1111/j.1755-3768.2008.01321.x

Construction of Quantitative Indexes for Cataract Surgery Evaluation Based on Deep Learning

Yuanyuan Gu[1], Yan Hu[2(✉)], Lei Mou[1], HuaYing Hao[1], Yitian Zhao[1], Ce Zheng[3(✉)], and Jiang Liu[1,2]

[1] Cixi Institute of Biomedical Engineering, Ningbo Institute of Materials Technology and Engineering, Chinese Academy of Sciences, Ningbo, China
[2] Department of Computer Science and Engineering, Southern University of Science and Technology, Shenzhen, China
huy3@sustech.edu.cn
[3] Department of Ophthalmology, Shanghai Children's Hospital, Shanghai Jiao Tong University, Shanghai, China
zhengce@me.com

Abstract. Objective and accurate evaluation of cataract surgery is a necessary way to improve the operative level of resident and shorten the learning curve. Our objective in this study is to construct quantifiable evaluation indicators through deep learning techniques to assist experts in the implementation of evaluation and verify the reliability of the evaluation indicators. We use a data set of 98 videos of incision, which is a critical step in cataract surgery. According to the visual characteristics of incision evaluation indicators specified in the International Council of Ophthalmology's Ophthalmology Surgical Competency Assessment Rubric: phacoemulsification (ICO-OSCAR: phaco), we propose using the ResNet and ResUnet to obtain the keratome tip position and the pupil shape to construct the quantifiable evaluation indexes, such as the tool trajectory, the size and shape of incision, and the scaling of a pupil. Referring to the motion of microscope and eye movement caused by keratome pushing during the video recording, we use the center of the pupil as a reference point to calculate the exact relative motion trajectory of the surgical instrument and the incision size, which can be used to directly evaluate surgical skill. The experiment shows that the evaluation indexes we constructed have high accuracy, which is highly consistent with the evaluation of the expert surgeons group.

Keywords: Cataract surgery assessment · Deep learning

1 Introduction

Cataract is the most common cause of vision loss and blindness in the world, and the number of cataract-caused blind people will reach 40 million in 2025 [1].

© Springer Nature Switzerland AG 2020
H. Fu et al. (Eds.): OMIA 2020, LNCS 12069, pp. 195–205, 2020.
https://doi.org/10.1007/978-3-030-63419-3_20

Surgical removal of the cataract remains the only effective treatment available to restore or maintain vision. Given the growing incidence of cataracts, learning to perform cataract surgery with a lower complication rate is a universal and essential aspect of residency surgical training in ophthalmology [10]. The technique of cataract surgery is associated with a significant learning curve and complication rates in surgery are affected by the experience and surgical skills of the surgeon [6]. Many residency programs are looking for ways to improve their surgical training, which include better assessment of surgical performance, identification of patient risk factors, surgical simulators, and structured curriculum.

To improve surgical training, the Accreditation Council for Graduate Medical Education (ACGME) has recently put forth 6 core competencies to assess the achievement of a certain level of competency during residency. The first two ACGME milestones for cataract surgery are described as follows: at level 1, the resident can describe indications for surgery, at level 2, the resident can perform selected portions of surgery including wound creation and microsurgical suturing [8]. To facilitate assessment and teaching of surgical skill, the ICO-OSCAR: phaco for ophthalmic surgery [11]. Surgical procedures are broken down into individual steps and each step is graded on a scale of the novice, beginner, advanced beginner and competent. Unfortunately, such assessments are subjectively and time-consuming. Automated algorithms, especially deep learning approach, may play a role in assessment trainee cataract surgery efficacy, in which it is critical to quantify surgical steps like wound creation objectively.

In recent years, extensive work has been carried out on the automatic evaluation of surgery skills [3,4,9]. The majority of existing evaluation methods focus on endoscopic surgery. For example, Jin et al. introduced an approach to automatically assess surgeon performance by tracking and analyzing tool movements in surgical videos, leveraging region-based convolutional neural networks [5]. However, there were few articles on the evaluation of cataract surgery, and they mainly focus on the capsulorhexis. Kim et al. separately modeled instrument trajectories and optical flow using temporal convolutional neural networks to predict a skill class(expert/novice) and score on each item for capsulorhexis in ICO-OSCAR: phaco [7]. However, this study only evaluated this step through the trajectory, movement rate, and movement direction of surgical instruments, but failed to achieve quantitative of multiple important indicators such as a cortical tear, resulting in low evaluation accuracy. Besides, due to the complexity of the surgical process scene, some indicators can only be reflected by sensors and tactile sensations, which are still difficult to achieve accurate automatic evaluation. Thus, we proposed to quantify the evaluation index in ICO-OSCAR: phaco through deep learning technology as key indexes to assist the comprehensive evaluation of doctors.

In this paper, we followed ACGME's milestones for cataract surgery and selected main wound incision as for the study object [13]. The use of sutureless self-sealing clear corneal main wound incisions has now become widely established in modern cataract surgery, like phacoemulsification, bimanual microincision cataract surgery. The unstable incision may cause severe clinical complications, such as anterior chamber instability, mechanical wound trauma, or

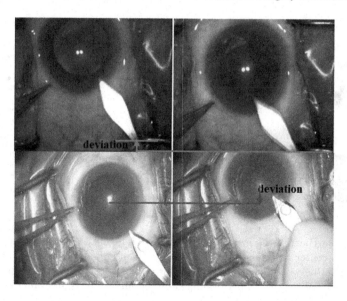

Fig. 1. Illustration of view field.

even endophthalmitis [14]. Thus, the accurate evaluation of cataract incision is of great clinical significance.

According to the ICO-OSCAR: phaco, we know that the assessment indexes of the incision mainly involve specific factors, such as the structure, location and size of the incision, anterior chamber leakage, and time. Referring to the motion of microscope and eye movement caused by keratome pushing during the video recording (Fig. 1), we propose using the deep learning network to obtain the keratome tip relative position and the pupil shape to construct the evaluation indexes, such as the relative trajectory, the size of the incision and the change of pupil scaling, so as to assist surgeons to realize the accurate evaluation of the incision. The deep learning networks used in this paper were ResNet [15] and ResUnet [16].

The major contributions of this work are summarized as follows: 1) We propose to obtain the keratome tip relative position and pupil shape to solve the problem of inaccurate evaluation indexes, which caused by a microscope or eye movement during video recording. 2) Through the visual features of the incision video, we construct objective and quantitative indexes for cataract surgery evaluation based on deep learning technology.

2   Proposed Method

In the following section, we describe our technical approach using deep learning networks (ResUnet and ResNet) to objectively assess surgical skills using intraoperative incision videos. Videos of incision provide us rich information, like a change of scene, action, and motion of surgeon. In our method, First, we

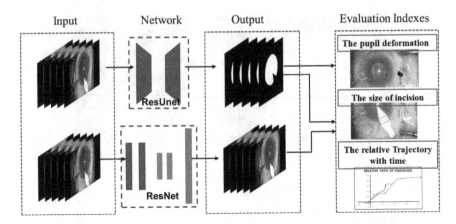

Fig. 2. The flowchart of the proposed method. We segment the pupil by ResUnet and calculated its center and axis length. The position of surgical instruments is located through ResNet network. Then, the above information is used to construct quantitative indicators to assist doctors in performing cataract surgery incision evaluation.

use the ResUnet model segmented the pupil, which is simulated as an ellipse to calculate the center point and the axis length. Second, based on the ResNet model we obtain the coordinates of the surgical tool tip through linear regression calculation, which is prepared for the construction of the motion trajectory and other evaluation indexes. As Table 1 shows we construct the corresponding relationship between evaluation indexes of ICO-OSCAR: phaco and the quantitative indexes we proposed.

Table 1. The corresponding relationship between the evaluation index constructed by us and ICO-OSCAR:phaco indexes

Assessment indexes of ICO-OSCAR:phaco	Proposed evaluation features
The structure of incision	The relative trajectory
The size of incision	The size data of incision
Leakage and/or iris prolapse	The axis length of pupil

Finally, we use the information obtained from the network model to construct evaluation indexes. Taking the center of the pupil as the reference point, the relative motion trajectory is drawn and the incision width is calculated. The change of axis length is used as an evaluation index of anterior chamber leakage. Figure 2 illustrates the overall flowchart of the evaluation method.

2.1   ResUnet for Pupil Segmentation

Precisely segmenting the pupil is a key procedure of the task. ResUnet combines strengths of both U-net and residual neural network, whose combination brings two benefits:1) the residual unit ease training of the network; 2) a neural network with few parameters can achieve comparable ever better performance on semantic segmentation. The ResUnet comprises three parts: encoding, bridge, and decoding. The first part extracts image feature information. The last part obtains the semantic segmentation. The bridge connects the encoding and decoding part. All of the three parts are built with residual units which consist of two $3 * 3$ convolution blocks and an identity mapping. In our work, the loss function is combined with the mean squared error (MSE) and Dice similarity coefficient (DSC), which gives better results for the pupil segmentation of cataract surgery images. The MSE between the label values and the predicted results, defined as:

$$MSE(y, y') = \frac{\sum_{i=1}^{n}(y - y')}{n} \tag{1}$$

where y and y' represent the labeled value and the predicted value of the model, respectively. The DSC is a set similarity measurement function, usually used to calculate the similarity of two samples (the value range is [0,1]). DSC defined as:

$$DSC(A, B) = \frac{2 \mid A \cap B \mid}{(\mid A \mid + \mid B \mid)} \tag{2}$$

where A and B represent the real results and predicted results respectively. When the value of DSC loss is closer to 1, the prediction result is more accurate in the network. Based on the segmented pupil shape, we fit the contour of the pupil as an ellipse to get the center and the axis length of the pupil.

2.2 Pretrained ResNet for Keratome Localization

To obtain the position information of the keratome tip, we propose using the pretrained ResNet model to locate the keratome. The ResNet is composed of Basicblocks, and different blocks have different convolution. In the output of each block, the residual network is used to add input information, which ensures the sufficiency of feature information. After experimental verification, the accuracy by ResNet (34) is higher than that by ResNet (50), so we choose the ResNet (34) to train the model and test samples. In the network structure, the loss function is MSE. During the test, to visualize the distance difference between the marker points (L_x, l_y) and the predict points (O_x, O_y), we defined the test loss as Eq. 3, which directly reflects the accuracy of the model:

$$D = \sqrt{(L_x - O_x)^2 + (L_y - O_y)^2} \tag{3}$$

where D is the distance of coordinate between the real point and the predicted point in pixel.

2.3 Constructing the Evaluation Indexes of Incision

In our method, the evaluation indexes of the incision are mainly composed of the operation time, the relative motion trajectory, the size, structure and location of the incision, and the scaling change of pupil. We subtract the coordinate of the pupil center from the coordinate of the keratome to obtain the relative coordinate of each frame, which is used to draw the tool relative trajectory. Besides, The keratome is always in motion. When make an incision, the keratome passed through the inside and outside of it. We calculate the width of the incision by calculating the distance between the coordinates of the keratome just after the internal incision and the coordinate of the starting point of the external incision. The above two evaluation indexes obtained by this method overcome the systematic errors caused by microscope movement and eye movement. Finally, we use the axis length obtained from Sect. 2.1 to quantify the scaling of a pupil as an indicator to judge anterior chamber leakage and/or iris prolapse.

3   Experiment Results

3.1   Dataset

Our dataset is comprised of 98 cataract videos from an operating microscope, collected by our cooperated surgeons. For our research, the incision procedure is cut from the whole operation video, and the time duration is from 15 s to 90 s, which is determined by the surgeons' proficiency. The frame rate is 25 fps, thus the dataset is enough for us to train the segmentation and localization model. In the task, we randomly pick out 8000 frames labeled with the keratome's point, and 2000 frames images labeled with pupil, whose labels are provided by the professional surgeon. We use 70% and 30% respectively for training and test.

3.2   Model Settings

The proposed model is implemented using the PyTorch framework and optimized through the Gradient regression algorithm, training and testing involved identical learning parameters and convolutional neural network settings for all the experiments. During ResUnet model training, there are 2000 images sized 1920×1080 available for training and testing. We start training the model with a mini-batch size of 6 on an NVIDIA Titan1080 GPU, with the learning rate at 0.0001 and 1000epochs. ResNet is set with 5 residual convolution modules, 2 pooling layers, and a fully connected layer. We train the model for 300 epochs, with a learning rate of 0.00001. The images, which are resized to 224×224, and the label file of the corresponding keratome location are the input of ResNet to train a model.

3.3   Result and Discussion

After 2000 epochs, we get a stable segmentation model, whose DSC is 0.967, which means the proximity between the segmented pupillary area and the real pupillary area. After that, the contour of the pupil is simulated as an ellipse, then compute its center point and axis length. Meanwhile, we get the results from the labeled ellipse. We calculate the standard deviation of the center point between the predicted and labeled ellipse with 4.93 pixels. The Fig. 3 shows the location of the predicted center, which is close enough to the real center of the pupil.

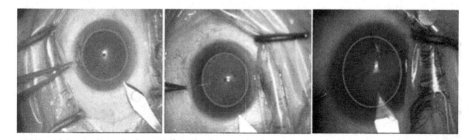

Fig. 3. Pupil segmentation results. The red ellipses are pupil edges, and green points are pupil centers. (Color figure online)

From the following images (Fig. 4) we can see the predicated tipping points of keratome. After 300 epochs, the positioning model shows excellent stability with the loss of 0.000042. The test result shows the standard deviation is 3.49 pixels, which means that the actual distance between marker coordinate and predict coordinate of tip point of a keratome is very small, which is acceptable for surgery assessment.

Fig. 4. Keratome localization results. The locations are marked by green crossess. (Color figure online)

It should be noted that we draw the trajectories before and after correction respectively with timing. In order to reflect the advantages of relative paths in the evaluation of surgical skills, we shift the absolute paths meaning uncorrected trajectories to around 0, and compared the motion tracks before and after correction in the same coordinate system. As can be seen from Fig. 5(b), the relative trajectories go into the second and the third quadrants, which means that the keratome passes through the center of the pupil and the keratome's wide edge enters the internal incision. Depending on the constant size of the keratome and pupil, from the above information, it can be determined that the shape of the incision formed is similar to a rectangle. Besides, we can judge whether the incision position is reasonable from the Angle between the starting point of the scalpel and the center of the pupil. The above information we can not be got from Fig. 5(a).

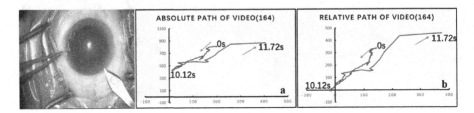

Fig. 5. The examples of relative and absolute tool trajectories. a: absolute tool trajectories; b: the relative tool trajectories

The size of the incision is an important indicator for evaluating whether the incision is appropriate. The width of the keratome in the video is 3 mm, and the clinical requirement is that the width-length ratio (W:L) of the incision should not be less than 2:3, which means that the actual incision width should not be less than 2 mm [2]. Only when the incision width is greater than or equal to 2 mm, it is clinically believed that a good path can be provided for the operation. Figure 6 shows the starting point of the external incision (a), the internal incision position (b), and the incision shape (c).

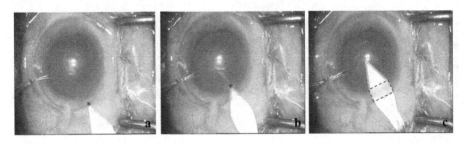

Fig. 6. a: The starting position of the external incision, b: Internal incision position, c: Incision shape

According to the ICO-OSCAR: phaco, anterior chamber stability, like no leakage and/or iris prolapse during surgery, is a key component to assess step of main wound incision. Therefore, we use pupil dynamics, like miosis or mydriasis, to monitor anterior chamber stability, as either anterior chamber leakage and/or iris prolapse can change pupil dynamics [12] from full mydriasis (fully dilation) to mid-dilated pupil or even miosis (fully constriction). Our previous clinical study had shown that length-axis reduces nearly 40% during pupil dynamics from mydriasis to miosis under physiological condition. Complete cataract surgery is usually performed within 20 min. After discussion with professional surgeons, we define warning feedback at 20% length-axis reduction in a continuous frame sequence, which indicated the pupil dynamics from mydriasis to mid-dilated pupil during main wound incision, and may indicate an anterior chamber leakage and/or iris prolapse. As can be seen from the Fig. 7 below, the axis length of the pupil in a continuous frame sequence is gradually decreasing, which means that there is a risk of anterior chamber leakage and/or iris prolapse in this operation.

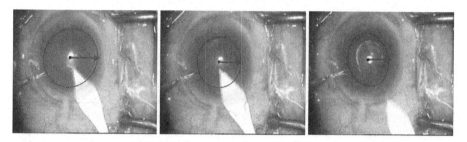

Fig. 7. An example of anterior chamber instability due to intraoperative complication. The blue arrows represent the pupil axis lengths which was suddenly shortens during the second and third image. (Color figure online)

Two surgeons, with more than 5,000 and 200 cataract surgeries experience respectively, rated seven cataract videos using the ICO-OSCAR: phaco. The video with inappropriate incision architecture, location, and size is awarded score 2, which we can judge by the relative trajectory and the size data of incision. The video of leakage and/or iris prolapse caused by local pressure is got score 3, and we can judge by the axis length of pupil. Incision either well-placed or non-leaking but not both are awarded score 4, which we can judge from the relative trajectory and the axis length of pupil. The video with appropriate incision size and well-placed, non-leakage and/or iris prolapse is got score 5. Based on the assessment indexes got from our method, we randomly select 7 videos, hiding the videos numbers, scrambling the sequence of the videos and their evaluation indexes, and then the doctors scored the videos and evaluation indexes respectively. Table 2 below shows that the evaluation results obtained by our method are highly consistent with the evaluation results of the expert group.

Table 2. Multiple comparisons of the same surgical videos.

Random video	Expert evaluation	Proposed evaluation
1	4	4
2	4	4
3	4	4
4	4	4
5	3	2
6	3	3
7	3	3

4   Conclusion

In this work, we proposed to segment the pupil through the ResUnet network, and the segmented pupil was fitted into an ellipse to calculate its center point and axis length. Then the position information of the keratome tip was obtained through the ResNet model. The above information obtained through the deep learning network was used to construct quantifiable and accurate evaluation indexes for cataract incisions. The experiment showed that the evaluation system we constructed has high accuracy, which is consistent with the evaluation of the expert group.

Complete cataract surgery includes incision, capsulorhexis, water separation, lens emulsification, etc., but our work is still limited to the first step. How to integrate all the procedures of cataract surgery into a complete evaluation system needs further efforts from us and doctors.

References

1. Al Hajj, H., Lamard, M., Charrière, K., Cochener, B., Quellec, G.: Surgical tool detection in cataract surgery videos through multi-image fusion inside a convolutional neural network. In: 2017 39th Annual International Conference of the IEEE Engineering in Medicine and Biology Society (EMBC), pp. 2002–2005. IEEE (2017)
2. Fine, I.H., Hoffman, R.S., Packer, M.: Profile of clear corneal cataract incisions demonstrated by ocular coherence tomography. J. Cataract Refract. Surg. **33**(1), 94–97 (2007)
3. Funke, I., Mees, S.T., Weitz, J., Speidel, S.: Video-based surgical skill assessment using 3d convolutional neural networks. Int. J. Comput. Assist. Radiol. Surg. **14**(7), 1217–1225 (2019)
4. Ghasemloonia, A., Maddahi, Y., Zareinia, K., Lama, S., Dort, J.C., Sutherland, G.R.: Surgical skill assessment using motion quality and smoothness. J. Surg. Educ. **74**(2), 295–305 (2017)
5. Jin, A., et al.: Tool detection and operative skill assessment in surgical videos using region-based convolutional neural networks (2018)

6. Johnston, R., Taylor, H., Smith, R., Sparrow, J.: The cataract national dataset electronic multi-centre audit of 55 567 operations: variation in posterior capsule rupture rates between surgeons. Eye **24**(5), 888–893 (2010)
7. Kim, T.S., O'Brien, M., Zafar, S., Hager, G.D., Sikder, S., Vedula, S.S.: Objective assessment of intraoperative technical skill in capsulorhexis using videos of cataract surgery. Int. J. Comput. Assist. Radiol. Surg. **14**(6), 1097–1105 (2019). https://doi.org/10.1007/s11548-019-01956-8
8. Leach, D.C.: A model for GME: shifting from process to outcomes. A progress report from the accreditation council for graduate medical education. Med. Educ. **38**(1), 12–14 (2004)
9. Levin, M., McKechnie, T., Khalid, S., Grantcharov, T.P., Goldenberg, M.: Automated methods of technical skill assessment in surgery: a systematic review. J. Surg. Educ. **76**(6), 1629–1639 (2019)
10. Mills, R.P., Mannis, M.J.: Report of the American board of ophthalmology task force on the competencies. Ophthalmology **111**(7), 1267–1268 (2004)
11. Swaminathan, M., Ramasubramanian, S., Pilling, R., Li, J., Golnik, K.: ICO-OSCAR for pediatric cataract surgical skill assessment. J. Am. Assoc. Pediatr. Ophthalmol. Strabismus **20**(4), 364–365 (2016)
12. Theodoropoulou, S., Grzeda, M., Donachie, P., Johnston, R., Sparrow, J., Tole, D.: The royal college of ophthalmologists' national ophthalmology database study of cataract surgery. Report 5: Clinical outcome and risk factors for posterior capsule rupture and visual acuity loss following cataract surgery in patients aged 90 years and older. Eye **33**(7), 1161–1170 (2019)
13. Weikert, M.P.: Update on bimanual microincisional cataract surgery. Curr. Opin. Ophthalmol. **17**(1), 62–67 (2006)
14. Woodfield, A.S., Gower, E.W., Cassard, S.D., Ramanthan, S.: Intraoperative phacoemulsification complication rates of second-and third-year ophthalmology residents: a 5-year comparison. Ophthalmology **118**(5), 954–958 (2011)
15. Wu, Z., Shen, C., van den Hengel, A.: Wider or deeper: revisiting the ResNet model for visual recognition. Pattern Recogn. **90**, 119–133 (2019)
16. Zhang, Z., Liu, Q., Wang, Y.: Road extraction by deep residual U-Net. IEEE Geosci. Remote Sens. Lett. **15**(5), 749–753 (2018)

Hybrid Deep Learning Gaussian Process for Diabetic Retinopathy Diagnosis and Uncertainty Quantification

Santiago Toledo-Cortés[1](✉) ⓘ, Melissa de la Pava[1] ⓘ, Oscar Perdomo[2] ⓘ,
and Fabio A. González[1] ⓘ

[1] MindLab Research Group, Universidad Nacional de Colombia, Bogotá, Colombia
{stoledoc,medel,fagonzalezo}@unal.edu.co
[2] Universidad del Rosario, Bogotá, Colombia
oscarj.perdomo@urosario.edu.co

Abstract. Diabetic Retinopathy (DR) is one of the microvascular complications of *Diabetes Mellitus*, which remains as one of the leading causes of blindness worldwide. Computational models based on Convolutional Neural Networks represent the state of the art for the automatic detection of DR using eye fundus images. Most of the current work address this problem as a binary classification task. However, including the grade estimation and quantification of predictions uncertainty can potentially increase the robustness of the model. In this paper, a hybrid Deep Learning-Gaussian process method for DR diagnosis and uncertainty quantification is presented. This method combines the representational power of deep learning, with the ability to generalize from small datasets of Gaussian process models. The results show that uncertainty quantification in the predictions improves the interpretability of the method as a diagnostic support tool. The source code to replicate the experiments is publicly available at https://github.com/stoledoc/DLGP-DR-Diagnosis.

Keywords: Deep Learning · Diabetic Retinopathy · Gaussian Process · Uncertainty quantification

1 Introduction

Diabetic Retinopathy (DR) is a consequence of *Diabetes Mellitus* that manifests itself in the alteration of vascular tissue. When an alteration in the correct blood supply occurs, lesions such as microaneurysms, hemorrhages and exudates appear [19]. These lesions can be identified in eye fundus images, one of the fastest and least invasive methods for DR diagnosing. Although early detection and monitoring are crucial to prevent progression and loss of vision [18], in developing countries approximately 40% of patients are not diagnosed due to lack of access to the medical equipment and specialist, which puts patients of productive age at risk of visual impairment [19,22]. Therefore, to facilitate access to rapid diagnosis and speed up the work of professionals, many efforts

© Springer Nature Switzerland AG 2020
H. Fu et al. (Eds.): OMIA 2020, LNCS 12069, pp. 206–215, 2020.
https://doi.org/10.1007/978-3-030-63419-3_21

have been made in the development of machine learning models focused on the analysis of eye fundus images for automatic DR detection.

For medical image analysis, deep Convolutional Neural Networks represent the state of the art. These methods work by means of filters that go through the image and exploit the natural structure of the data, being able to detect increasingly complex patterns. However, the success of these deep learning models depends on the availability of very large volumes of data, and this is not always the case for medical image datasets. For instance, one of the largest public-available image dataset for DR detection is EyePACS [5], which has 35126 samples for training. For this reason, training a deep learning model for this problem from scratch is not always feasible [9]. Instead, fine-tuning of pretrained models is preferred, as it allows the models to refine a general knowledge for an specific tasks. However, the number of specific sample images is not always enough to make a tuning that produces good final performances [9].

Classical machine learning methods such as Gaussian Processes (GP), on the other hand, were originally designed to work well with small data sets [6]. They have different advantages over deep neural network models, as lower number of parameters to train, convex optimization, modularity in model design, the possibility to involve domain knowledge, and in the case of Bayesian approaches, they allow the calculation of prediction uncertainty [20]. The latter would be useful in medical applications, as it gives to the final user an indication of the quality of the prediction [11].

This work presents and evaluates a hybrid deep learning-Gaussian process model for the diagnosis of DR, and prediction uncertainty quantification. Taking advantage of the representational power of deep learning, features were extracted using an Inception-V3 model, fine-tuned with EyePACS dataset. With these features we proceed to train a GP regression for DR grading.

Our framework shows that:

1. The performance of the proposed hybrid model trained as a regressor for the DR grade, allows it to improve binary classification results when compared with the single deep learning approach.
2. Gaussian processes can improve the performance of deep learning methods by leveraging their ability to learn good image representations, when applied for small datasets analysis.
3. The integration of GP endows the method with the ability to quantify the uncertainty in the predictions. This improves the usability of the method as a diagnostic support tool. Furthermore the experimental results show that the predictions uncertainty is higher for false negatives and false positives than for true positives and true negatives respectively. This is a high valued skill in computational medical applications.

The paper is organized as follows: Sect. 2 presents a brief review of the previous work related to the diagnosis and calculation of uncertainty of the of DR automatic classification. Section 3 introduce the theoretical framework for the experiments, which will be described in Sect. 4. Finally, in Sect. 5 the discussion of the results and conclusions are presented.

2   Related Work

Many approaches have been proposed for the DR binary detection, most of them based in deep neural networks [14]. Some of them combine deep models with metric learning techniques, as in [23], where an Inception-V3 is trained and embedded into siamese-like blocks. The final DR binary or grade prediction is given by a fully-connected layer. In [7], a customized deep convolutional neural network to extract features is presented. The features and multiple metadata related to the original fundus image are used to trained a gradient boosting classifier to perform the DR prediction. In [12] an Inception-V3 model is once again fine-tuned using a private set of eye fundus images, but not with binary labels, but with five DR grade labels. The results are reported using a subset of the Messidor-2 dataset [1,4]. This makes performance comparison impossible with many other results, including those presented in this paper. Better results were reported by Gulshan et al. in [8], where an ensemble of ten Inception-V3 models, pretrained on ImageNet, are fine-tuned on a non-public eye fundus image dataset. The final classification is calculated as the linear average over the predictions of the ensemble. Results on Messidor-2 were reported, with a remarkable 99% AUC score. In [17], Voets et al. attempted to reproduce the results presented in [8], but it was not possible since the original study used non-public datasets for training. However, Voets et al. published the source code and models, and details on training procedure and hyperparameters are published in [17] and [10].

Regarding the estimation of predictive uncertainty, the first work in this matter in DR detection models was proposed in [11], where bayesian inference is used for uncertainty quantification in binary classification of DR. Another approach is presented in [13], where stochastic batch normalization is used to calculate the uncertainty of the prediction of a model for DR level intervals estimation. In the work presented in [15], a dataset with multiple labels given by different doctors for each patient is used, which allows the calculation of uncertainty to predict professional disagreement in a patient diagnosis.

In relation to convolutional neural networks uncertainty estimation using GP, some work has been done specially outside the DR automatic detection context, as in [21], where a framework is developed to estimate uncertainty in any pretrained standard neural network, by modelling the prediction residuals with a GP. This framework was applied to the IMDB dataset, for age estimation based in face images. Also in [3], a GP on the top of a neural networks is end-to-end trained, which makes the model much more robust to adversarial examples. This model was used for classification in the MNIST and CIFAR-10 datasets.

To our knowledge, this is the first work that implements a GP to quantify the uncertainty of a model predictions of DR diagnosis.

3 Deep Learning Gaussian Process for Diabetic Retinopathy Diagnosis (DLGP-DR)

The overall strategy of the proposed Deep Learning Gaussian Process For Diabetic Retinopathy grade estimation (DLGP-DR) method comprises three phases, and is shown in Fig. 1. The first phase is a pre-processing stage, described in [17], which is applied to all eye fundus image datasets used in this work. This pre-processing eliminates the very dark images where the circular region of interest is not identified, eliminates the excess of black margin, and resizes the images to 299 × 299 pixels. The second phase is a feature extraction. An Inception-V3 model, trained with ImageNet and fine-tuned with EyePACS dataset is used as feature extractor. Each sample is then represented by a 2048-dimensional vector. The third and final task is the DR diagnosis, which is performed by a GP regressor.

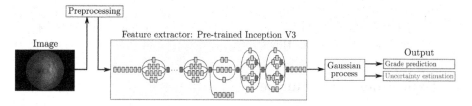

Fig. 1. Proposed DLGP-DR model. Fine-tuned Inception-V3 is used as feature extractor. The extracted features are then used to train a Gaussian process.

3.1 Feature Extraction - Inception-V3

Many previous works have used deep learning models for the diagnostic of DR. Recently, Voets et al. [17] attempted to replicate the results published in [8], by fine-tuning an assembly of ten pretrained Inception-V3 networks. While Voets et al. were not able to achieve the same results reported in [8], most of the implementation details, as well as the specific partitioning for the training and test sets are publicly accessible, and were used in this study in the fine tuning of an Inception-V3 model. Once trained, the feature extraction is achieved by defining the global average pooling layer of the network as the output of the model, and use it to predict all the images in the datasets. Thus, each image will be represented by 2048 features which are used to train and evaluate the GP model.

3.2 Gaussian Processes

Gaussian processes are a Bayesian machine learning regression approach that are able to produce, in addition to the predictions, a value of uncertainty about them [6]. The method requires as input a covariance given by a kernel matrix.

The kernel matrix would be the gram matrix computed over the training set with a Radial Basis Function (RBF). This RBF kernel depends on two parameters which will be learned during the training process. We performed a Gaussian process regression, where the labels are the five grades of retinopathy present in the EyePACS dataset. From the prior, the GP calculates the probability distribution of all the functions that fit the data, adjusting the prior from the evidence, and optimizing the kernel parameters. Predictions are obtained by marginalizing the final learned Gaussian distribution, which in turn yields another normal distribution, whose mean is the value of the prediction, and its standard deviation gives a measure of the uncertainty of the prediction. Thus, an optimized metric (attached to a RBF similarity measure) is learned from the data, used to estimate the DR grade.

This GP can be adapted to do binary classification. One simple way to do this is defining a linear threshold in the prediction regression results. The standard way however, consist in training a GP with binary labels and filtering the output of the regression by a sigmoid function. This results in a Gaussian Process Classifier (GPC). In any case, the predictions of a GPC are not longer subject to a normal distribution, and the uncertainty can not be measured. Therefore, the GPC will not take part in this study.

4   Experimental Evaluation

4.1   Datasets

Experiments were performed with two eye fundus image datasets: EyePACS and Messidor-2. EyePACS comes with labels for five grades of DR: grade 0 means no DR, 1, 2, and 3 means non-proliferative mild, moderate and severe DR, while grade 4 means proliferative DR. For the binary classification task, according to the International Clinical Diabetic Retinopathy Scale [2], grades 0 and 1 corresponds to non-referable DR, while grades 2, 3, and 4 correspond to referable DR. In order to achieve comparable results with [17], we took the same EyePACS partition used for training and testing (see Table 1). This partition was constructed only to ensure that the proportion of healthy and sick examples in training and testing was the same as that reported in [8]. EyePACS train set is used for training and validation of the Inception-V3 model. Then, the feature extraction described in Sect. 3 is applied. The extracted features are used for training the DLGP-DR model. The evaluation is performed on the EyePACS test set and on the Messidor-2, which is a standard dataset used to compare performance results in DR diagnosis task. Datasets details are described in Table 1 and in Table 2.

4.2   Experimental Setup

Fine-tuning was made to an Inception-V3 network, pretrained on ImageNet and available in Keras [16]. The model was trained for binary DR classification task.

Table 1. Details of Messidor-2 dataset used for testing. Class 0 correspond to non-referable cases.

Class	Test samples
0	1368
1	380

Table 2. Details of the subset and final partition of the EyePACS dataset used for training and testing. This is the same partition used in [17]. Grades 0 and 1 correspond to non-referable patients, while grades 2, 3, and 4 correspond to referable cases.

Grade	Train samples	Test samples
0	37209	7407
1	3479	689
2	12873	0
3	2046	0
4	1220	694

The data augmentation configuration for horizontal reflection, brightness, saturation, hue, and contrast changes, is described in [10], and it is the same used in [17] and in [8]. The top layer of the Inception-V3 model is removed and replaced by two dense layers of 2048 and 1 neurons. BinaryCrossentropy was used as loss function and RMSprop as optimizer, with a learning rate of 10^{-6} and a decay of 4×10^{-5}. The performance of the model is validated by measuring the AUC in a validation set consisting of 20% of the training set.

Once the model is trained, the average pooling layer from the Inception-V3 model is used as output for feature extraction. The extracted features from the Inception-V3 are normalized and used to train a GP regressor over the five DR grade labels, it means, to perform the DR grading task. RBF kernel plus a white kernel were used as prior for the Gaussian process, using the Scikit-Learn implementation in Python. RBF length scale parameter was initiated at 1.0, with bounds at $(10^{-2}, 10^3)$. White noise level parameter was started at 10^{-5}, with bounds at $(10^{-10}, 10)$. The output of the DLGP-DR is a continuous number indicating the DR grade.

Two baselines were defined to compare the DLGP-DR performance. Results reported by Voets et al. [17] constitute the first baseline of this study. The second baseline is an extension of the Inception-V3 model with two dense layers trained on the same feature test as the Gaussian process, which is called as *NN-model* hereafter.

4.3   EyePACS Results

DLGP-DR is evaluated in the EyePACS test partition. The results are binarized using a threshold of 1.5 (which is coherent with referable DR detection), and compared with baselines in Table 3. In addition, although uncertainty estimation is not used to define or modify the prediction, DLGP-DR uncertainty is analysed for false positives (FP), false negatives (FN), true positives (TP) and true negatives (TN). As mentioned before, referable diabetic retinopathy is defined as the presence of moderate, severe and proliferative DR. So, the false negatives are calculated as the patients that belong to grade 4 but are classified as grades 0 and 1. The false positives are calculated as the patients belonging to grades 0 and 1 but classified in grade 4. The results are shown in Fig. 2 and Fig. 3.

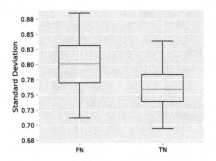

Fig. 2. Standard deviation for samples predicted as negative (non-referable) instances by DLGP-DR. FN: false negatives, TN: true negatives.

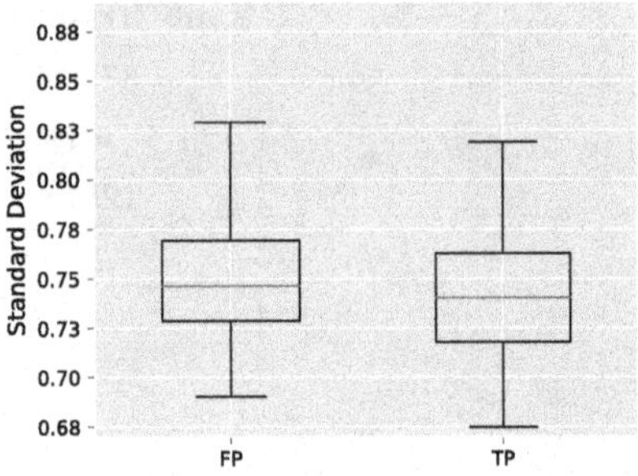

Fig. 3. Standard deviation for samples predicted as positive (referable) instances by DLGP-DR. FP: false positives, TP: true positives.

4.4   Messidor-2 Results

For Messidor-2 dataset, the predictions given by DLGP-DR are binarized using the same threshold of 1.5 used for EyePACS. Based on the results of the uncertainty measured in the EyePACS test dataset, those samples predicted negative for which the standard deviation was higher than 0.84, were changed to positive. The results are reported and compared with the baselines in the Table 4.

4.5   Discussion

Results reported in Table 3 shows that DLGP-DR outperforms specificity and AUC score of the *NN-model* and outperforms all the metrics reported by Voets et al. [17]. As observed in Table 4, DLGP-DR outperforms both baselines for specificity and AUC scores. Although Gulshan et al. have reported 0.99 for AUC score in Messidor-2 [8], as Voets et al. comments in [17], the gap in the results may be due to the fact that the training in that study was made with other publicly available images and with a different gradation made by ophthalmologists. Overall, this shows that the global performance of the DLGP-DR exceeds

Table 3. Comparison performance of DLGP-DR for binary classification in EyePACS test partition used in [17]. As it is not the standard EyePACS test set, comparison is not feasible with other similar studies.

Description	Sensitivity	Specificity	AUC
Voets 2019 [17]	0.906	0.847	0.951
NN-model	0.9207	0.85	0.9551
DLGP-DR	**0.9323**	**0.9173**	**0.9769**

Table 4. Comparison performance of DLGP-DR for binary classification in Messidor-2. Referenced results from [17] were directly extracted from the respective documents.

Description	Sensitivity	Specificity	AUC
Voets 2019 [17]	**0.818**	0.712	0.853
NN-model	0.7368	0.8581	0.8753
DLGP-DR	0.7237	**0.8625**	**0.8787**

that of a neural network-based classifier. In addition, in Fig. 2 and Fig. 3 the box-plot shows that the standard deviation is higher for false positives and false negatives. This means, that the DLGP-DR model has bigger uncertainties for wrong classified patients than for well classified. which provides the user a tool to identify wrong predictions. This behavior is especially visible for false negatives, which is the most dangerous mistake in medical applications, because a ill patient can leave out without a needed treatment.

5   Conclusions

In this study we took a deep learning model fine-tuned on the EyePACS dataset as feature extractor. The final task of DR classification and grading was carried out by means of a Gaussian process. For DR binary classification, the proposed DLGP-DR model reached better results than the original deep learning model. We also showed that a fine DR grade classification improve the binary classification performance of the original model.

Also, the DLGP-DR enables an uncertainty analysis. This analysis showed that the model could allow the identification of both, false negatives and false positives. The former are important due to the high cost of classifying a patient as healthy when it is not, and the later because they increase the costs of health care. The comparison between the Gaussian process and a neural network classifier for DR grades, showed once again that Gaussian processes are better tools for the analysis of medical images, for which datasets are usually far small to be analyzed entirely with deep learning techniques.

Overall, we demonstrate that the integration of deep learning and classical machine learning techniques is highly feasible in applications with small datasets, taking advantage of the representational power of deep learning and the theoretical robustness of classical methods.

Acknowledgments. This work was partially supported by a Google Research Award and by the Colciencias project number 1101-807-63563.

References

1. Abrámoff, M.D., et al.: Automated analysis of retinal images for detection of referable diabetic retinopathy. JAMA Ophthalmol. **131**(3), 351–357 (2013). https://doi.org/10.1001/jamaophthalmol.2013.1743
2. American Academy of Ophthalmology: International clinical diabetic retinopathy disease severity scale detailed table. International Council of Ophthalmology (2002)
3. Bradshaw, J., Matthews, A.G.d.G., Ghahramani, Z.: Adversarial examples, uncertainty, and transfer testing robustness in Gaussian process hybrid deep networks, eprint, pp. 1-33 (2017). arXiv:1707.02476v1
4. Decenciére, E., et al.: Feedback on a publicly distributed image database: the Messidor database. Image Anal. Stereol. **33**(3), 231–234 (2014). https://doi.org/10.5566/ias.1155
5. Diabetic Retinopathy Detection of Kaggle: Eyepacs challenge. www.kaggle.com/c/diabetic-retinopathy-detection/data. Accessed 15 Oct 2019
6. Ethem, A.: Introduction to Machine Learning, 3rd edn. The MIT Press, Cambridge (2014)
7. Gargeya, R., Leng, T.: Automated identification of diabetic retinopathy using deep learning. Ophthalmology **124**(7), 962–969 (2017)
8. Gulshan, V., et al.: Development and validation of a deep learning algorithm for detection of diabetic retinopathy in retinal fundus photographs. JAMA J. Am. Med. Assoc. **316**(22), 2402–2410 (2016)
9. Kaya, M., Bilge, H.: Deep metric learning: a survey. Symmetry **11**, 1066 (2019). https://doi.org/10.3390/sym11091066
10. Krause, J., et al.: Grader variability and the importance of reference standards for evaluating machine learning models for diabetic retinopathy. Ophthalmology **125**(8), 1264–1272 (2018). https://doi.org/10.1016/j.ophtha.2018.01.034
11. Leibig, C., Allken, V., Ayhan, M.S., Berens, P., Wahl, S.: Leveraging uncertainty information from deep neural networks for disease detection. Sci. Rep. **7**(1), 1–14 (2017)
12. Li, F., Liu, Z., Chen, H., Jiang, M., Zhang, X., Wu, Z.: Automatic detection of diabetic retinopathy in retinal fundus photographs based on deep learning algorithm. Transl. Vis. Sci. Technol. **8**(6) (2019). https://doi.org/10.1167/tvst.8.6.4
13. Lim, Z.W., Lee, M.L., Hsu, W., Wong, T.Y.: Building trust in deep learning system towards automated disease detection. In: The Thirty-First AAAI Conference on Innovative Applications of Artificial Intelligence, pp. 9516–9521 (2018)
14. Perdomo, O., Gonzalez, F.: A systematic review of deep learning methods applied to ocular images. Ciencia e Ingenieria Neogranadina **30**(1), 9–26 (2019)
15. Raghu, M., Blumer, K., Sayres, R., Obermeyer, Z., Kleinberg, R., Mullainathan, S., Kleinberg, J.: Direct uncertainty prediction for medical second opinions. In: Proceedings of the 36th International Conference on Machine Learning, PMLR 97, Long Beach, California (2019)

16. Szegedy, C., Vanhoucke, V., Ioffe, S., Shlens, J., Wojna, Z.: Rethinking the inception architecture for computer vision. In: Proceedings of the IEEE Computer Society Conference on Computer Vision and Pattern Recognition, December 2016, pp. 2818–2826 (2016). https://doi.org/10.1109/CVPR.2016.308
17. Voets, M., Møllersen, K., Bongo, L.A.: Reproduction study using public data of: Development and validation of a deep learning algorithm for detection of diabetic retinopathy in retinal fundus photographs. PLoS ONE **14**(6), 1–11 (2019)
18. Wells, J.A., et al.: aflibercept, bevacizumab, or ranibizumab for diabetic macular edema two-year results from a comparative effectiveness randomized clinical trial. Ophthalmology **123**(6), 1351–1359 (2016)
19. Wilkinson, C.P.P., et al.: Proposed international clinical diabetic retinopathy and diabetic macular edema disease severity scales. Ophthalmology **110**(9), 1677–1682 (2003)
20. Wilson, A., Nickisch, H.: Kernel interpolation for scalable structured gaussian processes (KISS-GP). In: Proceedings of the 32nd International Conference on Machine Learning. JMLR: W&CP, Lille, France (2015)
21. Xin, Q., Elliot, M., Miikkulainen, R.: Quantifying point-prediction uncertainty in neural networks via residual estimation with an I/O Kernel. In: ICLR 2020, Addis Ababa, Ethiopia, pp. 1–17 (2019)
22. Yau, J.W., et al.: Global prevalence and major risk factors of diabetic retinopathy. Diabetes Care **35**(3), 556–564 (2012)
23. Zeng, X., Chen, H., Luo, Y., Ye, W.: Automated diabetic retinopathy detection based on binocular Siamese-like convolutional neural network. IEEE Access **7**(c), 30744–30753 (2019)

Author Index

Printed in the USA/Agawam, MA
by Bookmasters

Printed in the United States
By Bookmasters